SD SOCSCI 15/21 £4

C000000647

Depression and the Self

Meaning, Control and Authenticity

Depression is widely recognised as the leading disability worldwide. Though classified as a medical condition, depression also contains very personal and social aspects which are integral to the experience – as those who have experienced it know all too well.

Drawing on research interviews with women who have experienced depression, this psychological study elucidates experiences of depression and the meanings attached to it. In so doing, Browne challenges current understandings of depression as a chronic and endogenous illness and stresses the importance of the perception of authenticity among depression sufferers. Written in plain language accessible to non-specialists, *Depression and the Self* argues that in depression, perceptions of control and the self are intertwined – and that this has important implications for diagnosis and recovery.

Tamara Kayali Browne, a bioethicist and philosopher of medicine, currently works as a lecturer of Health Ethics and Professionalism at Deakin University. She received her PhD from the University of Cambridge and a postdoctoral fellowship in Neuroethics at Novel Tech Ethics, Dalhousie University, following which she served as a lecturer of Bioethics at Sydney University and the Australian National University, winning three teaching awards. Her research in philosophical and sociological issues in psychiatry has been published in peer-reviewed journals, including *Philosophy, Psychiatry and Psychology*; *Medicine, Health Care and Philosophy*; the *Journal of Bioethical Inquiry*; and *Health, Risk and Society*. Her work has also appeared in the media, including *The Guardian, The Huffington Post, Psychology Today, The Globe and Mail, The Sydney Morning Herald, The Age*, and ABC radio.

Depression and the Self

Meaning, Control and Authenticity

Tamara Kayali Browne

Deakin University, Geelong

CAMBRIDGE
UNIVERSITY PRESS

CAMBRIDGE
UNIVERSITY PRESS

University Printing House, Cambridge CB2 8BS, United Kingdom

One Liberty Plaza, 20th Floor, New York, NY 10006, USA

477 Williamstown Road, Port Melbourne, VIC 3207, Australia

314–321, 3rd Floor, Plot 3, Splendor Forum, Jasola District Centre, New Delhi – 110025, India

79 Anson Road, #06–04/06, Singapore 079906

Cambridge University Press is part of the University of Cambridge.

It furthers the University's mission by disseminating knowledge in the pursuit of education, learning, and research at the highest international levels of excellence.

www.cambridge.org
Information on this title: www.cambridge.org/9781107138650
DOI: 10.1017/9781316481578

© Cambridge University Press 2018

This publication is in copyright. Subject to statutory exception and to the provisions of relevant collective licensing agreements, no reproduction of any part may take place without the written permission of Cambridge University Press.

First published 2018

Printed in the United Kingdom by Clays, St Ives plc

A catalogue record for this publication is available from the British Library.

Library of Congress Cataloging-in-Publication Data
Names: Browne, Tamara Kayali, author.
Title: Depression and the self : meaning, control and authenticity / Tamara Kayali Browne, Deakin University, Geelong.
Description: Cambridge, United Kingdom ; New York, NY : Cambridge University Press, 2018. | Includes bibliographical references.
Identifiers: LCCN 2017043599 | ISBN 9781107138650 (hardback)
Subjects: LCSH: Depression, Mental – Philosophy – Popular works. | Depression, Mental – Social aspects – Popular works. | BISAC: PSYCHOLOGY / Clinical Psychology.
Classification: LCC RC537 .B768 2018 | DDC 616.85/27–dc23
LC record available at https://lccn.loc.gov/2017043599

ISBN 978-1-107-13865-0 Hardback

Cambridge University Press has no responsibility for the persistence or accuracy of URLs for external or third-party internet websites referred to in this publication and does not guarantee that any content on such websites is, or will remain, accurate or appropriate.

For Mayada, Obada and Jason

Contents

Figures

Acknowledgements

I am grateful to many people who supported me throughout this project. First, I wish to thank the women who so generously gave their time to participate in this research and share their stories and experiences of depression and recovery. I learned so much from their insights and am truly in their debt.

This work was made possible by funding received from the Arnold Gerstenberg Studentship, as well as bursaries from Queens' College, Cambridge, and a Richard Stapley Grant. Thanks to Taylor & Francis Ltd. for permission to reprint Kayali, T., & Iqbal, F. (2012), Making Sense of Melancholy: Sub-Categorisation and the Perceived Risk of Future Depression, *Health, Risk & Society*, *14*(2), 171–189, in Chapter 5, and to Springer for permission to reprint parts of Kayali, T., & Iqbal, F. (2013), Depression as Unhomelike Being-in-the-World? Phenomenology's Challenge to Our Understanding of Illness, *Medicine, Health Care and Philosophy*, *16*(1), 31–39, throughout this book.

I am grateful to Martin Richards for supporting and believing in my research, as well as the lovely interdisciplinary environment of the Centre for Family Research at Cambridge University. I thank the good people at the Centre for Applied Philosophy and Public Ethics at Charles Sturt University who also provided a supportive intellectual environment and helpful feedback on one of the chapters.

Thank you to my family for their love and encouragement, and especially my parents, Mayada and Obada, who supported me in so many ways throughout my research. This book, and all the life-changing experiences that went along with it, would certainly not have been possible without them. Last but not least, thanks to my soulmate Jason for being a source of strength, joy, patience, kindness and love through it all. A true angel if ever there was one.

1 The Self and Related Concepts

The philosopher Immanuel Kant said, "Two things fill the mind with ever new and increasing admiration and awe, the oftener and the more steadily we reflect on them: *the starry heavens above and the moral law within*" (Kant, 2004 [1788]: 170). As a child I had fancied becoming an astronomer. Alas, those hopes were dashed when I learned that to become an astronomer, one must enjoy mathematics. So I turned instead (many years later) to the moral law within – the self – and in particular to autonomy and authenticity, being among the central concepts in bioethics and philosophy of medicine. Such concepts have, of course, been explored by philosophers for thousands of years, but I sought to understand what these concepts mean to people in real situations when those elements of the self are most acutely challenged.

As so much of our ideas concerning the self draw on our experiences and intuitions of what it is to have a self and to feel true to it, it seemed that while armchair theorising certainly has its function, even more can be learned from empirical studies. Moreover, although classified as a medical condition, depression also contains very personal and social aspects which are integral to the experience. Illuminating this human element of depression rather than just the clinical or the purely theoretical advances our knowledge of it in a way that may not be possible if scholarship is focused solely on theory (which may or may not have any bearing on reality), or on clinical aspects, or indeed solely on the experiences of individuals without relating the significance of those experiences to current theory. While physical illnesses do impact on the self in various ways, mental illnesses, by affecting one's thoughts, emotions and behaviours, directly impact the various elements which we take to form the self. Depression, being apparently the most common mental illness, seemed to be the perfect candidate for such an exploration into the self.

There is barely a person who either has not been directly touched by depression or does not know someone who has. Now considered the leading cause of disability worldwide and a major contributor to the

1

global disease burden, depression is said to affect staggering numbers of people – an estimated 300 million around the world according to the World Health Organization (2017). There is also a large literature on it to match – everything from scientific studies searching for causes and cures to autobiographical accounts written by those who continue to struggle with it or who have survived. This book is somewhat different in that it focuses on specific aspects of the self in depression.

Aside from the suffering inherent in depression, there is another difficulty which individuals who have experienced depression often face. Annette articulates this difficulty succinctly:

Annette: When you've done things or said things or thought things or behaved in an inappropriate way, you think, "Are people gonna see this as part of my personality? Is this part of who I am? Or you know, is this just how I behaved because my chemicals weren't right?"

As Annette describes, it is a question of where to assign responsibility for emotions, thoughts and behaviours which are normally considered to be part of one's sense of self but which, with a diagnosis of depression and subsequent treatment, now come under question. This problematises the way patients and the general public think about the self in relation to depression.

Prior research has presented accounts of patients on antidepressants who felt as though they went from an "old" to a "new" self, or had found their authentic self (Karp, 2006; Kramer, 1993). I sought to learn *why* some people feel like their true self while on antidepressants whereas others feel the opposite, why some describe depression as an illness ready to attack, while others describe it as a part of their self. I wondered if perhaps their views related in some way to their experiences of depression and treatment. Essentially, I sought to go beyond an examination of the effects of depression and psychiatric medication to see if individuals' reflections on their experiences of depression and treatment shed any light on our concepts of the self.

The women whose experiences I draw on in this book participated in a study conducted in England. The study aimed to investigate if and how aspects of women's experiences of depression, diagnosis and treatment relate to their perceptions of the self in depression and recovery. I included 37 women with different diagnoses and treatments in order to explore a broad range of experiences. As such, there were no limits placed on type, recurrence, duration or nature of depression (although minor depression was excluded) or type of treatment. In order to qualify for inclusion in the study, interviewees had to be female, be between the ages of 18 and 65, have been diagnosed with depression, have received treatment for it, and be feeling better (according to both the individual's judgement and her Beck score at the time of interview).[1] I included the latter condition in order to recruit individuals in a relatively stable condition so that they could reflect on their experiences of depression, treatment and recovery and to minimise the potential for emotional distress during the interview.

Seeking to focus on experiential aspects of depression rather than on the already well-studied gender and socio-economic aspects of depression, I realised this could best be done if I focused on one gender and on individuals with similar educational and socio-economic backgrounds. A number of studies have provided evidence of gender differences related to depression, citing both social and biological factors which could influence both the development of depression (e.g. Goodwin & Gotlib, 2004; Kessler, 2003; Kueher, 2003; Piccinelli & Wilkinson, 2000) and its course and responses to certain treatments (Barnes & Mitchell, 2005; Burt & Rasgon, 2004; Freeman & Gelenberg, 2005; Leibenluft, 1996, 1997). Studies have also documented female versus male narrative differences (e.g. Buckner & Fivush, 1998; Thompson, 1998), and there have already been several analyses of gender differences in depression experiences (Danielsson et al., 2009; Danielsson & Johansson, 2005; Danielsson et al., 2010; Emslie et al., 2007; Emslie et al., 2006; O'Brien et al., 2005). Setting aside gender differences thus allowed me to narrow the focus of my investigation onto other factors which may account for differences in individuals' accounts. This book is therefore not an investigation of the gender-related social issues surrounding the causes, diagnosis and treatment of women's depression. Rather, it is an investigation of how experiences of depression impact on certain aspects of the self.

I chose to interview women rather than men, firstly, because rates of depression are widely reported to be twice as high for women, as measured by both community surveys and diagnosed and treated cases (Angst et al., 2002; Bromet et al., 2011; Steffens et al., 2000), which meant it would likely be easier to find volunteers among the female population than among the male population. Secondly, I was aware that being of the same gender may enable the interviewees to identify with me and feel comfortable sharing their experiences. As Benney et al. (2003: 46) contend, "the least inhibited communication seems to take place between young people of the same sex". Being in my mid-to-late twenties at the time of the interviews, I also fit with the age range of most of the interviewees.

Given my research focus on different experiences of depression and treatment, it made sense to try to limit variation in other factors as much as possible. For this reason, I initially set out to select participants from one location. When recruitment within one city alone proved difficult and alternative means of recruitment other than through a psychiatrist were exhausted, I looked into additional locations from which to recruit. The two main study sites are unique due to their disproportionately educated, middle-class populations compared to many other parts of England. The sample of women who participated in the study reflects this and most were educated to university level. The sample was also predominantly white and fairly young – the average age was 32.8 years – and the largest age group by far was women in their twenties, with 18 of the 37 women in this age group. Although the characteristics of the sample limit the generalisability of the study's findings, it allowed me to focus on interpretive factors and the variety of experiences of depression, diagnosis and treatment rather than on the variety of experiences across gender, age, social class and ethnic groups which have been investigated in many other depression studies (e.g. Estroff *et al.*, 1991; Pilgrim & Rogers, 1993).

My focus on finding meanings within individuals' perceptions of their experience is patently a phenomenological investigation (Van Manen, 1984). As such, a phenomenological analysis was the most obvious analytic method for me to employ. Both descriptive and interpretative phenomenological analyses aim to capture the "quality and texture of the individual experience" (Willig, 2008: 57). Yet interpretative phenomenology recognises that such an analysis is always the researcher's interpretation of that experience. Moreover, rather than aiming to elucidate the general structure of how a particular phenomenon is experienced, as is the aim in descriptive phenomenology (Giorgi & Giorgi, 2008), my aim was more closely aligned with those of the interpretative branch in both its focus on perceptions (Kvale, 1996) and its attempt to interpretatively engage with material (whether they be texts or transcripts) to unravel the meanings within them (Smith, 1997). Its aim is to try to see the world through the participant's eyes and to take that insider's view as much as possible (Crossley, 2000). It does so by "allowing participants to tell their story, in their own words, about the topic under investigation" (Smith *et al.*, 1997: 68). As a result, interpretative phenomenology was a major influence on the analytic framework.

Defining Depression

Many people who have experienced depression say it is indescribable. My own perspective is as someone who has learnt about depression through reading studies and autobiographies, as well as speaking to others about their experience of depression. As I do not have a first-hand account of what depression is like, I speak as a bystander rather than as a survivor. My view, therefore, is as someone from the outside rather than within.

In addition to the experience of depression itself, the issue of the label the individual acquires may also have a significant influence on how the individual perceives depression in relation to herself. It is for this reason that I decided to use the clinician's diagnosis of depression, regardless of how accurate the diagnosis may be (or indeed, if a diagnosis is appropriate at all), as the criterion for inclusion rather than using other criteria such as the Beck depression scale or applying the diagnostic criteria in the *Diagnostic and Statistical Manual of Mental Disorders* (*DSM*). This allowed me to investigate the influence that the diagnosis itself has on how the individual conceptualises what it is she is suffering from and its role in her life and sense of self. As a result, rather than relying on so-called objective criteria for depression (which has the added risk of reifying the category), I embrace the subjectivity of the clinician making the diagnosis as a relevant and important part of an examination into the self and depression.

Defining the Self

In order to conduct an investigation into the self in depression, one must first be clear on what is meant by "the self". To this end, this section gives an overview (which is by no means exhaustive) of different definitions of the self to give the reader an impression of the landscape, before identifying which definition is given the most support by my empirical investigation. The term "self" is a concept which, as Epstein aptly describes, is "a slippery concept whose adequate definition is irritatingly elusive" (1973: 404), resulting in numerous definitions. *Merriam-Webster's Online Dictionary* defines the self as:

1 **a** : the entire person of an individual
   b : the realization or embodiment of an abstraction

2 **a (1)** : an individual's typical character or behavior "her true self was revealed"
   (2) : an individual's temporary behavior or character "his better self"
   b : a person in prime condition "feel like my old self today"

3 : the union of elements (as body, emotions, thoughts, and sensations) that constitute the individuality and identity of a person. (*Merriam-Webster's Online Dictionary*, 2010)

The New Shorter Oxford English Dictionary includes the following in its definition of the self:

A person's or thing's individuality or essence at a particular time or in a particular aspect or relation; a person's nature, character, or (occas.) physical constitution or appearance, considered as different at different times . . .
   True or intrinsic identity; personal identity, ego; a person as the object of introspection or reflexive action. (Brown, 1993: 2763)

These dictionary definitions give an indication of the variety of conceptions of the self. Within the literature, there is first a distinction between the self at the individual level and the self at the societal level (Ashmore & Jussim, 1997). At the individual level, authors usually distinguish between the self as subject (or agent) and the self as object (or observed entity) (Ashmore & Jussim, 1997). William James first referred to the distinction as "self as knower" and "self as known", or the "I" and "Me" or "subject" and "object" distinction, respectively (James, 1890). Several authors have attempted to identify the elements of the self as subject and object (e.g. Damon & Hart, 1982, 1986; Harter, 1983).

A second distinction within the concept of the self at the individual level is that between self-conception and self-evaluation: that is, between the evaluative and descriptive parts of the self (Beane & Lipka, 1980; Blyth & Traeger, 1983; Greenwald et al., 1988; Hogg & Cooper, 2003). A third distinction centres on the question of whether the self is stable or constantly changing. Some believe the self reflects time-specific and contextual factors – that it is socially constructed (Gergen, 1977; Linville & Carlston, 1994) – whereas others believe there is an underlying core self (Epstein, 1980; Markus & Kunda, 1986; Markus & Nurius, 1986).

On a societal level, first is the cultural notion of what defines a person, or "the shared conception of the person or individual" (Spiro, 1993: 114). Second is the cultural notion of what defines a self, or "the cultural conception of some psychic entity or structure within the person, variously described as 'pure ego,' 'transcendental ego,' 'soul,' and the like" (Spiro, 1993: 114). Third, and on a more practical level, there are "the bounds on the nature, content, and structure of individual persons and selves set by the current political, legal, economic, and informational institutions, as well as prevailing cultural values and accepted interpersonal processes" (Ashmore & Jussim, 1997: 8). Fourth, on a more specific level, there are the self-concepts of individuals within a given culture (Ashmore & Jussim, 1997). These four levels of the self, which of course are not discrete but overlap with each other, can be compared across societies, cultures and time. For instance, researchers interested in concepts of the self across different cultures usually study a society's conception of personhood (Spiro, 1993: 117).

Concepts of the self can also be divided along disciplinary lines. In philosophy, "the self" (or identity) is considered to be the locus of agency, responsibility and personal identity (Mackenzie & Atkins, 2008), but there is disagreement as to whether it is what constitutes an individual at a point in time, or at different points in time (Blackburn, 2008). Philosophers concerned with the self at one point in time contend that it is possible for more than one person to share the same body, so they ask what it is that gives us the impression that we are only one person (Locke, 1959). Philosophers concerned with what constitutes the self at different points in time note that we all change throughout our lives. We are different in some ways from the way we were, say, ten years ago, and may change again in another ten years. This raises the question of what evidence there is to say that I am the same person now as I was ten years ago. It is possible for someone else to have taken over my body in that time (Blackburn, 2008). Alternatively, my psychology may have changed drastically after an event, which problematises the extent to which I can be deemed to be the same person simply because my body has survived (Blackburn, 2008). Some of those I interviewed struggled with a similar issue, speculating as to whether depression had changed their self or whether they would have changed anyway with the passage of time, particularly when their history with depression spanned several years or even decades. Some felt so different during an episode of depression or mania, or when on medication, that they felt like a very different self, or not their true self.

Aristotle defined the self (which he termed the soul) as the essence of a human in the sense that it is the activity of the body. Specifically, it is the potential for rational activity that is the essence of a human self (Aristotle, 2001). In contrast, Ibn Sina (Avicenna) argued that the self is a substance independent of physical components. He postulated that if one was suspended in the air without any sensation whatsoever of external surroundings or even with one's own body, one would still have consciousness of one's self. As a result, the self is not dependent on anything physical (Goodman, 1992).

David Hume believed that the self does not have a constant, underlying essence, but is constituted of a variety of different, fluid elements which are interrelated. At any time, we are merely a bundle of perceptions that do not belong to anything. "We are never intimately conscious of anything but a particular perception; man is a bundle or collection of different perceptions which succeed one another with an inconceivable rapidity and are in perpetual flux and movement" (Hume, 2007 [1739]: I, IV, vi). Daniel Dennett argues that the self is not a physical substance but a "convenient fiction" like the centre of gravity. Especially when making sense of the world, the self is a convenient concept to invoke. But the fictional character at the centre of these stories is the self (Dennett, 1992). While this book cannot speak to the metaphysical question of "What is the self?" there are, nevertheless, instances when one's answer to this question influences one's ideas surrounding the concept of the self in depression. For instance, a dualist view of the self which conceives it as independent of the body may lend itself more easily to a biomedical view of depression as an illness, caused by a neurochemical imbalance, that is distinct from the self. As shown in Chapter 2, most of those who professed to hold such a view struggled to maintain it. Yet the view still exerts its influence on many, whether or not they actually espouse it.

Psychology focuses on the self at the level of the individual. William James, whom many consider to be the father of psychological and socio-logical analyses of the self (Ashmore & Jussim, 1997), was followed by Calkins (1900), who advocated for psychology to become a science of selves. Apart from those who emphasised the function of the ego and the id, psychoanalysts following Calkins largely ignored the study of the self for some time (Scheibe, 1985). The 1940s saw a revival of the study of the self when researchers created a self-report measure of self-esteem, and for the following 30 years this became a major arena in psychological studies of the self (Wylie, 1974). Apart from self-esteem, psychology has also become concerned with aspects such as self-states, self-motives, self-awareness, self-knowledge and self-image (Leary & Tangney, 2003). Psychological theories of self-discrepancy (Higgins, 1987), self-concept (Rosenberg, 1979) and psychotherapeutical consistency (Grawe, 2004) have also investigated the self.

As Ashmore and Jussim (1997) note, the terms "self" and "identity" within psychology overlap with concepts such as "personality" and "memory" which help to define the attributes and idiosyncrasies that make us who we are. For example, research into autobiographical memory has found certain personality features to be strongly connected to memories (McAdams, 1982, 1985; McAdams *et al.*, 1997; Woike, 1995; Woike *et al.*, 1999). Memories can also contribute to self-schemas (Habermas & Bluck, 2000; Markus, 1977), and certain memories have been called "self-defining" because they become crucial to the develop-ment of goals and mental well-being (Singer & Salovey, 1993). Memories can also contribute to generation identity (Conway, 1997; Conway & Haque, 1999) and the formation of a stable self-system (the individual's set of self-perceptions) (Beike & Landoll, 2000; Conway & Rubin, 1993; Conway & Tacchi, 1996; Fitzgerald, 1988, 1996). Conway and Pleydell-Pearce also note connections between memories and the working self, goals, emotion and the self-memory system (Conway & Pleydell-Pearce, 2000). On the other hand, Erikson distin-guished between "the self" as a continuous *ego identity*, "personal iden-tity" as the set of idiosyncrasies that make each person unique and "social identity" or "cultural identity" as the social roles a person plays (Wallerstein & Goldberger, 1998). According to Harré, the self is "that inner unity to which all personal experience belongs as attributes of a subject" (1987: 42).

Although the women I spoke with recalled memories associated with their depression during the course of their interviews, it is important to distinguish between these accounts and those of autobiographical memory and the self in that; rather than investigating the nature of their memories and their specific connections to aspects of the self, I examine whether simply perceiving the presence or absence of memories of events or circumstances in close connection with depressive episodes is meaningful to how one conceives one's future self. Allowance for the possibility of the absence of memory being meaningful in itself is thus a key methodological difference between this investigation and those concerned with autobiographical memory.

In anthropology, Hallowell is the main figure recognised as having begun an anthropological study of the self (Ashmore & Jussim, 1997).[2] Hallowell (1955) believed that the self is "culturally constituted", meaning that the individual's sense of self and the way she evaluates her self is a product of her culture. Potter and Wetherell (1987) argue that cultural discourses frame the way we talk about ourselves, and in turn our experience of personhood. As discourses differ between cultures, individuals in different cultures would experience being a "self" differently. In a similar vein, Harré contends that the structure of our language frames our beliefs about the self (Harré, 1985, 1989).[3] In contrast, Spiro (1993) argues that Hallowell believed in certain universal ideas about the self commonly held among cultures, and Baumeister (1987) builds on this notion by suggesting what those ideas may be. Burr (2003), on the other hand, believes it is the *concept* of self that is universal. These anthropological concerns should be kept in mind given that the views of the self among those I interviewed may differ with the views of the self expressed in other cultures.

The above discussion provides a rough "lay of the land" on which to appreciate where this investigation is situated within the broader picture. The definition of the self used in this book overlaps with its meaning within a particular branch of psychology (as presented in the next section).[4] I am particularly concerned with how the individual incorporates (or doesn't incorporate) depression into her concept of self (i.e. what attributes do and do not constitute her true self/authenticity in her eyes), how she compares her present self with her past self and future self (which can be viewed as self-states), her medicated self with her non-medicated self (also self-states) and what she considers to be her true self and why (again, attributes of the self). However, the way I investigate the self uses tools found in sociological studies of the self in illness.

Although I do not focus specifically on self-esteem, the issue arises indirectly in many interviews, especially with regard to the individual's faith in her ability to manage or overcome depression, and her view of herself in general as both a product of and causal factor in her development of depression. The individual's beliefs regarding her true self also tie in with her self-esteem. Susan Harter conducted a study which showed that the repeated performance of a false self lowers one's self-esteem, which in turn contributes to depression (Harter, 1997). However, the relationship could also perhaps be inverted, with depression and low self-esteem causing the individual to believe that her true self is not good enough and must be masked by a false self. Although I do not investigate this relationship per se, I explore issues surrounding authenticity and the selves which those interviewed choose to describe and present.

Deci and Ryan's (1991, 1995) self-determination theory postulates that competence, relatedness and autonomy are essential to the self. Competence is conceived as mastering particular skills and considering oneself capable and effective. Relatedness is the need to interact and connect with others, and autonomy is defined here as a need to act in ways that derive from the self. As Baumeister (1999: 13) explains:

Failing to fulfil the need for competence leaves the self feeling helpless, useless, and incompetent, whereas failing to fulfil the need for autonomy leaves the self feeling that its actions are dictated by external forces.

Kasser and Ryan contend that happiness and well-being depend on these "intrinsic needs". Their research found that people who focus on gaining "extrinsic goals" such as money and fame have a lower well-being (as measured by factors such as levels of anxiety, depression, self-actualisation and vitality) and that true self-esteem is based on a quest for competence, autonomy and meaningful relationships (Kasser & Ryan, 1993, 1996). This book examines the relationship between the self, control and well-being (specifically depression) from the opposite perspective. Rather than examining the self and control and measuring what effects different states of control have on well-being, this book focuses on one state of well-being – depression – and examines the relationship between the self and control vis-à-vis that state.

The Self in Existential Psychotherapy

The concept of the self that is most relevant to this investigation is that found within a particular strand of existential psychotherapy. Existential psychotherapy is based on the belief that the root of most psychological problems is when the individual comes face-to-face with the "givens of existence", resulting in an inner conflict (Yalom, 1980). According to Yalom, these givens (or ultimate concerns) are (1) death, (2) isolation, (3) meaninglessness and (4) freedom. I have changed the order in which they are normally presented in order to provide a brief overview of the first three themes before discussing the theme that arose repeatedly in the interviews – freedom.

(1) Death

According to Becker (1973), to be constantly aware of death would be too overwhelming, so one must be aware of death yet not be over-powered by this awareness. There are several mechanisms with which people deal with the reality of death. Becker (1973) and Yalom (1980) use the concept of the hero, in which people seek to become a hero (i.e. doing something that they think is valuable and will be remembered) in the hope that by doing so their memory will live on, and symbolically they will never die. Paul Tillich (1952) contends that facing death should mean not only facing the end of physical life but also the possibility of nonbeing. According to Tillich, nonbeing is another way to avoid death, as some people believe that if they do not really live, they will not really die. Avoiding relationships (interpreted as being) in order to avoid the pain of rejection (nonbeing) is one example of this.

Death also symbolises that over which humans have no knowledge and no control. Kierkegaard's view on this subject is taken from the biblical story of the Fall of Adam and Eve from the Garden of Eden. Here, humans emerge from instinctive animal action into a con-sciousness of our individuality, but simultaneously a consciousness of our death and decay. According to Kierkegaard, it is our awareness of our own death which is our greatest anxiety (Kierkegaard et al., 1980).

(2) Isolation

In existential therapy, isolation does not refer to interpersonal isolation (isolation from others) or intrapersonal isolation (isola-tion from parts of the self), but a deeper isolation (Yalom, 1980). No matter how close we can become to each other, we cannot escape the fact that we each enter the world alone and leave it alone. May and Yalom succinctly capture the point made by Mijuskovic (1979) that

there is a fundamental loneliness; the individual cannot escape the knowl-edge that (1) he or she constitutes others and (2) he or she can never fully share his consciousness with others. (May & Yalom, 1989: 378)

An inner conflict then exists between our awareness of this isolation and our wish to connect with others, to be protected and to be part of something greater than ourselves (May & Yalom, 1989). According to Heidegger, the desire for the security of being part of a group can motivate some to forego their individuality (Heidegger, 1962). Yet humans also find meaning for their lives through relationships (Buber, 1958).

(3) Meaninglessness

Meaning is a common thread throughout existential topics, as existential theory assumes that we always seek meaning in order to make our existence bearable (Becker, 1973). The question is whether we seek meaning (i.e. there is meaning in the world which we aim to discover) or whether we create it (i.e. our existence is devoid of meaning except the meaning we create). Thus, our inner conflict derives from being creatures who seek meaning thrown into a world apparently devoid of meaning (Yalom, 1980).

Jean-Paul Sartre maintained that "existence precedes essence" – that is, humans exist before they have a meaning in life. According to Sartre, there is no God to envisage a purpose for us before He brings us into existence, so we come into existence first and create a meaning for our own lives later (Sartre, 2007 [1947]). Viktor Frankl argued that meaning cannot be invented but must be discovered. He believed that meaning is so crucial that he based his "logotherapy" on the principles that life, no matter how wretched, always has meaning; our main motivation to live is to find this meaning; and we always have the freedom to discover meaning. According to Frankl, we can find meaning in life in three different ways:

1. by creating a work or doing a deed;
2. by experiencing something or encountering someone; and
3. by the attitude we take toward unavoidable suffering. (Frankl, 1959: 176)

(4) Freedom

Although freedom is usually seen in a positive light, in existentialism it is something to which one is "condemned" (Sartre, 1956). The individual is the architect of her own life, choices and behaviour, and with this freedom comes responsibility. For Jaspers, Kierkegaard, Nietzsche and Sartre, freedom means a complete freedom to define the self. Yet if it is true that we define ourselves and our world, then there is nothing to anchor or ground us – there is only an abyss or a void (May & Yalom, 1989). Our inner conflict arises from our awareness of this freedom on the one hand and a wish for something to ground us on the other hand (May & Yalom, 1989).

Karl Jaspers (1971), however, believes our freedom is limited by "boundary situations", which include death, suffering, guilt, chance and conflict. Otto Rank (1989) believes that the more an individual is unaware of the factors which limit his freedom, the more he is controlled by them. Yet, as Frankl (1959) found, even in circumstances when one's freedom is cut down to the minimum, such as it is in a concentration camp, one still has the most basic freedom – to decide the attitude one takes towards one's fate.

With freedom comes the responsibility that is then associated with the choices one has freely made. As Sartre (2007 [1947]) states, we are our choices, and must accept the responsibility that accompanies them. Encapsulated in this statement is the notion that the self ultimately consists of what we have control over. As Tillich states, "[m]an's particular nature is his power to create himself" (1960: 11). R. D. Laing, who is said to have been influenced by Sartre's existential theories, believed that society undermines individual freedom, and that people who have been diagnosed as mentally ill are simply victims of a "double-bind" in which society has placed them. These are situations in which the individual is left with an impossible choice and something becomes compromised – usually one's psychological stability (Laing & Esterson, 1970). Laing also believed that this double-bind occurs in families which place conflicting demands on their children. In *Sanity, Madness and the Family*, Laing and Esterson (1970) provide case studies which show how lies become perpetuated within families, making it difficult for a child to break out of their "bind" and reach the truth of their situation.

Cooper, Esterson, Foucault, Laing and Szasz led the antipsychiatry movement, rejecting the medical model of psychiatric disorder and arguing instead that they are simply labels placed on individuals who do not conform to societal norms and views of reality (Graham, 1986). In *The Divided Self* (1959), Laing proposes that psychiatric illnesses all have a psychological origin, and that medical treatments interfere with the natural course of the condition, which should cure itself. Here, Laing also attempts to get "inside the mind" of a schizophrenic and finds that if one listens carefully, a schizophrenic person's thoughts and behaviours are understandable, but they have an extreme insecurity which makes mundane circumstances seem threatening. In *Self and Others* (Laing, 1961), Laing further suggests that schizophrenia should be understood not as something which takes place inside one's head, but as a process which takes place between people, called the family interaction model.

Although Laing and the antipsychiatry movement provide an interesting application of existentialism to the practice of psychiatry, my analysis does not – and cannot – extend to lend support or otherwise to the larger claims made by antipsychiatry. Rather than attempting to ascertain the causes (psychological or otherwise) of depression, to question the psychiatric categories (although several interviewees certainly did) or to propose a new understanding of these categories, the analysis presented in this book of how experiences of depression may illuminate perceptions of the self reveals a striking resemblance to the Sartrean branch of existentialist philosophy which emphasises the importance of being aware of, and embracing, one's freedom to choose how one is to be. Nevertheless, Laing's approach has some relevance to this investigation in that the potential influence of social and family dynamics on the development of mental illness flags them as potential triggers for depression, of the sort discussed in Chapter 5. More than any other existential "given", those I interviewed repeatedly returned to the "given" of freedom and control in all aspects of the self explored throughout this book. Specifically, it is Sartre's emphasis on the optimism brought about by an awareness of one's freedom which implicitly arose within the interviews. By revealing how pivotal a sense of control is to views of the self – particularly to how one views one's future self – those I interviewed lend support to this aspect of Sartre's existentialism.

In contrast to other views such as the Socratic, with its emphasis on self-examination and understanding oneself (Nehamas, 1999), or the psychological view, in which authenticity means to live according to the values of one's "inner being" rather than one's society or upbringing (Wood *et al.*, 2008), interviewees viewed themselves as most "authentic" when they felt a greater degree of self-determination (or freedom). Ledermann, whose book explores existential therapy, expresses the notion thus, "[t]he person striving to achieve a greater freedom is also aiming at a greater degree of authenticity" (Ledermann, 1984: 3). The necessity of attaining a sense of freedom to attaining a sense of authenticity will become apparent in Chapter 4.

Situating the Book within Studies of the Self

Charles Taylor (1989: 34) asserts that "[w]hat I am as a self, my identity, is essentially defined by the way things have significance for me ... To ask what a person is, in abstraction from his or her self-interpretations, is to ask a fundamentally misguided question, one to which there couldn't in principle be an answer." It is for this reason that the phenomenology of people's experiences of depression, its significance for them and their self-interpretations can progress our understanding of the self. In pursuing this path, one must bear in mind that "the way things have significance" for the individual is necessarily informed by the gender and culture which the individual occupies. For instance, Carol Gilligan (1982) found that women define the self much more in terms of their relationships (mother, daughter, wife, etc.) than do men, who define themselves more in terms of independence and individuality than in terms of connection.[5]

Taylor (1989) highlights how the modern concept of the self is always rooted in terms of what is morally valued as good. This, in turn, differs from historical concepts of the self because what was valued was different, and there existed different narrative forms and different understandings of social ties. He also contends that, similarly, notions of "the good", narrative forms and understandings of social ties which are present in different cultures translate into different concepts of the self. As what is deemed valuable by the community is entwined with what is of significance to the individual, Taylor contends that culturally and historically embedded notions of morality are necessarily entwined with concepts of the self. Different concepts of the self are indeed evident across cultures (Cousins, 1989; Geertz, 1973; Kondo, 1990; Lienhardt, 1985; Markus & Kitayama, 1991; Triandis et al., 1993). Indeed, Geertz (1979) argues that the concept of the self is specific to the Western world. Any study of the self which incorporates people from different genders and cultural backgrounds would then need to take such factors into consideration to account for differences in notions of the self. Interviewing middle-class women in a Western society thus minimises the role that gender and cultural differences would have in explaining the different notions of the self which are presented.

Ascertaining how an illness affects the self helps us to learn more about the self. Sociological investigations of the self revolve around notions of congruence, coherence, consistency and discrepancy (Rogge, 2011), and much mental health research assumes self-consistency and self-congruence to be essential to the self (Grawe, 2004). While self-congruence has been the focus of many relatively recent sociological studies of the self in mental health (e.g. Ball & Orford, 2002; Burke, 1991; Kaufman & Johnson, 2004; Paul & Moser, 2006), other sociological studies have focused on the meanings of life events to individuals (e.g. Charmaz, 1983; Ezzy, 2001; Francis, 1997; Reynolds & Turner, 2008) as the ways in which individuals make sense of their social reality interconnects with their notions of self. It is with the latter focus that Chapter 5 is concerned, although, as the reader will see, I take a slightly different approach, focusing on the individual's perceptions and attributions of meaning. Rogge believes that, especially when teamed with qualitative methods, such an approach is "capable of providing a detailed account of an individual's concerns, meanings and life worlds. The neglect of inter-individual variance, for example as seen in life event research in positive psychology, can be countered by this approach" (Rogge, 2011: 61).

Initial sociological studies of chronic illness centred on Parson's (1951) sick role theory and labelling deviance (e.g. Gerhardt, 1989). More recently, approaches to this area have built on the work of Glaser and Strauss from their grounded theory perspective (Glaser & Strauss, 1967) with the aim of elucidating the meaning of the chronic illness experience to the individual. One influential idea within this literature is Bury's (1982) concept of chronic illness as a "biographical disruption". The literature has since developed this notion of disrupted biographies. Strauss and Corbin (1987) divide it into three aspects: biographical time, conception of self and bodily capacities. This book is concerned with the second of these aspects.

As several authors have found, chronic illnesses and acquired disabilities impact on and challenge the self, especially as they occur after an adult identity has been established (Bleuler, 1950; Brooks & Matson, 1987; Bury, 1982; Charmaz, 1991; Corbin & Strauss, 1987; Fine & Asch, 1988; Freud, 1958; Kraepelin, 1904; Schneider & Conrad, 1983; Sullivan, 1940). Such illnesses force the individual to come to terms with this challenge in a society which regards deviances from the norm as indications of both moral and physical inferiority (Weitz, 2001).

As Hydén (1997) notes, chronic illness changes the relationship of the individual with her body, the world and her self. The disruption of the individual's life also means a disruption of the individual's identity (Bury, 1982), as individuals are forced to adjust their life narratives and identities in relation to the illness (Hydén, 1997). Toombs (1988: 207) expresses the idea well when he writes that "[i]llness is experienced by the patient not so much as a specific breakdown in the mechanical functioning of the biological body, but more fundamentally as disintegration of his 'world'". This is evidenced by the way in which interviewees tell their story, for, in both my study and Hydén's, individuals do not talk so much about their symptoms before and after treatment but rather about what happened to their "self" before and after (Hydén, 1995). This idea is also demonstrated in the literature on narratives, in which recovery is presented as realising the authentic self (Maslow, 1976; Stevenson & Knudsen, 2008), restoring or reconstructing the self (Kohut, 1977; Williams, 1984), regenerating the self (Hawkins, 1990), creating a new self (Ridge, 2008; Schafer, 1992) or discovering a newborn self (Hawkins, 1993).

The notion of "stories" and "narratives" becomes useful here as a way of portraying the meanings present in these transformations (McAdams,

2001). Bruner (1986), McAdams (2001) and Polkinghorne (1988) suggest that the issues under discussion here are best understood through the "language of narrative". This is because, as Widdershoven (1993) contends, a life and its story are inseparable, as its meaning resides within the story. Life stories examine a life, or part of it, through the eyes of the individual, and are essentially narratives as they are underpinned by narrative discourse (Bertaux, 1981). However, life stories are usually recounted in a storytelling format, giving their narratives the "flavour of fiction, or of fictional accounts of what happened in a person's life" (Denzin, 1989: 42). They also refer implicitly to "the totality of a person's experience" (Bertaux & Kohli, 2009: 43).

Riessman (1993) emphasises the connection between life stories and identity, as individuals essentially *become* their autobiographical narratives. Giddens also states that "[a] person's identity is not to be found in behaviour, nor – important though this is – in the reactions of others, but in the capacity *to keep a particular narrative going*" (1991: 54). In contrast, others such as Strawson (2004) believe that identity need not take a narrative structure. While the "language of narrative" will at times be useful in this book, I do not wish to say that identity, or the experiences recounted by the interviewees, is only to be understood through this language, as experience can occur in different registers.

Research into life stories shares a connection with autobiographical memory, as the latter also uses a life story to help define the self (McAdams, 2001). Although this book elicits memories from interviewees as they recount their "illness narratives", there are some important differences between it and studies in autobiographical memory. First, although an investigation into the individual's account of how her depression fits into her past, present and future self involves uncovering memories which are key to her account, I do not presuppose that memories must be associated with meaningful aspects of the self and depression, whereas studies in autobiographical memory do not allow for the absence of an associated memory as a meaningful possibility. Second, autobiographical memory constitutes a wide range of personal experiences and information, whereas life stories are more limited in their scope, made up of a series of "temporally and thematically organized scenes and scripts that together constitute identity" (McAdams, 2001: 117). This point of difference is even further accentuated in the following chapters, which work within an even more delimited set of "scenes and scripts" known as "self stories".

Self stories, in contrast to life stories, focus on the self in relation to a particular experience. Although they, too, are personal narratives, they are recounted by the individual in relation to a certain type of experience (Denzin, 1989). Denzin, for example, examined how alcoholics represent themselves to each other through their self stories in Alcoholics Anonymous meetings (Denzin, 1989). In seeking women's stories of their depression and recovery and their representations of their self in relation to depression, I elicit self stories rather than life stories. In doing so, I not only focus on the self specifically in relation to depression rather than their life as a whole but also embrace the "multiplicity, variability, and context specificity" of the small story level which allows for the multiple identities that can emerge in a conversational context (Bell, 2009: 282). As Georgakopoulou writes, big stories represent a "long-standing privileging of ... a unified, coherent, autonomous, reflected up and rehearsed self" (2006: 128), whereas small stories are a new trend in narrative " ... that allows for, indeed sees the need for a scrutiny of fleeting, contingent, fragmented and multiple selves" (2006: 128). Here, the image of the "bricoleur" (Lévi-Strauss, 1966) becomes useful, as the self within these self stories is constructed from the available material or "story lines" at hand in society (Hydén, 1995), such as those within the media, literature, friends, family and practitioners. As in self stories, the self in the "bricoleur" metaphor is "ineluctably local" (Geertz, 1983), as our biographical work consists of pulling together facets of our personal history for our current purposes (Gubrium & Holstein, 1995; Gubrium & Holstein, 1998; Gubrium et al., 1994).

This book's slant towards a small story approach is driven by my desire to avoid the temptation to mould the data into a coherent narrative and instead to allow for the possibility of insight that can be gained from the shifting and sometimes contradictory positions that individuals can take. See, for example, Singh's (2005) study of parents of children diagnosed with Attention Deficit Hyperactivity Disorder (ADHD) which, in presenting the contradictions in parents' dosing decisions, reveals their underlying ideas concerning authenticity. The small story approach is thus well suited to examining the self through the lens of depression.

Within qualitative studies of health and illness, the "work-of-living" with health and disease has been categorised into five phases by Jensen and Allen (1994): (1) recognising the threat; (2) defending and protecting the self; (3) reconciling the change; (4) learning to live again; and (5) living again. Alternatively, Morse and Johnson (1991) have categorised the trajectory into four phases: (1) uncertainty; (2) disruption; (3) striving to regain the self; and (4) regaining wellness. Within studies of the impact of chronic illness on the self, the majority of the literature is split between describing it either as a biographical disruption (Bury, 1982), a loss of the self (Brody, 1994; Charmaz, 1983), a deconstruction/reconstruction of the self (or narrative reconstruction) (Davidson & Strauss, 1992; Hydén, 1995; Sells *et al.*, 2004; Williams, 1984; Williams, 1997), or as the self becoming redefined or reshaped (Romano *et al.*, 2010; Wisdom *et al.*, 2008).

Although I draw on this literature to inform and contrast with my analysis of the interview material, particularly in Chapter 2, I refrain from framing the significance of depression to the self entirely within the frameworks described above as such frameworks risk imposing certain assumptions onto the material. For instance, is depression necessarily experienced as a biographical disruption? As shown later, this is not always the case. By the same token, narrative reconstruction, which, as Williams (1997: 209) describes, is "an attempt to reconstitute and repair ruptures between body, self, and the world by linking-up and interpreting different aspects of biography in order to realign present and past and self with society" was not undertaken, or seen as necessary, by some of the women I interviewed as they did not consider that there was anything to "repair".

Chapter 2 focuses more specifically on the ways in which depression is described in relation to the self. Given this focus, the themes identified in the chapter differ slightly to the themes identified in the literature on the self in chronic illness more generally. Sometimes, the difference in themes is more of a difference in name than in thematic content; for instance, the following quotation is presented by Wisdom *et al.* as an example of the "loss of self" theme:

[Bipolar disorder] is a disease that for me, literally steals me from myself – a disease that executes me and then forces me to stand and look down at my corpse. It is what the criminal lawyer in me calls a medical examiner's antithesis: life by strangulation (Hartmann, 2002). (As quoted in Wisdom *et al.*, 2008: 491)

The quote could also be considered an example of the "enemy of the self" or "illness" themes presented in Chapter 2. The chapter draws on some of the themes present in the literature on the self in depression rather than in the literature on chronic illness more generally, for three reasons: (1) the former themes have been developed specifically in relation to depression narratives; (2) not all interviewees were of the view that their depression is a chronic illness, which challenges the degree to which themes in narratives of the self and chronic illness are applicable to depression; and (3) the themes within the literature on the self in depression align more closely with the terminology that interviewees used to describe their depression.

Defining Authenticity

Just as there are many ways to define the self, so it is with authenticity. I will here present a few contrasting definitions of authenticity (which are by no means exhaustive of the variety) before presenting the definition I will be working with in this book. This book is not concerned with what comprises authenticity in a metaphysical sense. Rather, it is concerned with authenticity in the existential sense – that is, the sense in which it is invoked in discussions of responsibility and moral psychology. That is, what it is to think, feel and act in a way that expresses what one truly is. As Bernard Williams explains, it is "the idea that some things are in some sense really you, or express what you are, and others aren't" (Guignon, 2004: viii). Another connotation, according to Monica Betzler, is "being oneself". As Betzler (2009) notes, if the term is not to be interpreted superficially, it must mean that it is possible to not be oneself in the sense of betraying or failing oneself.

While these descriptions allude to what it is to be true to oneself, several scholars have also linked authenticity closely with autonomy such that one of the conditions of autonomy is authenticity (e.g. Betzler, 2009; Dworkin, 1976; Meyers, 1989; Ryan & Deci, 1999). For instance, Carver and Scheier (2000: 285) describe how part of what constitutes autonomy is not only to be free from external impediments but also to act authentically, according to what one truly values. They write:

In an early draft of our commentary, one of us wrote that self-determination can be exercised by stepping onto a busy highway without looking, but that's not right. Internal perceived locus of causality could (we assume) be reflected in such an act, if the impetus to act originates inside the person's mind. So could self-governance, in the sense that the decision to act is made on one's own with no outside interference (the dictionary definition of autonomy). The act could be freely chosen. But upon further review, such an act probably would not be autonomous in the Deci and Ryan view, because it fails to advance a value of the true self, and indeed may conflict with an important value of the true self (desire for self-preservation).

One problem with definitions of autonomy and authenticity such as these is that they are conceived as asocial, giving the impression that the true self is either disconnected from, or in opposition to, outside agendas. This view of authenticity is in stark contrast to Taylor's, in which authenticity is not just an individualistic struggle but one which must involve a connection with one's social and moral context and with projects larger than oneself in order to derive meaning (Taylor, 1991a). In other words, external influences can be viewed as part of the dynamic and mutually influencing relationship between a person and her environment. The

human mind, brain and behaviour are socially embedded and it is difficult, if not impossible, to separate them from the social context in which
they operate.

Another problem with determining authenticity is that it may be difficult
to distinguish one's authentic self from one's ideal self (if an authentic self
even exists). That is, the desire to view oneself as authentic in certain mental/
emotional/behavioural states and not others may be motivated by the desire
to present one's ideal self or best self as authentic, which may or may not
coincide with one's true self. Relatedly, Loe and Cuttino (2008: 309) write:

> If an individual's goal is always "authenticity," the phenomenological emotional
> experience of feeling true to oneself (Taylor, 1992; Vannini, 2006), then medicine
> can create a sense of inner conflict as the gap widens between perceived "authen-
> tic" and "ideal" identities.

Chapter 4 not only provides support that this sense of inner conflict
indeed exists among some individuals but also goes some way towards
unpacking *why* it exists – that medication's perceived challenge to self-
determination lies at the heart of this conflict.

In the chapters that follow, my empirical investigation explores what
the phenomenology of authenticity and the self in different states
(depressed, medicated and so on) might tell us about these concepts.
The potential for the phenomenology of these concepts to further our
knowledge of them is particularly salient in the case of authenticity
because what it is to *be* authentic is often understood to be intimately
tied with what it is to *feel* authentic. In fact, as mentioned above, several
authors regard authenticity as an affective state of feeling true to oneself
(e.g. Erickson, 1995; Gordon, 1989; Harter, 2005; Salmela, 2005;
Schwalbe, 1993; Turner & Schutte, 1981). Asking individuals about
the states in which they feel they are their "real self" and why they feel
that way reveals a common thread within what authenticity means to
them. If we take authenticity to be intimately tied to feeling true to
oneself, then these accounts support certain facets of the way authenticity
has been defined thus far while challenging others.

The concept of authenticity I support is one which allows for the
influence of society and morality, and places autonomy (or self-determination) front and centre, such that the state in which the individual possesses
autonomy determines the state in which one is authentic.[6] (In fact, according to Trilling (1971: 122), one connotation of the Greek for authenticity
(*authentheo*) is "being in control".) Such a definition implies that an action
can be considered my own and authentic even if it is not consistent with my
best intentions, as long as I retain control of my actions. Such an account of
authenticity also allows us to say that one need not be reflective in order to

be authentic. As long as the individual is in control of her actions, she can be considered to express her authentic self, regardless of whether she reflects on her self-state or not, and regardless of whether her actions are in line with her ideal, or even best, self. This is the definition of authenticity I favour and which is suggested by, and consistent with, the empirical evidence in this book. Chapter 4 provides support for, and suggests an added nuance to, the relationship between autonomy and authenticity.

Defining Control

The interviews contained in this book advance our knowledge of the self and authenticity by providing empirical support for particular aspects or interpretations of these concepts. The individuals I spoke with made it apparent that their sense of self depends upon their sense of control. In other words, individuals indicated that differences in how they view their self depend on differences in their sense of control. A sense of control was invoked in different ways depending on the context. For instance, when speaking of authenticity, the sense of control that the individual invoked was self-determination. When speaking of one's future self, individuals invoked a sense of control over future episodes of depression as being significant. As such, it does not make sense to provide a hard definition of control here as I have done for the self and authenticity in order to show how the empirical evidence corroborates or contrasts with such a definition. Instead, I will clarify the different senses in which "control" is invoked by the interviewees in order for the reader to understand the nature of this crucial lever.

It was clear from the context of the interviews and my follow-up questions that those I interviewed used "control" in slightly different ways depending on the subject of discussion. In Chapter 2, there were those who described themselves as being an "out of control self" when depressed or manic, and those who felt that depression was out of their control. Some professed to feeling both ways at different times. In either case, their sense of control was used to explain their view of depression. First, "control" is used in a similar sense to "self-control", meaning an ability to control their thoughts, emotions and behaviours such that they would not become *depressive* thoughts, emotions and behaviours. Berkowitz's (1982: 225) definition of self-control as "the ability to intentionally manipulate covert mental events, most notably inner speech and images, in order to regulate one's own behaviour" is the most relevant definition here and is common to many other understandings of self-control. "Control over depression" was also invoked by the individual as an ability to change her environment or to take action such that she would not become depressed. Chapter 5 also invokes both these senses of control – either the ability to control one's thoughts, emotions and behaviours such that they would not become *depressive* thoughts, emotions and behaviours; or the ability to change one's environment such that one would not become depressed.

Closely linked to both these senses of "control" is "self-determination" or "autonomy". Chapters 3 and 4 rely on this nuance of the concept more so than the other chapters. The more the women felt they could determine aspects of their self (i.e. their choices, actions, behaviours and so on), the more they felt authentic. Conversely, the more they felt that another force (e.g. a biochemical imbalance or an antidepressant) was determining these aspects of their self, the less control they felt they had over them. This is congruent with the dictionary definition of autonomy being the ability to act, choose, etc. without external impediments. Autonomy has also become closely intertwined with what it means to be authentic, so what these women say about authenticity also has implications for its relationship with autonomy.

Overview

A typical journey through depression moves from its first appearance, to diagnosis, to treatment (medical or otherwise) and finally to recovery or stabilisation. The journey may not be linear and may go back and forth or skip a step or two, but the women I spoke to had been diagnosed with depression, had undergone treatment for it and felt better. They were therefore in a position to provide insight into the impact of each stage of depression and recovery on their self. What emerges is a relationship between perceived control and the self. Each chapter elucidates the contours of this relationship as it arises within each stage of depression and recovery.

Chapter 2 presents the different ways that depression is viewed by the individuals I spoke with and is in keeping, as much as possible, with the ways in which it is described by the individuals themselves. It also examines the contexts in which those views are presented, the ways they are frequently combined and the reasons why individuals choose one theme over another or a combination of themes. Chapter 3 focuses on how individuals first react to their diagnosis and what impact it has on their sense of self. Prior explorations of how individuals react to being diagnosed with depression have documented shock, fear, relief and denial. While these reactions were also voiced by the women I spoke to, my exploration of why they reacted in the way that they did shows that their reactions were premised on a biomedical understanding of depression at the point of diagnosis.

In Chapter 4, I examine how individuals view the role of medication in relation to their responsibility for recovery, as well as their reflections on the notion of an authentic self, what they believe to be essential for authenticity and how/whether psychiatric medication presents a challenge to it. In meta-syntheses of the literature in this area conducted by Malpass *et al.* (2009) and Khan *et al.* (2007), control has been recognised as an important issue in treatment for depression, influencing how individuals feel about their medication as well as their self on medication. I shall also propose that perceived control (*qua* self-determination) plays a pivotal role in individuals' views of authenticity, adding detail to the part it is understood to play within individuals' perceptions of the self in depression.

Chapter 5 demonstrates that an individual's beliefs about how depression began can be significant for her views of depression and its role in her life – particularly its role in her future self. I shall show that those who considered most of their episodes to have been triggered by events or circumstances in their lives were more likely to believe that their depression could in future be overcome, whereas those who did not consider most of their episodes to have been triggered were more likely to believe their depression to be chronic. The final chapter will then present the implications of the previous chapters for our understanding of the self and the way depression is treated.

2 The View from Inside
The Variety of Views of Depression

Overlapping Views

J.K. Rowling describes depression as "[t]he absence of hope. That very deadened feeling, which is so very different from feeling sad" (Bennett, 2013). She embodied that description in the characters of the Dementors in her Harry Potter novels. Winston Churchill is said to have described it as his "black dog". When examining the phenomenology of depression, one soon realises that depression is experienced in different ways by different people. We also know that individuals may have more than one, sometimes even contradictory, set of views of depression. Yet what is less known is *why* individuals come to espouse a particular view, or set of views, of depression.

Most of the women I spoke with expressed more than one view of depression. This finding contrasts with the emphasis that some biographical and narrative researchers have placed on narrative coherence – particularly thematic coherence – of self-narrative (McAdams, 2006). Yet as several such as Rogge (2011) note, individuals vary in the extent to which they are consistent in the narrative they use, and specifically the extent to which they view their diagnosis as biographically disruptive (Richardson *et al.*, 2006). This chapter will explore these differences within individual narratives in more detail. In particular, possible reasons for the frequent blending of views of depression among the women I interviewed are discussed towards the end of the chapter where the most commonly used combinations – that of "depression as an illness" and "depression as a part of the self" – are examined in more detail.

The Venn diagram in Figure 2.1 represents how the views of depression are interrelated. It shows which views overlapped with each other, and (roughly) the extent of overlap. For example, the degree of overlap between "part of the self" and "illness" circles reflects the number of interviewees who viewed depression as a part of their self as well as an illness. Some even viewed depression in three ways – a part of the self, an illness as well as a catalyst for change.

It is possible that women tend to use more than one way of describing depression because one view of depression is the individual's preferred

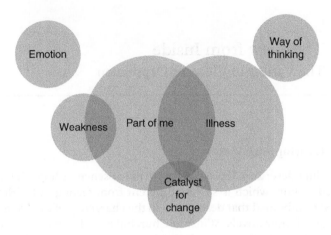

Figure 2.1 Overlaps in views of depression

view whereas the second (or third) is invoked either for convenience or ease of reference. Alternatively, individuals may change their view over time, and their expression of these different views during their interview may be a testament to both their old and current views. One interpretation of the most common combination of "illness" and "part of the self" is that depression is seen as an illness which resides in the self and, owing to the extent of its influence on and duration in the individual's life, is inseparable from it. Yet another interpretation of this combination of views is that depression is seen primarily as an illness, but one which has a significant impact *on* the self. Finally, an illness versus part of the self viewpoint sees the two views at odds with each other and is often seen in the context of the interviewee trying to decide where to assign responsibility for certain behaviours. The last section here explores why and how interviewees combine the two views or pit them against each other.

Depression as an Illness

There is a range of reasons for why women describe depression as an illness. Some of those I spoke with stated that their view of depression as an illness was probably influenced by their clinician, others they had spoken to or the literature they had read. A few women said they described depression as an illness because depression made life harder for them; a few said it made them depart from what they considered to be their normal mode of function; and a few others saw it as an illness because (or when) it affects one's physical health. Some described depression as an illness because for them it shares the quality of feeling out of their control as other illnesses do.[1]

Most of the interviewees who described depression as an illness were diagnosed with bipolar depression and stated that they had a family history of depression. In contrast, the majority of those who described depression as a part of their self were diagnosed with unipolar depression and only half said they had a family history of depression. This relationship may be the result of a number of factors. First, as the chapter on diagnosis (Chapter 3) discusses, the public tends to view bipolar depression as "more serious" or "more biomedical" than unipolar depression, and those I interviewed expressed similar views. Second, if a particular trait is believed to be inherited, it can take on a deterministic element and come to be seen as inevitable. Thus, if an individual believes her depression to be inherited, this may well cause her to view depression differently. This trend within those who described depression as an illness, in contrast with those who described it as a part of their self, may thus be a reflection of how difficult it is to disentangle an individual's beliefs about her diagnosis, knowledge of her family history and views of her condition.

Some interviewees said they preferred viewing mental illness as akin to physical illnesses because they felt that this view avoids the shame associated with the former:

Heather: At the time, I felt like depression made me a failure, but having come out of the other side now I see it as you get ill, you go to the doctor, you get better. Why should it be any different for having a mental illness as opposed to a physical illness? So I'm not ashamed of it anymore.

Women such as Heather self-reflexively stated that describing depression as an illness is a way of giving it the same status as physical illnesses. In their view, this legitimises depression such that it makes as much sense to blame the sufferer of depression for her condition as it is to blame a sufferer of influenza. As a strategic move, as well as one often encouraged by the medical profession, the illness view is supposed to establish depression as a condition which is reified beyond the self, separate from "normal" sadness and worthy of medical attention (Helman, 1988; Lester & Gask, 2009). This view removes any reason for shame, because as an illness, depression is represented as "beyond rational mastery", with its representation "relegated to the realm of the body over which we have no conscious control" (Kokanovic et al., 2008: 464). The prevalence of this view among the women interviewed, and its instant association with the sick role and all that goes with it, demonstrates the power of the biomedical narrative within the illness view. As Estroff describes, "[t]he clear association of medical/clinical models with self-labelling also suggests that the mantle of medicalisation or the 'no-fault' provisions of having an illness (Parsons, 1972) are embraced by many" (Estroff *et al.*, 1991: 361–362).

This perception of course ignores the fact that the individual to some extent can still control many illnesses. The risk of acquiring lung cancer, for instance, can be greatly reduced by not smoking. The risk of acquiring heart disease can be minimised by maintaining a healthy diet and lifestyle and so on. The illness view avoids seeing depression as a judgement of character or an indication of moral failure. It thus appears to succeed in separating depression from the moral self but, as described later, in practice does not succeed in dissociating depression from the self completely. Moreover, as discussed in Chapter 4, the relief of some responsibility afforded by the simple illness view is a double-edged sword, for a reduction of responsibility also means a reduction of control.

The term "illness" as it was used in the interviews was a flexible one, and was adopted for a variety of reasons. A number of researchers have found that individuals diagnosed with depression find it helpful to view it as a biomedical illness (as Zoe says below), but that commitment to this view is stronger during the initial stages of depression and is more likely to be combined or replaced by another view later (Badger & Nolan, 2006; Givens *et al.*, 2006; Holt, 2007; Knudsen *et al.*, 2002). Alternatively, individuals can simply be conflicted in their views. Most of those I interviewed indeed viewed depression in more than one way. As I probed their reasons for adopting the illness view, I began to see the nuances behind this depiction of depression.

Zoe is one of the interviewees who views depression as an illness because she feels it shares that "out of control" quality with physical illnesses. At the same time, Zoe implies that depression is unlike other illnesses because it straddles both the biological and the psychosocial sphere in its likely causes, symptoms and treatment more than other illnesses:

So why wouldn't you expect to have control over [your depression]?

As an illness, I suppose it's just easier to think about because you can't really blame anything but it just makes the most sense to think of it like that. Yeah and then there's not much control you have over lots of illnesses. But like other illnesses, there's things you can do to help. But it is difficult because it's at the interface between biology and social interactions and how it works.

That's an interesting point. So it helps to see it as an illness. Do you think that's an accurate way of seeing it?

I mean, but that's not to say that I don't think I have any responsibility to help myself, if you see what I mean. It's not just saying it's an illness and there's nothing I can do about it. So I think because it's at the interface, it's an illness that you can also tackle with psychological techniques. But then it's still an illness, it's just that it can be tackled with thoughts as well.

Whereas women such as Zoe relied on a flexible definition of illness which includes both mental and physical symptoms, a few women supported their view that depression is an illness because it has physical as well as mental effects. This justification implies that unless a condition has physical symptoms, it is not really an illness. Wendy provides an example of this view as she makes a sharp demarcation between the mental and the physical in her definition of when depression becomes an illness:

Have you ever heard people describe [depression] as an illness? And what do you think about that?

[...] I think the physical aspects that can be cured, like not being able to walk or hold a pen and write, that is an illness and it can be cured by drugs or whatever. Talking in that case wouldn't exactly help, but the way of thinking and the different way of thinking – that's not an illness. That just *is*.

So are the physical things an illness because they are physical?

I'd say actually yes I'd say so, because you really can't . . . I mean not being able to walk when there's nothing wrong with your legs, that's not normal. Whereas for me, thinking in a particular way, that *is* normal for me, whereas not being able to walk is *not* normal for me.

Wendy also touches on another justification used by a few other women for the illness model of depression, which is that it departs from their normal mode of function. This view is similar to the definition of disease as whatever departs from "normal species functioning" (as described by Christopher Boorse (1977)).[2] Ingrid provides an example of this view:

You know normal people don't sleep in bed all day. They go to work. I want a job. I don't want to be in bed all day. I don't want to be sitting at home. I want to be out there like everybody else. That's how I see it as an illness.

Wendy and Ingrid are among those who make such a distinction between illness and non-illness, and it is one that appears analogous to the distinction made by medical sociologists between "disease" and "illness" – disease being the medical pathology/objective state of the body (i.e. something we can measure) and illness being the subjective experience of disorder (physical, psychological and social). Fredrik Svenaeus summarises it thus:

[t]he line of demarcation between normal being-in-the-world and abnormal being-in-the-world certainly cannot be determined with the precision of the sphygmomanometer (with which one measures blood pressure) or the sensitivity of a tissue biopsy (with which one can detect the presence of cancer). This fact should come as no surprise, however, given the nature of phenomenological investigations, and the characteristics of mental illness in general. Recall the DSM-IV criteria for a depressive episode quoted above: the episode should cause "clinically significant distress or impairment in social, occupational, or other important areas of functioning." This is a life-world matter, dependent not only upon how things "really are," but also upon how the person and people around him (including family, friends, and the doctor) interpret them to be. In the domain of illness, in contrast to the scientifically more objective domain of disease, the question of normality is in the end always anchored in normative judgments. (Svenaeus, 2007: 161)

While Wendy and Ingrid use the term "illness" instead of "disease", what that term refers to, for them, is a state which deviates from what is normal for the species (on Ingrid's definition) or what is normal for the individual (on Wendy's definition). In either case, they seek to anchor depression within "the scientifically more objective domain of disease" as distinct from the more subjective "life-world matter". Of course, the problem with such a distinction is that while sphygmomanometers and biopsies may take accurate measurements, the point at which a result is deemed to be problematic, and therefore classified as disease, still involves a normative judgement and is not always clear-cut. The difference may be that for certain conditions, such as a broken bone, there is much more agreement as to what the problem is and how it should be fixed than is the case for other conditions, such as mental illness (Hughes & Ramplin, 2012). In other words, there are values inherent in all diagnoses, but there is more agreement concerning the values inherent in some diagnoses compared with others. Moreover, something may deviate from "normal species functioning" but not necessarily be problematic. Regardless of the ease with which we can separate fact from value, or disease from illness, it is noteworthy that some of the women draw on such a distinction in order to separate depression from their self.

An alternative interpretation of the illness view is that it functions as a mechanism to separate, and in doing so protects, the individual's core self from her malfunctioning body (Czuchta & Johnson, 1998; Register, 1987). An anonymous mental health service user, for example, writes that recognising that he had an illness enabled him to then look to the part of his self which he considered separate from the illness in order to regain hope of moving on (Anonymous, 1989). Deegan also writes that "the most important vocation for persons struggling with mental illness is the work of becoming one's self *in spite* of one's illness" (Deegan, 1989: 143) (emphasis added). Yet individuals espouse diverse definitions of "depression as illness" and, as described later, do not necessarily believe that the "illness" and the "self" are mutually exclusive. It is a finding which also problematises any attempt to apply the notion of "biographical disruption" to such cases. As Fox (1993: 146) observes, the focus on biographical disruption "serves to 'fabricate' a subject who is effectively 'trapped' within her/his 'pained' body and is required to 'adjust' or 'adapt' to the limitation this engenders". For those who were able to separate the "illness" from the "self", it could indeed be said that the self was experienced as having to adjust to the disruption wrought by the "illness". However, most of those interviewed did not consistently hold to this concept. Hence, it is difficult to say whether, and to what extent, the individual's biography had been disrupted.

Depression as a Part of the Self

About a third of those I interviewed viewed depression primarily as a part of who they are.[3] Of these, half felt that depression had gradually developed at the same time that their character was forming, rendering it difficult to distinguish whether depression had caused certain mental, emotional and behavioural tendencies to develop, or whether the direction of influence went the other way. Yet what they felt was almost certain was that it was now difficult to extricate depression from their self – whether it was seen as an established character trait which flared up now and then, or an "old friend" or partner who feels like part of them simply because it has been with them for so long, or a warning sign that not all is well with their life and something had to change.

Some women felt that depression is a part of who they are due to the length of time they had experienced it or the number of times it had recurred. A couple of the interviewees were similar to those in David Karp's book *Speaking of Sadness* in that at first they did not think what they had was an illness, but rather a personal failing. Yet when their low mood persisted after they felt the reasons for it had disappeared, they came to the conclusion that it must be an illness related to a lack of serotonin. Karp and most of those he interviewed came to the conclusion that because any external reasons for depression had disappeared, the cause must be biological (Karp, 1996). Among those I interviewed, however, there were also individuals who had the opposite view – that because external reasons had disappeared, the cause might lie within the self. This finding became apparent during interview analysis, and the sample size for each view was too small to be able to speculate as to why some saw the persistence of depression despite the absence of external reasons as an indication of a biochemical problem at its root rather than a sign that they needed to reassess themselves or their lives.

I will, however, present Barbara's story as she was one of the few women whose recurrent experiences of depression caused her to rethink its possible causes. Rather than thinking of depression as something transient, she began to consider whether the recurrence of depressive thoughts was a reflection of some deep-seated belief.

So has your impression of [depression] changed over the years?

Yeah I guess [...] I saw it as really I guess like a medical thing. I guess like "Oh it's just a chemical imbalance in the brain and sometimes I feel depressed so I shouldn't worry about it." I think that just meant that I didn't really deal with any of the issues that were making me feel bad.

So how did that change?

And that changed more when I started to get more depressed and then I couldn't really work out ... because it went on for longer and it was worse ... I wasn't really able to say to myself, "Oh this is just something that happens sometimes and it'll go away", because I started to see, "Well actually these are the things that I really think. *Maybe I really think these things.*" So maybe which part of it is really me? (emphasis added)

Here, Barbara expresses how the internal conflict between viewing depression as a chemical imbalance versus viewing it as part of the self can manifest itself. For women such as Barbara, a realisation that something more serious was wrong caused them to look inward to examine the cause. As Barbara indicates, this inward search was a process of self-discovery. Perhaps not surprisingly, most of the women who viewed depression as a catalyst for change also fell into this category. Insight achieved through counselling or other means often made them conclude that at the root of their depression was a mistaken or ill-founded belief about themselves or the world, as Barbara again illustrates:

The main thing that helped me improve I would say was counselling and feminism [...] It was really helpful talking about some of the things and the hang-ups that I'd had that I'd never really talked about. And it was weird because it wasn't like I hadn't talked about them because I'd actively not wanted to talk about them, it was just because I hadn't consciously thought about them enough.

And loads of stuff from my course – like I was doing an anthropology class on colonialism and learning loads about how social stereotyping works and different social pressures and loads of analyses about different power relations. It just made me realise that all the things I'd been feeling, I'd been blaming it all on myself but actually I'd been insecure, but all of the things that have been coming out has been the result of me picking up social stereotypes as well and feeling like I had to be this way.

Of those who viewed depression as a part of who they are, it is telling that only two viewed it solely as such. That is, the vast majority of those who primarily viewed depression as a part of their self also incorporated views such as the illness model, or the catalyst for change model, into various aspects of the way they view depression.

Depression as a Catalyst for Change

Just over a quarter of the women I interviewed said they felt that depression prompted them to gain insight and to change aspects of themselves or their lives. However, only a few women focused on this aspect as their primary view of depression. These women saw the changes they made as a result of having had depression as more than just minor additions to their lives. Instigating change, they believed, was depression's primary function. Predictably, this is why all the women who viewed depression as a catalyst for change said they would not choose to permanently remove depression from their lives. To them, it is their mind or their body's way of telling them that something is wrong and needs to change, or forces them to come to terms with aspects of themselves or their past. Gail describes this idea here:

Do you think, if you could press a button, theoretically, that would ensure that you would get rid of depression forever, would you press it?

No, because that's the best way to know how you kind of get away from your true self again. If you don't get any signs on the way, then you can really go a long way from who you're supposed to be, and then maybe you realise when it's too late. So I would not do it, no.

This idea is mirrored in the literature by authors such as Siegel (1990) who hypothesise that individuals become ill because they "need" their illness, or who attribute their achievements and personality changes to their illness (Butler & Rosenblum, 1991; Higgins, 1992). Alternatively, Hydén (1995) would describe such a psychological change as a switch from being merely a character in one's own life to becoming the author.

Williams might describe this group as having lost their "personal *telos* and sense of identity" through their depression experience, as he describes a case of a woman with rheumatoid arthritis who "saw her illness as the bodily expression of a suppression of herself" and "the stress of events and the suppression of herself as merely components in the social process of being a wife and a mother" (Williams, 1997: 199). Yet a loss of identity only describes half the story for women such as Gail, because having recognised that they had lost "who you're supposed to be", they described that this recognition then catalysed them into changing course or "regaining their self". Gail's view is instead akin to what Frank (1991) describes as a "dangerous opportunity", whereby the destruction of the self caused by depression provides an opportunity to create a more authentic self. The catalyst for change view can also be understood in terms of Radley and Green's (1985, 1987) concept of secondary gain, which Herzlich (1973) refers to as "illness as liberator". Although in reference to the liberation from the usual burdens of work afforded by an illness, and the alternative avenues of fulfilment which can result, the phrase is nevertheless apt here. Other authors would portray this transformation as a new meaning to life and a change in values which emerges from the struggle to make sense of the illness experience (Cobb & Hamera, 1986; Hall, 1990; McLean, 1991).

A variation on this way of thinking but which I still consider part of the "catalyst for change" viewpoint is the view that it is not depression as such but the difficult *life experiences* that individuals had which acted as catalysts for their character development. According to this type of "catalyst for change" view, reflecting on and recovering from their hardship caused them to learn, grow and strengthen their personality. An extract from Anne's interview is provided here to illustrate this view:

So do you think it's a part of your character, or just a passing thing, or an illness or ... ?

What? Which aspect?

Depression.

Hmmm. That's a good question. No I don't think it's a part of my character. It's a passing thing. It's because of the circumstances mostly [. . .]

Ah that's very interesting. So do you think depression has changed you as a person?

I don't know if it's the depression or the experience that I had – going through difficult periods in my life and getting through these periods – it teaches you a lot. You feel more experienced and now I think I'm more ... I have more resistance to shocks coming from the outside.

As there are some like Anne who differentiate between the experience of depression and the difficult circumstances which they believe prompted their depression, this differentiation adds a nuance to the "catalyst for change" view of depression, and one which has not appeared in accounts of depression so far. The difference may appear slight, but it is meaningful, because what Anne is saying is that she feels more resilient now, such that she would probably not dip into depression in response to a stressful period in the first place. Whereas for Gail, a depressive mood serves as an indicator for her that something in her life must change.

Those who described their depression primarily as a catalyst for change were diagnosed with unipolar depression and felt they tended to experience something in their lives that triggered their depression. They were also much more hopeful and optimistic about their future than any other group. Some of the women outside this group who did not experience a trigger felt guilty because, in their eyes, not experiencing a trigger meant that they had no right to be depressed, or that experiencing one would have at least made it easier to explain and justify their depression to others. In a similar sense, a trigger provides for a narrative that weaves into the individual's life. Their depressions are easier to understand, and hence easier to relate to, than those whose depressions arise seemingly out of nowhere. But when depression causes the individual to discover something about herself, to learn something new, to rethink her past or her future, her goals and values or the way she lives her life, then it goes beyond simply providing her with a neater narrative – it begins to serve a purpose. There is then even more cause for optimism because not only did the individual learn from and overcome depression in the past but if it happens again then, according to this view, it would probably happen for a reason.

For women who view depression as a catalyst for change, depression ceases to be something to fear and instead becomes an indicator that something in their lives or their selves must be changed. This point of view can only come with insight. Those who gained insight into themselves or their lives as a result of depression were not confined to the "catalyst for change" group, but very few of this group described depression as an illness overall. On the other hand, at least a third of those who viewed depression as a part of their self indicated that they gained some insight or learnt something valuable about themselves from having had depression. Having said this, depression was by no means seen as an easy lesson or a welcome event. The insights that depression, or the hardships surrounding it, gave were painfully won. Kleinman summarises this notion in his description of lessons learnt from chronic illness: "[f]or the seriously ill, insight can be the result of an often grim, though occasionally luminous, lived wisdom of the body in pain and the mind troubled" (Kleinman, 1988a: 55).

Depression as a Way of Thinking

Of all those I interviewed, only one woman described her depression as a way of thinking. This woman was Wendy. Raised in a rural setting,

Wendy felt isolated and restricted until she grew old enough to move away. At school, there were few students with whom she could relate and she found it a lonely experience. Despite these contributing factors, Wendy felt her depression was something inbuilt – that although those social factors contributed to her depression, she suspected she might have been depressed regardless of her social situation.[4] When I asked at what age she believed her depression began, she stated that her thinking and behaviour had been what most people would probably consider to be depressed since at least the age of seven. She explained that she came to this conclusion by contrasting the way she used to think and behave before and after she began taking antidepressants. The change, she explained, was so great that she stopped taking them after just a few months.

So why did you take yourself off that [medication]?

[...] It completely alters the way you think and behave and everything and that's so disturbing.

So what kind of things for example?

[...] The way you think about the world. The way you perceive ... I don't know because it's just ways of thinking. Basically the way I thought was normal was basically depression. And okay by that stage it was bad enough for me to notice that I couldn't function, so I had to go on medication because that's the only way to fix it, but I can't remember but I knew that I was completely different to what I was used to. I suppose it's like being on any mind-altering drugs. You think different thoughts and perceive things differently.

The change was akin to what Kramer (1993) describes in *Listening to Prozac* as a complete personality change. But unlike Kramer's patients, Wendy was not happy with this new personality because it was so alien to her. To Wendy, depression is a paradigm which is part of her sense of self – her unique way of seeing the world. She does not accept society's conventions – its "Western corporate material culture" – and does not relate to the mainstream with its emphasis on appearance, money, marriage and having children. At university, she was finally able to find others who related to her attitude. Until then, she had felt alone in her unease with society's values.

However, it was not until her late teens that a very low mood began to accompany this frame of mind and eventually had an impact on her body. She had thoughts of committing suicide and could no longer walk properly or even pick up a pen. Realising that something was very wrong, she went to a doctor and was prescribed antidepressants. Wendy explained that the antidepressant restored her mood and physical function, but also altered her thinking. It was its effect on her thinking which she found to be an especially unsettling experience. Yet despite the elevation in her mood and physical function, she was not tempted to stay on the antidepressants because of how strange and artificial they made her feel. In this respect, she was resisting society's bias against dysthymic individuals – a bias which can push such individuals to take medication they might otherwise prefer not to take (Weisberger, 1995). She describes her experience on antidepressants as "like being on a constant high" or on "mind-altering drugs".

Unlike many others I interviewed, Wendy does not use medication to help her define what constitutes the "illness" and what does not. Doing so would mean that everything which was altered by the medication, including her way of thinking, was part of the illness. To Wendy, it felt as though everything had been changed by the medication. Accepting a definition of illness as everything that was altered by medication would thus entail a loss of self to the illness. Instead, she chooses the definition of illness to be whatever deviates from her normal state of functioning. So the physical and mental changes which occurred during the worst stages of her depression are what she considers "illness". On the other hand, she does not consider her attitude, which others might consider to be a depressive outlook, to be part of the illness because it is her normal mode of thinking.

Wendy thus incorporates two different descriptions of depression into her viewpoint. At its worst stage, depression, to her, becomes an illness worthy of treatment with antidepressants. In its milder form, it is a way of thinking which is part of her self and of which she has no desire to be rid. She still calls the latter "depression" because it was also transformed by the antidepressants and because she understands that society would consider her way of thinking to be a form of depression. However, she describes it as an attitude or way of thinking which could be seen as a subset of the "part of self" view which nevertheless has some unique characteristics. In contrast with other accounts of the self in chronic illness (e.g. Davidson & Strauss, 1992), Wendy's sense of self was not threatened by depression because she believes it has always been part of her self, hence there is nothing to "rediscover" or "reconstruct". Instead, Wendy's case could be seen as supporting Jensen and Allen's notion that "individuals could conceivably experience disease as wellness by accepting disease as an integral part of themselves" (1994: 361).

Several women who felt that the condition is now a part of their self were not proud to say so. Their tone was mostly one of conceding that having experienced depression as a part of their life for so long, or lacking any other satisfactory explanation for its occurrence, they feel inclined to admit that it must be a part of their self. Like it or not, they simply cannot imagine who they would be without it. Wendy, on the other hand, is proud and defiant. Simply deviating from what is considered a normal attitude by the rest of society does not make her ill. Illness, to her, is what deviates from *her* normal mode of function.

Christopher Dowrick (2009: 101) argues that "the major driver behind the concept of depression as a medical diagnosis is a more fundamental set of cultural perceptions in Western societies, where our expectation that happiness is the natural way of being leads us to see negative emotional states as intrinsically deviant from normality". The difference between Wendy and Ingrid's accounts reinforces this point, as Ingrid accepts the societal expectation that happiness is a natural way of being, whereas Wendy rejects it. To return to Jensen and Allen's point, Wendy thus defines what society calls "disease" as "wellness" (or rather, "illness" and "wellness") as far as her personal biography is concerned, and simultaneously challenges the belief that what is called depression should be "negatively evaluated" (Dowrick, 2009: 121). Bill Fulford asserts that "we are concerned, typically, with desires, beliefs, emotions, motivations, and so forth, areas of experience and behaviour in which human values are, characteristically and legitimately, *diverse*" (2001: 82). Perhaps, given Wendy's case, we should take this assertion more seriously.

Depression as a Weakness

Views of depression overlap with each other, and the view described here is no exception. At least two women described depression as a weakness or a tendency alongside another description of depression. For Evelyn and Frances, depression is a set of weaknesses or sensitivities which, if ignited, can set off a depressive episode. Frances illustrates this view here.

But do you yourself see it as an illness or something else?

I feel like you have weaknesses and tendencies that build up over a long period of time [...] I've had a reasonable upbringing and so on, but I mean terrible losses and painful horrible things have happened to me around my sense of self I suppose and my safety and my self esteem and all that kind of thing. I think you get weaknesses and it's like fault lines in a volcanic area or an earthquake area. And then there's a trigger. Now I don't consider that that is an illness, but that is a weakness. Maybe it's a bit like having a heart condition where you take this medication and be a bit careful, you know, but you're not ill, you know? So I don't know. It's hard isn't it?

The weakness view, however, is quite fraught. It is quite close to describing depression as a weakness of character, leaving individuals open to having their struggles dismissed as simply needing to "buck up".[5] Yet this was not what Frances and Evelyn were saying. Describing depression as a vulnerability that can be triggered did not in any way diminish its seriousness. Rather, it appeared to be a way of normalising depression while still recognising their distress, in much the same way that the teenagers of Mervi Issakainen's (2014) study sought to escape the views of depression as a mental illness and the view of depression as "a matter of pulling oneself together" by framing it instead as "a normal but serious affliction". Such a move can be quite strategic when considering the fact that the biomedical model of depression actually contributes to, rather than alleviates, stigmatisation (Angermeyer *et al.*, 2011; Lafrance, 2007). Richard Bentall explains that this is because the biomedical model promotes a view "that humans belong to two sub-species: the mentally well and the mentally ill" (Bentall, 2016).

It may be tempting to characterise the "depression as a weakness" view as an offshoot of "depression as a part of me", but Frances was resistant to this idea:

Did you ever have any of your therapists or doctor describe it to you as an illness or sort of in terms of chemical imbalances? And what do you think of that?

Well they do I suppose call it a chemical ... Well [doctors] call it [bipolar disorder] a personality disorder don't they actually? Which really scares me. I mean I don't accept that. I had a great personality thank you and still do and I'm not a danger. I mean I really object to that.

Thus, distinguishing the "weakness" view from the "part of self" view allows for more detail and a more accurate reflection of the individual's representation of depression within her narrative. The perception of having an underlying weakness that is triggered by a circumstance or event was common to both Frances and Evelyn and occupied a crucial role in their narratives, just as triggers for depression played a crucial role for those who espoused the "catalyst for change" view. However, in the "catalyst for change" view, understanding a trigger for depression offers insight, whereas in the "weakness" view a trigger offers no such insight.

Depression as an Emotion

One of the women I interviewed did not describe depression in any of the ways mentioned so far. She held steadfast to the belief that depression is an emotion, pure and simple. For Penny, depression is not a disease that one can get rid of simply by swallowing a pill. In contrast to the "illness" view, Penny emphasises individual responsibility and describes depression as an emotion which the individual can control and think oneself out of by thinking positively. Penny's description of depression as "just something that you feel" makes it sound deceptively mild. Yet given her story, depression was anything but mild. She firmly believes the main cause of her depression was her parents' violent rows, their divorce and the resulting instability. This view is interesting because at the age of three she was deemed hyperactive and placed on Ritalin, which she says did not work but made her depressed. As a result, she was taken off Ritalin and placed on antidepressants. She then took antidepressants from the age of 6 until 13, culminating in a suicide attempt, until she and her mother decided she should stop taking antidepressants. It is interesting that although she believes Ritalin played a role in causing her depression and that the antidepressants did not only fail to help but actually made her worse, she does not blame the medication for causing her depression but sees the main cause as having been in an unstable family environment.

This view is consistent with her story that although coming off the antidepressants helped, her family life was still unstable and she was still withdrawn as a teenager, going through weight gain and six months of bulimia. Consequently, her depression improved a great deal more when she left home. The resulting stability and independence she gained, as well as meeting the man who became her husband and the continuing support from her mother, provided her with more strength and influence to be able to "view things positively" (in her words). Since leaving home, she has been able to reflect on past events. She puts her improvement down to working through her feelings about her parents' separation, taking up yoga, support from her husband, resisting antidepressants and, in her words, "relying on herself". Combining support with self-reliance seems to have empowered her to the point where she can control how she feels about events that take place in her life fairly well.

Penny's view of depression is similar to "depression as a catalyst for change" in its emphasis on depression as something which is not a disease but a life problem that can only truly be solved by insight. In fact, Penny shares many characteristics with the majority of those who described depression as a catalyst for change: she believes her depression was triggered by circumstances in her life, that it was caused by environmental or life stress rather than biology, is not comfortable with taking medication for depression, feels she has a fair degree of control over her mood, believes that her depression is a temporary rather than a chronic condition and was diagnosed with unipolar (not bipolar) depression. Like the "way of thinking" and "weakness" views, the representation of depression as "an emotion" is quite a rare one. On the face of it, the rarity of this view may seem counter-intuitive given the very emotional form that depression can take in many individuals. Yet this rarity may be a result of what Abram de Swaan (1990) describes as "protoprofessionalisation", in which the lay person accepts and, to some extent, internalises the professional accounts. As Michael Power and Tim Dalgeish (1996) note, psychiatric texts devote a great deal of attention to "affective disorders", yet hardly any to the nature of emotions. Even when emotions are discussed in such texts, the discussion usually occurs in a separate sphere from discussions on psycho-pathology (Pilgrim & Bentall, 1999). Nevertheless, Penny's "depression as an emotion" view provides support for Simon Williams' proposition that it might be

better to think in terms of *emotional health* (as a fully embodied phenomenon), than a sociology *of* "mental" health. Appeals to emotional health, echoing the above points, help to: (i) avoid the medico-centric and/or dualist ring of mental health; (ii) put embodiment centre-stage; and (iii) bring emotions to the fore in all discussions of health, including the "afflictions" of inequality. (Williams, 2003: 151–152)

Combinations of Views

Despite encouragement by the medical establishment to view depression as an illness that is separate from the self, many people tend to question this distinction. Most of the women I interviewed who at some point in the conversation spoke of depression as an illness also described it as a part of their self, and vice versa. Perhaps, then, there is some truth to Horacio Fabrega and Peter Manning's (1972) assertion that what separates mental illness from other illnesses is the impossibility of separating the self from the condition. There were different senses in which depression was invoked both as a part of the self and as an illness. Roughly half of the interviewees said they had difficulty categorising certain traits or quirks as an illness because the traits or quirks felt too much like a part of their personality. Imogen was one such person:

But the most frightening thing I read recently was about a sort of chapter in this book about manic depressive illness and it was about personality and interpersonal rela-tionships. And I read it and I just thought, you know, you think of yourself as an original person, and I read it and just thought, "Oh my God, there's so much of it there that's completely how I'm like". [...] It said something about how bipolar people can be very ... they sort of fall in love really easily and have these really passionate sort of affairs and really sort of love people to extremes, like to a complete extreme – almost possessiveness and quite horrible ways really. And I read it and just thought that's probably me. Oh dear. You know, and I was kind of horrified to realise that there are these patterns of behaviour that are quite common between people with the illness [...] And even now I kind of think, "Is that just me or everybody goes through things like that? Or how far is it the illness and the depression?"

Another way that the women I interviewed invoked both "depression as an illness" and "depression as a part of the self" views was simply to refer to it as an illness at times and as a part of their self at other times. Take Layla, for example:

When I was a bit younger, I would have been too scared to tell someone [that I have bipolar] because I'd think that they'd think, "That's a bit rubbish. What are you talking about?" Whereas now I feel a bit stronger and a bit more in control to tell people that that's what I've got. It's just me. It's part of my personality.

Later in the interview:

So do you think your idea about bipolar disorder has changed over the years?

Yeah definitely. I think I used to think people who had things like that were crazy and couldn't lead normal lives [...] But I also see it more as like a medical illness I think.

For some women, describing their condition as a part of the self at certain points during the conversation and as an illness at other points produced contradictions in their narrative, whereas for others it did not. The reasons for this discrepancy in views of depression also varied. Sometimes the interviewee resisted calling depression an illness because it sounded "like something was wrong" with her, made her feel like an invalid or because she did not buy into the biomedical causation model. At other times the individual might reconsider depression to be an illness after all by virtue of its response to medical intervention. An antidepressant is supposed to fix a chemical imbalance in the brain. Since it worked, they reasoned, a chemical imbalance must have been at least one of the problems, as Karen articulates:

Do you think biology plays a part in it?

[...] I mean, biology has a part because if biology doesn't have a part then Seroxat shouldn't work, and it does. And I definitely know that because ... I don't know. Either the power of placebo is so great that you go from a point where you can't imagine your life anymore, you can't imagine living, to a point where you're back to normal.

Sometimes the discrepancy between viewing depression at times as an illness and at other times as a part of their self seemed to be between a conscious and subconscious viewpoint. For example, when I asked directly, the interviewee might say that to her depression is a part of her self, and yet at other times during the conversation she would refer to depression as an illness, sickness, condition or similar "medical" language. About half of those I interviewed believed a description of depression as something other than an illness to be more accurate, but it was sometimes referred to as an illness nonetheless as it may have simply been easier to refer to as such. For example:

Do you think depression has given you anything positive?

Karen: It might. The ability to, like I said, empathise with others, to help others, may be something positive. Besides what I know about depression? No. Nobody likes to be sick.

Is it like being sick?

Karen: No, not really. It's . . . When you are depressed it is because nobody can see it . . . .

This phenomenon could be interpreted as shifting between what Hydén (1997) calls speaking in the "illness voice", which is to describe the illness "from the inside" as someone still suffering (which in this case would be describing depression as part of the self), versus speaking in the "healthy voice" as someone whose life has been invaded by something external (which in this case would be depression as illness) or something that was in the past. I suggest two slight modifications to this perspective. One modification is that those supposedly speaking "from the inside" (although it sounds incongruent to describe those depicting depression as a part of their self to be speaking in the "illness voice") did not necessarily see themselves as "still suffering" (or indeed "suffering" at all). Second, those who described it in the so-called "healthy voice" did not necessarily believe it was in their past. For instance, some who described depression as a part of their self felt it was probably now over, but insofar as it formed a crucial part of their past, it contributed to their current self.

An Illness that Is Part of the Self

The combinations and permutations of the different descriptions of depression I came across provide rich territory to explore. One of the permutations of the "depression as illness" and "depression as a part of the self" combination is the view that depression is an illness that *is* part of their self. The most common reason that interviewees gave for this view was that depression seemed entrenched either in their personality or their family history (or genetic makeup), or both. Most of those who espoused this view said their family had a history of depression and felt their depressive episodes were usually not triggered by anything. Miriam is a typical example of this combined "illness that is a part of the self" view. She grew up in a family in which most of the members have suffered from depression in one form or another. At times she described depression as an illness, but at other times described it in the following way:

I'd always felt at that stage that if I was a ball, the depression was at the centre, but it had a switch so I could switch it off. That's what I felt. And at the end of the counselling, I was still a ball with a much smaller centre and that was fixed. And I kind of felt instinctively then that if I took that away I would be hollow. I felt like it was deeply ingrained – just part of who I am. I couldn't take it away any more than I could take away being able to see or hear or taste. So I don't know. I mean my brain just interpreted that as it being hard-wired in, rather than a case of nurture. [...]

Why do you think it's so much a part of you?

I think partly because it's a part of everyone in our family. So subconsciously my idea of a person has always included this little kernel of depression, either treatable or not.

Miriam's account sounds very much like biographical reinforcement (Carricaburu & Pierret, 1995). In their study of HIV-positive haemophiliacs and gay men, Carricaburu and Pierret describe how the diagnosis of HIV for men simply reinforced aspects of their identities which had centred on haemophilia or homosexuality. For example, for men with haemophilia, it simply confirmed their lifelong illness experience. For gay men, it reinstated their personal and political struggle. In a similar fashion, the diagnosis of depression seemed to confirm Miriam's idea of what constitutes a person, or at least what constitutes herself. However, Miriam's is an example of a family in which nearly everyone had suffered from depression, so the other women may not have experienced biographical reinforcement to the same extent. Nevertheless, the others who described depression in a similar way expressed a sense of depression as being deeply entrenched in their personal makeup despite not knowing of any family history of depression. Instead, they felt it was something they were simply born with, just as they were born with a particular disposition. For such women, they had felt a tendency to become depressed for as long as they could remember, even if a "full-blown" depression did not manifest until much later in their lives. Often they would describe depression as an illness as well at another point in the interview. Theresa, who was diagnosed with bipolar disorder, provides an example of this view:

Do you think bipolar has changed you?

Yes in a way, but not like ... I don't know, it's difficult. I'm still kind of ... I don't think so. I think I can't say it's changed me because I think it *is* me. It's part of me so I can't see it as having changed me. It's changed thought processes and it's changed how I see things and how I react to things and how I deal with things, but not kind of you know ...

Later:

So if you could theoretically press a button that would get rid of bipolar forever, would you press it?

Oh absolutely! Straight away! Yeah of course.

Why is that?

There's no reason that you'd want to hold onto it, you know? You can sit and talk rhetoric about the positives about it, like it affects how you see people and whatever, but of course if you could get rid of it ... It's an illness.

Belinda, on the other hand, views bipolar depression as inseparable from her self based on the influence it has on the way she reacts to people and situations in life. Without these unique reactions, she reasons, she would not be who she is. Yet at the same time she refers to what she has as an illness.

I think I'm more than just bipolar illness but by the same token I don't think you can separate me from bipolar disorder because so much of the way I behave and the way I interact with people and all that sort of stuff is influenced by the fact that I have much more intense reactions to things.

These three examples reflect a range of different viewpoints within those who felt that depression is simultaneously a part of their self as well as an illness. While Miriam and Belinda said that if given the choice, they would not choose to be rid of their depression, Theresa used the illness view as a justification for why she would choose to be rid of it. After all, why would anyone want to hold onto an illness? Yet it is also something she does not consider to have changed her because she believes it has always been part of her. For Theresa, depression is an illness which has always had a significant impact on her self. The two concepts are not in contradiction. Yet the inference is that if she had been born without it, she would have been a different person and, she implies, would probably have been better off.

While Miriam's particular account of depression is a case of biographical enforcement, the "illness that is part of the self" view as a whole could be understood as a variation on biographical continuity. In Pound *et al.*'s (1998) study of stroke in older people, illness was seen as inevitable in later life. As a result, older people, especially those from working-class backgrounds, were more accepting of hardship. In this way, stroke was almost biographically anticipated. In a slightly different manner, women who view depression as an illness that is part of the self demonstrate an element of biographical continuity insofar as depression is at least not articulated as a biographical disruption but is worked into their narrative. Their self had been developed by, and with, depression. As Theresa explained, "I can't say it's changed me because I think it *is* me." As such, depression is experienced as a biographical continuity – if nothing else, for the inability to conceptualise what the self would have been like without depression.

Part of the Self Developed by the Illness

A few of the women I spoke to felt that depression is a part of their self that has been formed or altered by the illness. Being an intense experience, as well as a sometimes long and protracted one, these women felt that depression had left its mark on their character in one way or another, often by learned behavioural or cognitive habits. Ursula illustrates a version of this view:

It's easier to think of [depression] as part of me, but it's probably better to think of it as an illness [. . .]

And which one do you think is more true?

They're probably both true because it is an illness but it's part of me as well because it's a part of my experience and part of my past experience of what has formed me. So in that sense it's part of me as well.

The experience of depressive or bipolar-related symptoms for long periods of time without being diagnosed also compounds the problem of separating personality from pathology:

Gina: I do find that difficult to distinguish between symptoms and my own character, especially because I was undiagnosed and untreated for a very long time and I feel like my personality and my character developed while I was sick . . .

Gina explained that even when she is not experiencing depression or hypomania, she has a tendency to behave as though she is depressed or hypomanic, implying that these tendencies belong to the illness but that force of habit has imbued her behaviour with characteristics of the illness – characteristics which were not originally her own.

Even for those who adamantly described depression as an illness, it was impossible to neglect the impact it had on their personality. Diana said she sees depression as an illness largely because of the literature she has read, but also expressed how she had felt "disappointment to see myself changing into someone else that I don't even like". Although she placed depression squarely in the illness category, she was painfully aware of its reach into her personality. Lisa Robinson defines the self as "the thinking, knowing, feeling part of the human organism which deals with the world" (1974: 19), and Donna Czuchta and Barbara Johnson (1998) recognise that it is precisely because mental illness affects those human aspects that it is capable of shaping the self. This is why depression cannot be *just* an illness, as it affects how an individual thinks and feels about him or herself, the world and his or her future. Of course, more physical conditions and illnesses can also affect these aspects of the self, but the effect can be quite pervasive in the case of depression as it directly impacts an individual's thoughts, feelings and behaviours – the very stuff that the self is made of.

I could certainly understand why these women came to view depression both as an illness and as a part of their self in nuanced ways. Yet these women were a subset of the whole, so I wanted to delve deeper into their stories to see if there was something that might have helped to draw them towards this particular view rather than another. I found the answer in their family history, or at least their interpretation of it. Nearly all of those who view depression as "an illness that is part of me" and all those who view it as "a part of me developed by the illness" said they had some family history of depression or bipolar disorder.[6] On one level, it is not surprising that a family history of depression or bipolar disorder might lead one to these viewpoints. When I asked if they believed that genetic factors played a causal role in their depression, many cited whether or not another family member had also been diagnosed with unipolar or bipolar depression as a justification for their belief. As family history can be seen as closely linked to inherited genetic factors, and genetics in turn is implicated in the biomedical model of depression, it is easy to see how a family history of unipolar or bipolar depression can lead one to view it as an illness.[7] Indeed, the majority of those I interviewed who described unipolar/bipolar depression mainly as an illness reported that they had some family history of it. Earlier, Miriam invoked her family history as a reason for why she views depression as both an illness and a part of her self (although family history was sometimes also used to justify a view of depression as an illness that is separate to the self rather than part of it). For women such as Miriam, Wendy and Bridget, locating depression in their genes, chemicals or hormones was seen as integrating, rather than isolating, depression as part of the self. Miriam illustrates this view:

So has your view of depression changed over the years?

[. . .] I've always felt that it's just a part of me – that it's hard-wired. It's like having a hand [. . .] it feels as solid as any part of my body . . . there is a little chemical bit that's just part of my brain that's not fixable.

Joseph Dumit (2003) makes a demarcation between "genetic" disorders and "brain" disorders, claiming that individuals are more inclined to see the latter as part of their self than the former. However, women like Wendy, Miriam and Bridget challenge this demarcation as they include both their genes and their brain within their self-concept.

Genes and the brain were not the only physiological aspects that influenced the individual's self-concept. Bridget cited the number of episodes she experienced and her reactions to physiological and psychological stresses as reasons for why she feels that depression is so much a part of her self:

I know different people will react to a situation in different ways. Some people will go through things I've gone through and not get depressed and I'm not one of those people. And I think it's something to do with the way I react to psychological stress, but also I think physiological stresses. Because I think, to me it's really interesting that hormone changes with both my children and pregnancy changes, the hormone changes in pregnancy, or that's what I think it is, have always triggered my depression. Although maybe it's the physical effects of being pregnant – you know, the morning sickness. But even when the morning sickness goes the depression doesn't stay so . . .

So I guess despite the hormonal triggers or physical triggers, you think it's still a part of your persona as you say?

Yeah, I honestly don't think it's just chemical. I don't think it's purely chemical that I get lower levels of serotonin and noradrenalin and that means I get depressed and you give me tablets and I get better. I don't think it's that simple.

Bridget could easily have viewed depression as an illness that is separate to her self, having linked her depressive episodes to her pregnancies so strongly. Yet what struck me about Bridget's explanation was that the self, for her, is both physiological and psychological:

I think [depression is] part of who I am, I think, much as I'd like it not to be [. . .] I think it's a part of my physiological and psychological persona [. . .]

   I don't think, you can't say there's a medical physiological model, for me anyway, or there's a psychological model. I think it's an interplay of factors [. . .]

In this way, Bridget resists the mind–body dichotomy. It is not new to conclude that a unique reaction to events or circumstances may point to a locus of depression within the individual. However, to conclude that a unique reaction to physiological stresses indicates the same thing (rather than that the depression is a result of a "biochemical imbalance" that is separate from the self) implicates both the mind and the body in the concept of the self, rather than separate in the Cartesian sense. Bridget's view, as well as the view expressed by Miriam and Wendy earlier, departs from the Western tendency to conceptualise the body as separate to the self. Instead, they include the physical, not just the spiritual, as intrinsic to the self.

Is It Me or the Illness?

It is striking that most of the women I interviewed spoke candidly about how they struggled with whether certain aspects of their thoughts, feelings and behaviours belong to themselves or to depression or bipolar disorder – that is, they would often raise the issue of whether those characteristics were simply manifestations of their "illness" or a part of who they are, without any prompting. They confided that at times they were unsure whether they were really entitled to feel guilt-free for behaviours which they have been told or read are symptoms of depression or mania and whether the biomedical explanation was simply providing them with an escape from responsibility.

Thoughts, feelings and behaviours which have been labelled as part of a psychiatric illness can also be seen as part of the self. As discussed earlier, many interviewees expressed this view. However, the terms "illness" and "self" were sometimes used as though they are mutually exclusive. Classifying characteristics as either belonging to illness or to the self may have implications for responsibility. The struggle to categorise certain thoughts, feelings and behaviours usually raised a slew of issues surrounding control and responsibility, the self and what defines an illness. Participants openly expressed their difficulties in assigning responsibility for their actions, or indeed, in calling their actions their own, and in taking credit for their recovery. They expressed doubts regarding the biomedical narrative for depression and its implied separation of physical processes, which cause the illness, from the emotional/mental processes, which supposedly constitute the self. Gina is one of those who struggled to distinguish one from the other:

Why do you think it was harder to come to terms with the bipolar diagnosis than the depression [diagnosis]?

[. . .] When I got bipolar diagnosed, I thought there's a whole new set of symptoms – there's a whole new raft of information that I need to learn now. I think it felt like I didn't know myself anymore. I think that was the difficulty. It felt like I didn't know myself anymore and it felt like I didn't know what was me and what was the disease. I think that was another big difficulty and another thing that I found actually really difficult for a very long time was actually teasing out what was personality and what was pathology. And I still have quite a hard time with that.

Many of the women I interviewed tried to identify why they had difficulty distinguishing the self from sickness, or indeed why they felt the need to make such a distinction in the first place. While their explanations varied, there were some common themes throughout. The most popular reason for questioning whether depression can be separated from the self was that the interviewee felt she had had depression for so long that it was difficult to determine whether her character had changed due to depression or simply due to the passage of time. This dilemma may be emphasised by the fact that the average age of onset of depression for these women was during adolescence, when it is not unusual for an individual's character to change as they entered adulthood. For some women, it was also difficult to establish exactly when depression began in the first place, and therefore where the line is between the self and sickness – if there even is one at all. Evelyn is one of the many women who articulated this uncertainty:

Do you think depression has changed you as a person?

Well given that I couldn't really say when it began … Would I be different if I didn't have negative thoughts? Well yes, but that would be a change of personality. It would be a change in how I dealt with things, how I related to people.

Some women stated that sometimes they make a conscious distinction between what belongs to the self and what belongs to the illness based on personal preference. The following quotations are from women who have chosen what constitutes part of their self and what does not, acknowledging that the views they espouse do not necessarily reflect some underlying truth but are rather a reflection of what they would rather own and disown. Quite often, their preference was to shunt certain less desirable traits and behaviours away from the bounds of the self and into the confines of the illness (here understood as separate from the self) in order to dissolve allegations of personal responsibility for their behaviours. By doing so, they render it just as nonsensical to blame the individual for these "symptoms" of depression or mania as it is to blame an individual for getting the flu. Bridget and Miriam illustrate this view:

Do you think depression has changed you as a person?

Bridget: [. . .] I actually think I'm much lazier as a consequence of being depressed over the years. But I might just be blaming it because it's easy to blame it. It could just be me, you know.

Do you think biology plays a part in it?

Miriam: I wanted [depression] to be something chemical that could be fixed. Or that could not possibly be construed as my fault.

In this way, many struggled to try to separate their depression or mania from their self and felt that assigning more blame to biology was a way of avoiding guilt for their behaviours. That this struggle with responsibility was seen across the board, and often with little prompting, highlights it as a major issue in an individual's experience with depression. The struggle has also been highlighted in studies such as that conducted by Jennifer Wisdom and colleagues, who stated that such women experienced a "duality of selves" whereby conceptions of "their real, authentic selves" were presented as dichotomous to their "alternate selves" which "were seen as part of who they were, but were separated as parts that they did not much like or were ashamed to show the world" (2008: 491). However, I see these narratives as more than an expression of a "duality of selves", but as an expression of doubt about the biomedical narrative. Interviewees articulated this struggle regardless of whether they view depression as an illness or as something else. Even those who purported to espouse the biomedical narrative of depression showed that they were not entirely convinced of its division between the self and sickness when it came to depression and self-determination. This resistance to the biomedical narrative was also apparent in Simone Fullagar's study, in which she reports that ". . . despite the dominance of biomedical accounts, very few women attributed their recovery solely to medication or understood depression as singularly caused by a chemical imbalance" (2009: 403). Instead, views of the self within depression are constantly being negotiated and in flux or, as Dumit states, "they have entered into a relationship with their brain that is negotiated and social" (2003: 46).

In *Speaking of Sadness*, David Karp sees the struggle between the self and illness more as one in which people attempt to explain their depression as biologically or environmentally caused. He writes, "[i]n the end, nearly everyone comes to favour biomedically deterministic theories of depression's cause [. . .] This is partly a result of their gradual commitment to a medical version of reality. It is also a result of the intrinsic nature of depression itself" (Karp, 1996: 31). He then goes on to describe an experience also described by several of the women I interviewed – that once the depressive thought pattern is set in place, biology seems to take over and maintain the cycle. Although Karp's study is now somewhat dated, it is worthwhile presenting it here to show how these previous views contrast with those I encountered. I suggest three modifications/updates to Karp's statement. First, although the nature versus nurture debate did figure in my interviews to a certain extent, the choice was not always between the two. It was not uncommon for the individual to state that the main cause of her depression was probably her personality, and this was not necessarily situated in her biological makeup or blamed on her upbringing – it was simply something she was born with but also subject to change. Second, biomedical deterministic theories of depression's cause were certainly not favoured by the women I interviewed to the extent that they were in Karp's. This may be a reflection of the change in lay beliefs between then and now, or the different geographical locations, or both. The biomedical theory, rather than being favoured as the primary cause of depression, was in the majority of cases tentatively invoked as the preferred cause when the question of where to assign responsibility was raised. Perhaps it is now simply a rhetorical device, but certainly, one must not ignore the moral work that the illness model does, and which several women openly acknowledged, in exonerating the individual of responsibility for certain behaviours. Third, while the feeling that one's mood had gained a momentum which felt out of one's control may provide a clue as to the underlying workings of depression, it does not serve as evidence for an "intrinsic biomedical nature". That, unfortunately, still remains a mystery. Some of the differences between those I interviewed and those whom Karp interviewed may be culturally informed. Both Ilina Singh (2002) and Natasha Mauthner (2002) report that biomedical narratives of depression were much more popular among their US interviewees than their UK counterparts.

Debbie's statement hints that there is a degree of self-fashioning involved in creating a narrative of depression:

What do you think has changed you?

I think, oddly, it's just as simple as having to talk to other people about it has changed me, because like I said, it made me rationalise it more and it made me see it as something which is separable from me. Even though I see it as very much a part of me, when it gets to be too much I can kind of step out of myself. It's like you can pick and choose. I know that that's probably not the most sensible thing to do, but yeah I don't know. It kind of is part of me and it isn't part of me. When it gets out of control, I'd rather it wasn't.

Experiences of depression have a social reference point, and the retelling of these experiences reflects this. A similar point is made by Arthur Kleinman, who highlights that narratives of illness are part of a life story and play a particular role within it. Narratives can create sense of loss, or act like a myth that reaffirms one's core values in the face of adversity (Kleinman, 1988a). Nevertheless, Debbie and Annette were aware of the moral work that their particular narrative was doing. As Kleinman, notes, their reflexivity is not something we often expect of patients:

[t]he chronically ill are caught up with the sheer exigency of their problems; what insight they possess into its structural sources and consequences they are not expected to voice. This is a social fiction of the illness role. The patient, in order to

legitimately occupy that role, is not expected to be consciously aware of what she desires from it, what practical uses it has. (Kleinman, 1988a: 119)

Not only do the women I spoke with show how reflexive patients can be, they also show what roles their particular views of depression play in their life story and view of their self.

I now turn to another area in which the inner conflict of the self versus the illness becomes apparent. After listening to accounts of how some of the women experienced mania, I was struck by their similarities with schizophrenia and Dissociative Identity Disorder (DID). One such case was that of Annette, a softly spoken young mother who described how she suddenly and unexpectedly began to hallucinate. What then followed was, as Annette described, "an absolute hell" of delusions and paranoia:

I couldn't sleep for about four days, couldn't eat anything, I became delusional. I thought I was God, I thought my husband was the devil, I was screaming and shouting, doing things that I wouldn't normally do. My husband got some old friends of ours up to help because he was obviously finding my behaviour hard to cope with because it was totally out of character. I remember taking all my clothes off in front of one of our friends, which I wouldn't normally do ... or shout abuse or scream, you know. I wouldn't normally behave like that. I was out of control.

Following medication, Annette recovered from her manic state and struggled to understand what had happened. She felt ashamed and embarrassed and was at a loss as to how to explain behaviour so out of character. At one point she describes who she was during her manic state as "an out-of-control Annette", but at another point says that she was not really herself.

Jeanette Kennett and Steve Matthews, in their paper *Identity, Control and Responsibility: The Case of Dissociative Identity Disorder* (2002), also note the similarity between certain forms of bipolar disorder and DID and would argue that the person during the manic phase was an "out-of-control Annette". In an exploration of whether it is one self or multiple selves at the heart of these mental illnesses, Kennett and Matthews present an argument that individuals who behave badly in one of these alter ego states are still the same self but in a deluded state. They liken it to the common view that acts committed while drunk are still committed by the same person, but in an altered or deluded state. The differences are first that this alter state is perhaps more extreme in cases of schizophrenia, DID and certain cases of bipolar disorder; and second, that the agent has no control over when the switch between the "normal" and alter state occurs.

Yet the debate surrounding responsibility need not be framed such that if there are multiple selves involved, one cannot be held responsible for actions that the "other self" committed; or that if there is only one person involved, he or she can be held accountable (Kennett & Matthews, 2002). Instead, those suffering from such conditions are the same self but in a deluded state such that even though their actions are their own, they are no more morally responsible for them than the actions of someone while sleepwalking. It is worth quoting the following extract from their paper as it summarises the point quite well:

Even if DID sufferers are not morally responsible for the bad actions they perform in an alter state it is fitting that they should feel some measure of concern and responsibility for those actions, in much the same way as we expect the truck driver to feel particularly bad about the death of a child who ran into his path even though he could not have helped hitting the child [...] The point is that neither the truck driver nor the DID sufferer is in the same position, morally speaking, as a bystander: we will find it disturbing if either moves too quickly to distance or excuse themselves. (Kennett & Matthews, 2002: 523)

Within this framework, there is still room for individual responsibility. Once the individual is aware of his or her condition, the onus is then on him or her to seek treatment and take precautions to prevent, as much as possible, "bad acts" from occurring again in the future. This idea was expressed by some of the women I interviewed, but the range of views regarding perceived control in recovery was on a continuum, from those who felt they had surrendered control to the medication all the way to those who felt very much in control throughout their recovery, or that medication was simply one of the tools in their toolbox for recovery and prevention.

Interpreting the Views

It is clear that despite psychiatry's efforts to promote the illness view of depression, the view is far from unilaterally accepted by those diagnosed with it. Most individuals are aware of the moral work it does (i.e. the deflection of personal responsibility for depression), and this awareness prevents them from adopting the view wholeheartedly. The illness view works as a defensive shield against attacks on their character, yet is subject to doubt upon introspection. Furthermore, the illness view does not portray the complexity of the condition and its effect on so many aspects of the individual's life and sense of self. As a result, many individuals prefer either to describe depression in another way or to combine the illness view with another view.

The biomedical model of depression views it as a medical illness that is caused by a biochemical imbalance in the brain that precedes the psychological symptoms – an imbalance that is best treated with antidepressant drugs (Essom & Nemeroff, 1996; McGrath *et al.*, 1990). Although the women I spoke with had been through the clinical process of diagnosis and treatment, the biomedical model did not dominate their views of depression. They reported that the media, literature (usually in the form of textbooks, handbooks or autobiographies), friends and family had influenced their views of depression too, which may at least partly explain some of the variety of views described in this chapter. Yet many of those who did not describe their depression as an illness still made reference to the illness view or described their view in marked contrast to it. Take Penny, for example, who described depression in the following way:

Anything that you think people should know about depression?

That depression is not a disease, basically. It's just something that you feel. It's an emotion that comes over you and needs to be dealt with. Because people always think it's a disease and it's not. It's just an emotion and it can be solved by something or someone can solve it. Doctors, anyone, can solve it [...]

As mentioned earlier, Penny's view is not a reflection of a mild depression. Her experience of depression included self-harm, bulimia and a suicide attempt.

The narratives that those diagnosed with depression use to describe it reveal the relationship between the self and responsibility that these individuals decided to espouse. As Gareth Williams (1997: 187) explains, "an individual's account of the origin of that illness in terms of putative causes can perhaps most profitably be read as an attempt to establish points of reference between body, self, and society and to reconstruct a sense of order from the fragmentation produced by chronic illness".[8] The illness view of depression, for example, assigns a significant portion of blame for depression on genes or chemicals. The other views, on the other hand, place less emphasis on the role of biology and more emphasis on the role of the individual. The way the individual chooses to see depression in relation to her self thus has implications for personal responsibility. Likewise, the individual's feelings regarding her responsibility for, and role in, depression influence how she chooses to view depression in relation to her self. This point becomes more striking when the issue of responsibility is placed in doubt, usually resulting in a clash between the "illness" view and the "part of self" view.

At this point, it is important to recognise that an individual's view of depression is embedded in her cultural and socio-economic context. Cultural comparisons make this point more apparent. Some cultures do not even have a description for depression (Bhugra & Cochrane, 2001; O'Connor *et al.*, 2002; Russell, 1991), and in others, the illness view of depression does not surface. For instance, the Black Caribbean women who Dawn Edge and Anne Rogers (2005) interviewed rejected the label "postnatal depression" and depression as illness, and instead normalised their suffering, emphasising the need to be strong and to deal with their problems themselves rather than resort to medical help. June Brown and colleagues (2011) found that Black African women in Britain showed an even greater tendency towards demedicalised beliefs about depression than White British and Black Caribbean people.[9] Western countries outside the United Kingdom may also produce different responses. For instance, Natasha Mauthner's (2002) study of women diagnosed with postnatal depression found that the biomedical model held more sway in women's descriptions and explanations of depression in the United States compared with the United Kingdom. Age and gender also have an effect on how individuals view depression. In a study conducted in Sweden, men spoke more readily of physical pain whereas women spoke more of emotional pain (Danielsson & Johansson, 2005). A study in the United States also found that teenagers, like adults, described depression in terms of an "illness trajectory" (Wisdom & Green, 2004), whereas a study of elderly people in England did not feel their depression was an "illness" but rather a result of the circumstances associated with their age (Burroughs *et al.*, 2006). In these respects, the women I spoke to viewed depression in ways very much in keeping with those of their social and cultural context.

Developing a coherent view of the self may be difficult, if not impossible, to construct. So too, it seems, is a coherent view of depression. For in narrating their views of depression, there is a degree of self-fashioning involved of which many individuals were aware. Each of their views speaks to certain aspects of the individual's experience while possibly ignoring or negating others. Given the often complex and multi-layered nature of depression experiences, one view of depression alone was often not enough to speak for their whole experience. Thus, most women invoked two or more views of depression which sometimes resulted in contradictions, and sometimes did not.

Conclusion

The issue of moral responsibility for depression and the individual's behaviour while depressed arose across the board. Even those who experienced what they described as severe depressions or psychoses, whom one might imagine would find it easier to contrast the depressed/psychotic self from the "well" self, struggled to identify what traits and behaviours they can say belong to their self and what belong to the "illness", if indeed the illness is separate to the self. This uncertainty means more than simply whether the individual feels she is letting herself "off the hook", but also has implications for what she feels is within her power to control and what is not. The views of these women are echoed on a larger scale, with those in the "recovery movement" promoting hope and empowerment for the ability to overcome depression, whereas those in the "chemical imbalance" camp see otherwise. As such, it is not just a philosophical dilemma but also a practical one: Is the individual's responsibility confined to taking her medication when she is instructed to (if antidepressants are useful for her) and monitoring and reporting any changes in mood, or can more be done?

Further, this chapter reveals the difficulties that interviewees faced with either espousing or consistently maintaining a view of depression solely as an illness in keeping with the biomedical model. It is telling that there is also a lack of scientific evidence to support the serotonin deficiency hypothesis (e.g. Murray & Lopez, 1996; Üstün et al., 2004), and pharmaceutical companies appear to have ceased promoting it. The fragility of the chemical imbalance/biomedical model is thus underscored not only by the ambivalence felt by many individuals towards it – with many who say they espouse an illness view nevertheless struggling to maintain its separation from the self – but also by the scientific evidence (or lack thereof). The persistent reference to the chemical imbalance hypothesis within the interviews despite its instability is then particularly striking. One may posit that it is indicative of the narrative's mythical status. The persistence of the biomedical model despite its fragility is illustrated even more so in the next chapter.

3   Going for Help
The Impact of Diagnosis on the Self

First Impressions

In symbolic terms, diagnosis represents the naming of a set of experiences; a formal move from health to illness; grappling with and negotiating the sick role; and usually the first step into the medical world of doctors and treatments.[1] Diagnosis impacts on how individuals view themselves, but individuals also apply their own meaning and interpretation to their diagnosis.[2] If an individual's interpretation of her diagnosis throws her responsibility for certain thoughts, emotions and behaviours into doubt, then the place of those thoughts, emotions and behaviours as part of the self also comes under question.

In contrast with the variety and complexity of views of depression presented in the previous chapter, when I asked my interviewees how they initially reacted to their diagnosis, it became apparent that whether they were relieved or resigned, accepting, rejecting or nonchalant, their reaction was premised on a biomedical view of depression. It should be noted, however, that this medicalised view does not occur all the time and across the board. An individual's account of her view of depression at the point of diagnosis can be in stark contrast with her view of depression at the time of interview.

Views of depression not only vary at different points in time within the individual but also among different groups of people. For instance, those who have not been diagnosed with depression tend to place more weight on non-medical explanations of the cause of depression than do those who have been diagnosed (Kuyken et al., 1992; Ogden et al., 1999; Thwaites et al., 2004; Tully et al., 2006). Nevertheless, this is not to say that lay views of depression in the West are decidedly non-medical. Jorm and colleagues (2000) found that people in Western cultures are more comfortable with professional models of depression and medical treatment than those in Eastern cultures – a finding which is perhaps not surprising given the prevalence of medical discourse in Western culture (Shaw, 2002).

Not only do people who have not been diagnosed with depression tend to view it in more demedicalised terms than their diagnosed counterparts, but even physicians find it difficult at times to maintain a medicalised view of depression over a demedicalised view. In their study of 20 general practitioners (GPs) in the United Kingdom, Susan McPherson and David Armstrong (2009) found that when speaking about patients for whom antidepressants were ineffective, GPs tend to demedicalise depression. That is, GPs seem to attribute the ineffectiveness of medication in such patients either to the likelihood that the patient instead suffers from a personality problem (either a personality disorder, or is simply a difficult patient), which detaches the label "depression" from the patient, or to the view that antidepressants are no better than placebos anyhow, which demedicalises the treatment. GPs are also more likely to demedicalise depression in underprivileged areas (Chew-Graham et al., 2000) and in the elderly (Burroughs et al., 2006), tending to perceive it as a normal reaction to stressful circumstances. The result is that patients can not only be medicalised but also demedicalised (McPherson & Armstrong, 2009). This demedicalisation of depression among physicians can extend to causal explanations. For instance, Roanne Thomas-MacLean and Janet Stoppard's (2004) interviews with 20 primary care physicians in Canada found that their medicalised views of depression conflicted with their recognition of the role played by the individual's life context. Physicians spoke of depression as both "normal" and "wrong". However, if something is "wrong" with the patient, it should not simply be a normal reaction to stressful circumstances. If it is a normal or understandable reaction to stressful circumstances, it is the situation or the environment that is "wrong". Depression, of course, need not be viewed in this either/or dichotomy. The plasticity of the brain means that trauma and stress, by impacting on one's psychology, can alter the brain's neural circuitry.[3] Yet a strict biomedical model states that changes to neural circuitry or brain chemistry *precede* the psychological state. Whether or not this causal model fits with their experiences of depression, the women I spoke with felt that what it gave with one hand, it took with the other.

The Biomedical Model: A Double-Edged Sword

The biomedical model underlay almost all interviewees' initial reactions to their diagnosis, either as an explanation for their feelings of relief or doubt, their fears about stigma or their feelings of being labelled. Debbie, for example, felt that her diagnosis (bipolar depression) was bound up with the biomedical paradigm:

So then how did you feel when they first gave you the diagnosis?

I felt kind of invaded, because they'd attached something to me which seemed very clinical and scientific.

Gail, the only interviewee who did not have a biomedical view of the diagnosis, had gone directly to a psychotherapist for treatment with Chinese herbs because she did not subscribe to the biomedical narrative of depression and her memory of her mother's treatment for schizophrenia made her determined to avoid Western medical treatment. Gail's relief upon being diagnosed was instead predicated on her feeling that "I felt I knew I was facing a problem and the problem had a clear name. And because the problem had a clear name, there must be a clear solution to it."

The biomedical model of depression clears the individual of responsibility for her condition but also has the potential to condemn her to something chronic, for according to the model there is no cure – no "exit" from the depression career – only ways of managing it. This is seen as being especially true of bipolar depression, with numerous websites and articles reinforcing the message that bipolar depression is a serious, chronic and incurable illness (e.g. Arehart-Treichel, 2002; Everyday Health, 2010; Keitner *et al.*, 2009; Melbourne MediBrain Centre, 2009; Torpy, 2009). Layla clearly articulated the sentiment that many others voiced concerning the prevailing opinion that bipolar depression is more serious than unipolar depression:

It sounds really silly, but I feel like if you say to someone "Oh I've got bipolar", then they take it slightly more seriously. But if you say "I've got depression", then they think "Oh, you're really sad". [laughs] "Poor you", or "You've got PMT" or something. Whereas if you say you've got bipolar, I think people take it a bit more, "Oh that's an illness. Oh that's a disease."

Those who initially felt relief upon being given a diagnosis (such as those who felt it meant depression was not their fault, that they were not going insane) and those who felt that they didn't know themselves anymore were reacting to the former aspect of the biomedical model which they seemed to associate with the diagnosis – that is, responsibility for their condition and associated behaviour lies with their chemicals, not with society or their selves. Miriam illustrates this view:

So how did you feel when [the doctor] made that diagnosis?

Relieved. Because I had wondered if I was going insane. Because it's not normal to get upset because you've forgotten to put the water in the fridge or something like that. And I was aware – very aware – that it wasn't normal. And I wanted it to be something chemical that could be fixed. Or that could not possibly be construed as my fault. So the diagnosis of depression was a relief.

That such relief is predicated on a biomedical understanding of depression carries with it risks that have been identified by several scholars thus far. Fredrik Svenaeus uses the phenomenological notion of "bodily resonance" (in depression, a sense that one is out of tune with the world) as an explanation for serotonin's relevance to feelings and the wider context in which the body is situated and cautions against an over-reliance on the biomedical model:

... we enrich our biological accounts by providing them with this phenomenological dimension, by relating them to patterns of meaning constitution; otherwise, we risk mystifying biology – risk transforming it into something foreign to problems of everyday life. Discussing serotonin deludes us into blaming our brains, rather than ourselves and the societies we live in (Valenstein, 1998). (Svenaeus, 2007: 162)

Nikolas Rose (2007) argues that subjectivity has increasingly become understood in biological terms, thanks to the biomedical model – an argument that builds on Foucault's (1998) notion of biopower as a way of managing groups through the use of technology. In this case, it is people's emotions that are being managed through the use of medication. As Simone Fullagar elaborates:

[t]he neurochemically deficient self is one such figure who is required to exercise responsibility and self-control to restore and maximize their life potential via biomedical expertise [...] we can see the seductive power of biomedical explanations that reconfigure the problem of unsuccessful womanhood as a neurochemical problem that can be expertly and rationally managed. (Fullagar, 2009: 403–404)

By negating any role that problematic social norms and cultural practices can play in causing depression, the biomedical model also plays into the patriarchal interest in turning attention away from sexist norms and practices that disproportionately affect women. Simone Fullagar, Michelle Lafrance and Janet Stoppard have all emphasised the gendered power relations within the societal problems that the biomedical model ignores.[4] Many have also criticised the biomedical model for reducing the individual's experience to a set of physical causes and symptoms (e.g. Aronowitz, 1998; Eisenberg, 1977; Lafrance & Stoppard, 2007; Scheper-Hughes, 1990; Taussig, 1980) as well as being individualistic and gender-blind (Nicolson, 1998; Pilgrim & Bentall, 1999; Stoppard, 2000). The biomedical model thus performs several duties within diagnosis. It negates self-blame, but also negates the social and psychological factors within which depression is also situated.

As Miriam illustrated earlier, the initial reactions interviewees had to their diagnosis – such as feeling labelled, not knowing who you are anymore, relief and fear – were reactions to this biomedical model of depression. It is a testament to how influential the biomedical model has become that it has imbued itself within lay perceptions of what a diagnosis of unipolar or bipolar depression means, or at least what it means when one first hears the diagnosis applied to oneself.[5] Various factors channel the individual towards a particular internalisation of her diagnosis. David Pilgrim and Anne Rogers note that there is disagreement as to which factors have the most influence, but that diagnosis exerts power over the individual's identity is generally agreed upon among labelling theorists:

[f]or Scheff (1966) it is psychiatrists; for Goffman (1961) it is the family plus professionals plus the total institution. However, there is an agreement that, once labelled, this significantly alters the person's identity and social status. Once a person is seen to have lost their reason, then they will never be quite the same again in the eyes of others (Garfinkle, 1956). They are stripped of their old identity and a new one takes its place in what Goffman calls a "status degradation ceremony". Part of such a process then leads to the labelled person internalizing the new identity ascribed to them. (Pilgrim & Rogers, 1993: 17)

The widespread acceptance of the biomedical model, particularly for bipolar disorder, in turn acts upon the individual's expectations of her condition. Clinicians, the media, literature, friends and family all contribute to the individual's acceptance of her depression as chronic, such that it is difficult to tell whether depression is viewed as chronic because the individual has experienced it as severe and unrelenting, or because of the results of genetic studies she has read, or because the power of sociocultural attitudes and expectations influences and confirms a belief in its chronicity. Yet the women I spoke with described a mixture of reactions to the point at which a new identity was bestowed upon them, and certainly not all of them would have experienced it as a "status degradation ceremony". There were several, for instance, who felt relieved. Moreover, the new identity was not always internalised and was at times rejected. Frances, for instance, voiced serious doubts about her diagnosis of bipolar disorder. Without accepting one's diagnosis, it is hard to see how it can be internalised.

The reactions of the women I interviewed to their diagnosis show that they feel as though they have had a biomedical label thrust upon them – especially so for the diagnosis of bipolar depression. Bipolar depression's even heavier biomedicalisation in the eyes of the public is cemented by the belief that it is a genetic problem. That belief, in turn, contributes to the individual's view that it is not possible to overcome bipolar depression. By promoting genes as the centre of control of the condition, the biomedical model also renders it inescapable in the individual's eyes. As Zoe explains, "[i]f it's just biologically caused then it's not possible to cure, but it's possible to prevent or alleviate rather than to cure". Gina further explains, "I mean the problem is as long as the prevailing opinion is that it's hereditary or it's genetic, I don't think I'll be able to convince myself that I'm over it altogether".

Emphasising the biomedical view of depression deflects blame and is commonly thought to act as a defence against stigmatisation. The National Alliance on Mental Illness uses brain images and genetic tests to depict mental illness as biological, and that because it is biological, no one is responsible for it and it therefore does not deserve any stigma (Dumit, 2003)[6] (although recall that this approach turns out to have the opposite of its intended effect). Mike Bury (1982) argues that this is the biomedical model's advantage – helping individuals to maintain a sense of integrity in the midst of the illness. However, emphasising a genetic basis for depression can be a double-edged sword, with the moral seduction of the model counterbalanced by the sense of autonomy it asks the individual to relinquish. The journalist Tracy Thompson illustrates this dilemma when she writes about her diagnosis:

[s]o I was sick. But this was my brain I was talking about, not my gallbladder or my kidneys. It had some mysterious property called "consciousness". It produced behaviour, the sum total of which was somehow me. If I wanted to say simply that my brain was sick, I could stop there and disavow responsibility for that sickness – but if I did that, I would be giving up my idea of autonomy in the world. I would be simply a product of some chemical abnormality in a lumpy gray organ between my ears. (Thompson, 1995: 189–190)

Not only does the simplistic, popular notion of biochemical causation undermine perceived autonomy, but it can also give the impression that the condition is permanently ingrained and impossible to escape. Long-term follow-up studies indicate that positive outcomes in recovery are possible for individuals diagnosed with severe mental illness (e.g. Breier et al., 1991; Harrow & Jobe, 2010; Jobe & Harrow, 2010). Yet the biomedical model which has permeated popular perceptions of diagnosis paints a darker picture. As Comaroff and Maguire note, the biomedical model leaves us "especially bereft when we have to face events for which no rational explanation or remedy is forthcoming" (1981: 119). This point may explain why it is that although in theory a model of depression that places blame entirely on the individual's social environment should also have the effect of diminishing the individual's sense of control, in practice it is easier for individuals to view themselves as passive in the face of chemical imbalances than as passive in the face of social stresses. In the case of a depression caused by social stresses, there is at least potential for rational explanation, and hence the potential for gaining control. (I explore this point in detail in Chapter 5.)

However, as illustrated in the preceding chapter, many individuals do not hold to just one view of depression and the biomedical view can be incorporated into one's self-view in ways that do not necessarily contradict other views. This phenomenon is not unique to the women I interviewed. In a study conducted by Renata Kokanovic and colleagues (2013), individuals both adopted aspects of the biomedical view of depression and simultaneously resisted it – going to the doctor for help with personal problems (for lack of an alternative) and hoping for some relief of symptoms, but not anticipating that the doctor can help them solve the root causes of their problems which were situated in the social world. There is a similar tension when it comes to questions of agency. We saw that while some of the women I spoke with understood the biomedical model as a challenge to their ability to view themselves as agents, this was not the case for others. Suzanne McKenzie-Mohr and Michelle Lafrance (2011), in their study of women who had experienced depression or rape, also showed that women were eager to express agency while at the same time deflect blame for their experience. They understood themselves as both agents and patients rather than as either blameworthy or passive victims. In the same way, an initial understanding or impression of one's diagnosis in biomedical terms does not necessarily rule out a search for meaning or rule the person out as an agent in his or her journey out of depression.

On the one hand, the experiences recounted in this chapter support labelling theorists who contend that being labelled changes an individual's identity and her status in the eyes of society. On the other hand, their experiences emphasise that it is not the diagnosis per se but the individual's interpretation of that diagnosis which has the most salience for if and how it will be internalised. Sue Estroff and colleagues (1991: 361) make a similar point:

[o]ur data suggest that individuals' understandings of their problems, more than formal designations like a psychiatric diagnosis, have a strong influence on their views of themselves in relation to mental illness. Self-labeling, or seeing oneself as having a mental illness or being mentally ill, is clearly influenced by many factors, most of which are not clinical but contextual, experiential, and sociocultural [. . .] Labeling theory thus overestimates the importance of these formal biomedical

designations, while failing to consider adequately how aspects of the person influence label acceptance or rejection.

Estroff and colleagues recount the racial and gender influences on self-labelling. I suggest that the individual's beliefs regarding self-determination and responsibility also influence self-labelling. In both cases, what is apparent is that the overall impact of a psychiatric diagnosis on the individual is not a one-way process but the result of an interaction which occurs between the diagnosis and the meaning the individual ascribes to that diagnosis. This meaning in turn derives from the social interaction that the individual has with others (Blumer, 1969).

In the eyes of the women I interviewed, depression was viewed in medicalised terms at the point of being given that label. But the meanings the diagnosis has among different groups can be quite different, and the way an individual describes his or her symptoms can vary markedly from one culture to another. The Chinese, for example, are more likely to present with somatic symptoms than to speak about emotion (Kleinman, 1988b); in parts of India, they might be more likely to describe a fallen or painful heart (Pilgrim & Bentall, 1999); and in many non-Western countries, there is no word for "depression" (Kim, 2002; Marsella, 1980). Individuals may receive a different diagnosis (such as neurasthenia if they are in China) rather than depression (Kleinman, 1988b).[7] A biomedical model may never be implied or assumed, and hence never internalised by the individual. The implications of the diagnosis may thus have an entirely different impact on people in different cultures.[8]

Conclusion

The initial reactions of those I interviewed to their diagnosis revealed that they felt as though a biomedical model of depression was imposed upon them. As such, their reactions were based on what they felt the biomedical model meant for their sense of self. How and to what extent a diagnosis could impact on the individual's sense of self largely hinges on the degree of self-determination and responsibility the individual believes the depression allows. Those who believe the diagnosis exonerates them from responsibility for depression feel relieved by their diagnosis. In contrast, those who fear stigmatisation fear the blame they might receive from people who believe depression to be a personal failing, or something an individual should be able to control. Being labelled with what one understands (at least at the point of diagnosis) to be a biomedical disorder also has ramifications for the individual's sense of self by the implication that one has less self-determination. In theory, there is nothing to prevent certain thoughts and emotions from being both aspects of a psychiatric condition and aspects of one's personality. But in practice, learning of a diagnosis that is interpreted as removing one's responsibility for those traits also seems to challenge the place of those traits in one's self. Removing responsibility for certain traits and behaviours also effectively removes them from within the individual's control. As such, the biomedical model was a double-edged sword – removing responsibility for depression while simultaneously removing the prospect of having control over it.

Many scholars have criticised the biomedical model of depression for ignoring psycho-social factors surrounding and contributing to depression, and there is now scientific consensus that causes of depression are complex, not well understood and likely to involve a combination of biological, social and psychological factors (Murray & Lopez, 1996). This point even became the subject of Richard Bentall's open letter to Stephen Fry concerning his BBC documentary series *In the Mind* (Bentall, 2016). Yet the biomedical model does more than that – it also indirectly contributes to the view of depression as a chronic condition. It does so by both diminishing the individual's sense of self-determination and by putting forward a model of depression in which there are no exits. A belief that one has the ultimate power to change one's thoughts, emotions and behaviours appears to be a prerequisite to being able to identify them as truly one's own. This belief is influenced not only by how the individual interprets her diagnosis but also by how she interprets the role of medication.

4   Taking the Medicine
The Impact of Medication on the Self

Negotiating Medication and Its Side Effects

After being diagnosed, people usually move onto the next step in the clinical process – treatment.[1] But treatment for depression often causes more psychological introspection than treatment for more "physical" illnesses. This is understandable when we consider that treatment for depression targets our thoughts, emotions and behaviours – elements normally considered to be part of the self. During the course of the interviews, it was clear that medication's work is not confined to treating depression. Its stake in one's sense of autonomy and responsibility never went unnoticed, as the women either felt they had relinquished control of their mood and behaviour to the medication or incorporated medication's role into a narrative that made room for personal autonomy and responsibility.

We know that antidepressants can challenge our sense of autonomy and authenticity. In a questionnaire administered by Kessing *et al.* (2005) to 493 people diagnosed with unipolar or bipolar depression in Denmark, 42 per cent believed that when you take antidepressants you have less control over your thoughts and feelings and 43 per cent believed that antidepressants can change your personality. In another study, 22 people (mostly women) who had chosen to take St John's wort to treat their depression rather than prescription medication were interviewed. The authors found that one of the reasons why these people had chosen St John's wort rather than prescription medication was because they wanted to feel more in control in their treatment and recovery (Wagner *et al.*, 1999). Yet it is not clear why herbal remedies should be perceived to give the individual more control than conventional medication, unless the individual believes the herbal remedy is not as effective as conventional medication and therefore still leaves much of the work of recovery to the individual. Such a view first of all begs the question as to why one would want to use a particular medication because it is *less* effective, and secondly, there is no consensus as to the effectiveness of St John's wort for the treatment of depression. Studies such as these have clearly identified issues related to medication and self-determination – particularly between an increased psychological reliance on medication and a reduced sense of control. In this chapter, I examine *why* individuals feel the way they do about medication and the implications their views have for how depression is treated.

The process of being prescribed medication is of course not the same for everyone. However, in general the individual sees either a GP or is referred to a psychiatrist, who would usually diagnose and follow that by suggesting the patient try a certain medication. GPs are usually the first port of call, but if they feel that the patient's depression is severe or that she may have bipolar disorder, the patient is then referred to a psychiatrist. This process is seen as "best practice".[2] Those diagnosed with unipolar depression are normally recommended antidepressants along with talking therapy. Talking therapies range from cognitive behavioural therapy to counselling, interpersonal therapy and psychoanalytic psychotherapy. However, access to talking therapies can be challenging, as the waiting lists for them can be long. For this reason, antidepressants often become the first form of treatment a patient accesses. All but two of the women I spoke with had used prescription medication for their depression at some point. Of the two who did not, one used St John's wort and another used Chinese herbal medicine.[3] In contrast, those diagnosed with bipolar depression are usually given mood stabilisers either solely or in addition to antidepressants. Mood stabilisers appeared to be prescribed regardless of how frequent episodes of mania occurred or how much they bothered the individual. For example, Felicity explains why she would rather be treated solely with antidepressants:

Yeah they, I mean when you get a diagnosis of manic depression, it seems to me they want to put you on a mood stabiliser. So I was on sodium valproate *and* lithium but my hair started to fall out. So I eventually prevailed on them to let me come off the sodium valproate, and my hair stopped falling out. But lithium has got nasty side effects and I would sooner be on an antidepressant, but I just have to convince them somehow or other [. . .] My preferred scenario would be to go off the lithium and go on an antidepressant. But they like you to be on a mood stabiliser and they don't want you to be on an antidepressant as well because they think that will make me go high.

Yes. But you don't mind that so much.

No, no I don't [laughs]. Exactly.

A diagnosis of bipolar depression thus entails a different treatment regime and it is common for such individuals to be told that they will probably need to be monitored regularly and may need to be on medication for the rest of their lives. Further, all but one of those diagnosed with bipolar depression were on medication at the time of interview, whereas this was not the case for all those diagnosed with unipolar depression. These factors place those diagnosed with bipolar depression in a slightly different position as far as treatment is concerned, which could affect how they feel about their self and their degree of autonomy.

Most of the women I interviewed stated that side effects were a concern. They were such a concern for Debbie that she chose to use St John's wort instead of prescription medicine, viewing the former as a less problematic and more benign form of treatment:

So why did they decide to put you on St John's wort instead of other medication?

Well it was because I didn't want to have medication principally. I didn't like the idea of the side effects, and also you can't really treat a human problem I don't think with drugs, even though they say it's to do with chemicals in your brain and hormones and stuff. So I just wanted something natural which wouldn't have dreadful effects in other areas [...]

Here, Debbie expresses both a desire to avoid side effects and a notion that it is more apt to choose a "natural" treatment for a "human" problem. Presumably, herbal remedies, like prescription medicines, are taken in order to alter biological processes, but because they are herbal they are perceived to be "natural" and thus somehow better. But while the incidence of side effects for St John's wort is lower than for prescription antidepressants, St John's wort is not free of side effects either (Linde et al., 2008; Rossler et al., 2007).[4]

For many of the women I interviewed, using prescription medication meant putting up with side effects. Often, the side effects were outweighed by the perceived benefits of the medication. Yet at times, the side effects proved to be too much and the individual was then prescribed a different medication until a tolerable one was found. This process of trial and error often made the individual feel like a guinea pig, painfully aware that each medication was an experiment. Some found the side effects so horrific (which was just one of the adjectives used) and the process of trial and error so arduous that they stopped using medication for years, if not altogether.

Peter Kramer, author of the bestseller *Listening to Prozac*, describes how some psychiatrists consider the process of prescribing antidepressants to be not one of choosing that which is most likely to be effective but one of choosing between side effects (Kramer, 1993). Yet the side effects and the way in which people are expected to subject themselves to them in a sort of ongoing experiment can have a significant effect on whether the individual chooses to continue with medication or not. The women I interviewed reported side effects including weight gain, dizziness, low libido, intense aversion to sunlight (due to dilated pupils), difficulty with walking and coordination, difficulty reading and writing, severe headaches, hypertension, tinnitus, nausea, vomiting, hair loss, joint pain, muscle jerks, dry mouth, heart palpitations, symptoms resembling viral meningitis, excessive sweating, nightmares and "numbed" emotions (although some would argue that numbed emotions are not a side effect but in fact the aim of the medicine). These side effects are more than mere headaches and are also subject to the individual's perceptions of their importance. For instance, weight gain may not bother some women very much, but for others, self-image is such an important issue that they will avoid a particular medication entirely in order to avoid weight gain (Spijker *et al.*, 2004).

Of course, the patient is under no obligation to fill their prescription, but it may be due to the nature of the medical encounter that they tended to do so. Just over half of those I interviewed described the process of taking medication as a sort of "deal" they strike with themselves – weighing the pros and cons of taking the medication before deciding to go ahead with it, remain on it or stop using it. For example, Frances describes how she weighed the positive effects of her medication against the negatives:

So do you consider yourself better now?

I think so. I'm certainly on the right medication. I'm on Depakote. I mean it keeps me stable; it seems to deal with depression. I haven't had depression at all, although my circumstances could have prompted it [...] I'd say the saddest thing for me is that I just don't feel myself. I'm not myself. And I'm not bright as a button anymore. I'm not full of ideas anymore. I'm not creative like I used to be. I'm not sharp. I think I do have memory problems. I think I do have problems with spelling and vocabulary which I used to be absolutely fantastic at. I just don't feel *me* quite. I'm a bit sort of fatter, slower. I'm probably just a slightly different kind of a person but I'm okay. So it's really hard. I'd love to be how I am normally. I'd even like to be how I am a bit manic because I love it, you know? And sometimes that makes me a bit sad and when I meet people now and when they're only getting to know me for the first time I do sort of say, "Oh I wish she knew what I used to be like". [...]

So how much control do you feel you have over bipolar?

Well I feel a bit like it's been taken away in that I'm on the medication and that's a kind of deal. It's like okay, I don't want to take it but I will. And I'm on the lowest dose I can be on now, probably safely, and that's a horrible thought.

Why?

Well because it could be for life, and then if I don't want to take it, might it happen again? And how bad would it be and what might happen? I really don't wanna take it but I do, and that's the deal I've struck.

For Frances, the price she pays to keep her deal is a loss of creativity, eloquence and intellectual capacity. She also mentions weight gain, a possible lifelong reliance on medication and that she simply does not feel like herself. Experiences such as these attest to the fact that these medications are "dirty" drugs – that is, their effects are not specific but wide-ranging. Prozac and other Selective Serotonin Reuptake Inhibitors (SSRIs) were seen as a breakthrough for the treatment of depression at the time not because they were considered to be more effective but because they were considered to be "cleaner" than tricyclics (i.e. fewer side effects) (Kramer, 1993). But when it comes to assessing the benefits of a drug against its side effects, sometimes a patient's perspective can differ markedly from a psychiatrist's. For some of those I interviewed, the side effects of some of their drugs, such as mumbling or losing articulacy, were more disturbing than the condition the drug was aimed at treating. Convincing their psychiatrists that this was the case, however, was experienced as challenging. The subjectivity involved in such a cost-benefit analysis is even more apparent when we consider the following question: If the situation were to be reversed and a patient were to seek medical help to alleviate symptoms much like these side effects, would the doctor judge side effects such as mood fluctuations to be worth it in the cost-benefit analysis? I speculate that the trade-off may not necessarily be based on whether the symptoms are worse than the side effects but on what the patient is seeking medical help for, and what then becomes the focus of medical attention.

The Simple Narrative: When It's All about the Medication

Some of the women I interviewed felt that medication was the single most crucial factor in their recovery. Those who felt this way often invoked the illness model as an explanation for the likely cause and treatment of depression. These women reasoned that a fluctuation in biochemistry must have triggered the onset of depressive or manic symptoms, and this "biochemical imbalance" is what the medication corrects. Being a simple view and allowing the individual to take a back seat, the narrative had its appeal. But this also meant that recovery from depression was largely out of their hands:

So what do you think was the key to your improvement?

Annette: Medication. Definitely. Medication would probably be number one.

You were saying that having work and having friends to talk to and support really helps. Do you ever feel that that gives you some kind of control? Or is that something separate?

Annette: Yeah, I think it helps to build up your confidence again, but I think it's more about your character and your personality and your self esteem.

Helps to build up your confidence again. But in all honesty, I think it doesn't give you any control. I think if you took away the meds, no amount of going to work or talking to your friends or, what was the other one? I think that was it, wasn't it? No amount of that would prevent another episode.

Women like Annette consider their medication to be the most effective element in their recovery but struggle with the resulting loss of control they feel over their mind and emotions. Despite being grateful for the improvement afforded them by the medication, it is not enough to make them feel good about the prospect of remaining on it indefinitely.[5] Their ambivalence about taking medication stems from feeling dependent on something external to themselves in order to function. Malpass and colleagues (2009) summarise this feeling as a tension between "the need for self-determination and fear of relapse", or "a difference between symptoms 'being controlled' and 'feeling in control' of symptoms".

For some, the ritual of taking a pill serves as a daily reminder that something is still not right – that although they may be feeling better, they are still dependent on something to keep them well, and therefore do not feel completely recovered.

Would you want to come off the medication eventually?

Rebecca: I think I would, definitely [...] It's sort of difficult for me to accept the fact that I'm on medication because I guess as long as I'm on that, then it's an indication that I'm ill in some way and that there's something wrong with me. And that's not a nice thought. It's something I might have to accept at some level that I need this to feel normal – whatever normal is. And I mean, I know of people who are constantly on medication but it's not very nice because again you wanna be able to get through your life without that sort of chemical crutch or whatever ... And it's illogical because again especially if it's mainly physical then it can happen. It's like people who are constantly on antibiotics or whatever. But still it's a slightly frustrating thought that you need pills just to be able to function normally.

As Rebecca notes, there are individuals with chronic illnesses who need to take medication daily in order to stay well. Yet in the case of depression, staying "well" means staying "mentally well", which, as we have seen, has very personal connotations. There are also women such as Ingrid and Hazel who feel that it is not normal to have to take medication in order to feel normal, and who resent its symbolic reminder that things are not normal.

And how did you feel about taking the medication?

Ingrid: I hate taking medication. Even now still I don't like taking it because I feel I have to take tablets every day to feel normal. I still feel like that and I do it because I have to but I don't like it. I still wish that I could be medicine-free. My mother used to drink a lot and she was also on medication. I can't remember what they were called now but when she was drunk sometimes she used to take overdoses of tablets and to me taking tablets makes me feel I have a weakness and reminds me of her probably a lot. So I don't like taking them for that reason.

What's the symbolism in taking the medicines that bothers you?

Hazel: [. . .] [Taking medication] reminds me every day of what I did in the past – what experiences I had in the past. It's like – I can tell you a story. For example, a girl broke up with her boyfriend and she was trying to forget this guy. And she did this by marking on the calendar, "Okay today I'm going to forget him", and then the next day she would mark on the calendar, "Today I'm going to forget him." So what's the ending? So after a year, she is still thinking about the guy. It's like this – I won't forget.

For these women, the constant reminder that one is dependent on something seen as external to the self in order to keep depression away is, ironically, cause for a sense of sadness in and of itself. On the one hand, medication restores their sense of rationality and in that sense is viewed as indispensable. On the other hand, the more power attributed to the medication, the less control they feel over their state of mind – a sentiment which engenders fear. For individuals who feel they have relinquished some of their self-determination to medication, it is seen at best as a necessary evil and at worst as a danger. Without any other significant means of control over their episodes, and without an explanation for medication's role in recovery that incorporates the individual's capacity to help themselves, they feel reliant on medication on the one hand, but resentful of that reliance on the other, seeing that reliance as an admission of failure.

Barbara: It always felt like such a defeat to take antidepressants. It's like, "Can't you cope with life unless you take some drugs to make you okay?"

So do you want to eventually come off [the medication]?

Hazel: I'm quite ambivalent. On the one hand, I think for me I resent it sometimes because it's like still I think not being able to control it is a failure, so I still think there's some symbolism in the medicines. That's why I don't want to take them. I hate it. But on the other hand, I'm very afraid. I'm very scared if I didn't take the medicine what would happen. I'm really worried, because I've been on medication for such a long time now. It seems very shaky. It's like I'm walking on string if I don't get support.

Their mixed feelings were how a mother might feel after struggling in vain all night to calm her crying baby and finally handing it over to an experienced friend for help. On the one hand, there is relief that the baby is now calm, but on the other hand there might also be a feeling of inadequacy that she was unable to calm her child herself.

According to the biomedical view, depression is caused by an imbalance of brain chemicals (neurotransmitters) and treated with antidepressants, which restore the balance.[6] According to this view, the most important role the individual has is to take her medication at the times specified by her practitioner. This view, in its simplest form, exonerates the individual of responsibility in depression but at the same time allocates the largest share of responsibility for recovery to medication. This is the double-edged sword. There are, of course, some who find their medication effective and are happy to remain on it for the rest of their lives, having no qualms about relinquishing control to the medication. However, women such as Gina and Bridget realised the risk in which this placed them. Gina, who had found her latest medication almost miraculous in keeping her well, had begun to think she may even be cured and may never have to worry about having another depressive or manic episode again – until she had the following conversation with a friend:

[Friend] said, "How would you feel if you did have another episode?" and it really made me stop and think, because I had completely made up my mind that I was never gonna have another episode again. And then I just started thinking, "Well what impact would it have on my psyche if I did have another episode?" Like, I would be completely distraught if I did because I think it would feel like … Because at the moment I sort of feel like I'm cured. Like it's not there anymore and I don't have to worry about it. And that's how I want to feel about it because I don't want to have to go through life thinking, "There could be another episode just around the corner. Oh I have to be really careful. Oh what if? What if?" and agonising about my behaviour and being cared for by a mental health team. I don't want that. That's not how I want my life to be. I just want to live my life and not worry about it. But I can see now, having spoken to my friend last night, that there might be some danger in that because if I did have another episode I have no idea how I'd cope. I think if it gets worse – if I become resistant to my medication, if I start rapid cycling – I think I'll kill myself. I do think that I'll just kill myself because I can't live like that anymore. Like I've spent so many years of my life acutely depressed and I won't live like that in the future again …

I'm really afraid of living a sort of half-life, you know. Because again on these online support forums or whatever they're called, there's just so many people whose lives are just shattered and there's nothing they can do about it. You know, they can't hold down a job, their partners have left them, they don't have access to their children. They're not living. They don't have lives. They're, like, surviving. They're, you know, breathing but they're not living. They don't have lives and I don't see the point of enduring that kind of life, I really don't. I just think there's nothing positive in it and everything negative, so if that's how I end up, then I don't wanna know.

Is the faith in the medication very important?

Very important. Very important, yeah.

For Gina, the stark contrast between her situation on and off medication is at once a blessing and a curse. Unlike those such as Ingrid, Barbara and Hazel, Gina did not express concern with the level of control her medication seemed to have over her emotional and mental state or with sacrificing this sense of personal autonomy per se as long as she remained well. The difficulty only came when she realised how precarious her situation was and what the practical consequences were of relying so heavily on medication. That people can feel afraid of becoming psychologically dependent on their medication is well documented. However, Gina's feelings reveal more than just a psychological addiction or dependence on medication. It is not so much a fear of becoming dependent, but a fear that if the medication were to fail, all would be lost. Rather than feeling dependent on something that may or may not be important or effective, such a fear is predicated on the effectiveness of the medication itself. The difficulty, then, is with the repercussions of this effectiveness to their sense of control.

If we dig deeper and ask why medication's effectiveness can, ironically, be a source of unease, we find that the answer centres on medication's passive influence on the individual. Its workings are independent of any conscious control and so the individual feels it is the medication that is in control of her mind and emotions. Evelyn articulates this notion when she states:

I think the reason why I really resented the medication is because I felt *it was changing me in a way out of my control* in a sense. (my emphasis)

If the individual does not feel she plays a key role in her own recovery, she either resents or fears her vulnerability. For those who feel left out of their own recovery, it is clear that issues of autonomy and responsibility are more than just abstract philosophical concepts – they have a very real and personal significance for the person being treated but are largely not addressed during the course of their treatment.

The Complex Narrative: When Different Therapies Play a Role in Recovery

Many of the women I interviewed expressed other views of depression, or more complex versions of the illness view, which incorporate individual responsibility into their narrative. Diana, for instance, articulated one such view:

I think, because maybe I'm too much into this yoga and healing stuff maybe, what goes around your energy and your emotional life affects your body and your physical body. And then in turn, when there is something wrong with your body, in turn it also has an impact on your emotional life because if you ... Then if you have physical problems it will in turn affect your emotional life. And I see depression as a very good example for this. I mean, what's happening in your life, if you don't cope with them or just get over them, I mean. If you can't leave them behind just, you know, if you can't solve them in time, in time they will have an impact on your physical body like in your brain and everything. And then, that will have more impact again.

If one's physical and psychological states are both implicated in the development and maintenance of depression, it allows either of them to be legitimate targets for treatment. Both physical and psychological elements can then also be incorporated into the explanation of recovery, as women such as Nancy and Barbara illustrate:

And the pills help you with [getting pleasure from things]?

Nancy: Yeah. I think the pills start to lift your mood, and once your mood is lifted, you can do things that actually help yourself. But I did actually work through most of my depression ...

Barbara: I think antidepressants and stuff, they make you feel better but they don't solve your depression. They don't sort things out in a permanent way, they just make you more capable of thinking about the things without being scared of it.[7]

Another explanation which a few used to articulate the role of medication in their recovery from a depression was to compare it with socially accepted mood-enhancers such as tea, coffee or chocolate. What, they asked, is the moral difference between eating chocolate and taking an antidepressant in order to increase the level of serotonin in your brain? They argue that both have the same effect, but one is more socially accepted than the other.

So why would you want to come off [medication]?

Evelyn: I'm not sure. I guess because it doesn't feel like the genuine me. But comparing it to my cup of tea in the morning, I could inflict me at 7 o'clock without it on the world but I don't think that would be very nice for people! I suppose it's not normalised in society like a cup of tea is. It would be like going into an exam. There is no actual philosophical difference really between taking ... what is those anti-Alzheimer's drugs? I heard a radio article on them. There's not really that much difference between taking one of those and having a mug of coffee and a chocolate bar before you go in biochemically, it's just that society chooses to make one freely available to everyone and not the other. And some people probably need the concentration-enhancing drugs if they are the type that panics in exams and other people don't. Do they have a disability and should they be given the enhancing drugs? It's a bit of a non-question. You have to draw the line somewhere.

The comparison to chocolate, caffeine and other mood-enhancers relegates antidepressants to a category of substances which are not thought to override personal responsibility but to enhance alertness and concentration. For individuals with these more nuanced views of the role of medication, there is more room for individual responsibility. Responsibility here refers to their ability to control or overcome their depression. Yet rather than being a burden, the control and responsibility they feel they had were sources of empowerment. Barbara explains why:

So do you feel more in control of depression now?

Yeah yeah, much more. Much more.

You sort of know what you'd do if it happened again?

Yeah. Like I think going to counselling has allowed me to learn to think about things in a different way, and think things through a lot more and just have more of an open mind about stuff that I don't know about myself, as opposed to before . . .

Barbara's explanation, typical of those who placed less emphasis on medication as a key to their recovery, shows the direct connection individuals make between aspects of recovery which require active participation (such as gaining insight into their experience, changing their habits, keeping a regular routine and so on) and a sense of control over depression. There are yet more connections – some predictable and some not. While all of those who had a "simple narrative" to describe the role of medication also viewed depression as an illness (as one might expect), those who expressed a more complex narrative for the role of medication expressed a variety of different views of depression. That is, the complex narrative regarding antidepressants did not connect with a particular view of depression, but with a variety of views.

Medication and Authenticity

Treatment with antidepressants can cause many people to redefine their view of their selves. On the one hand, antidepressants can be viewed as enabling the individual to take control of his or her life or to feel more authentic. For instance, Anders Petersen writes that depression could be interpreted as the result of long-term pressure on individuals to attain "authentic self-realisation" in contemporary Western society. In reducing symptoms and assisting the depressed individual to overcome inactivity and social inhibitions, antidepressants can be understood as enabling the individual to achieve authenticity (Petersen, 2011). On the other hand, antidepressants can also be seen as undermining authenticity. The question that is then raised is, "Why would individuals adopt one view of their self over another?"

I suggest the answer lies in where control of the self is perceived to reside. Among all those I interviewed, it became clear that what is important for questions regarding authenticity is not whether the individual feels authentic on medication but *why* she feels that way. To illustrate this point, below are the three ways in which the relationship between antidepressants and authenticity arose among the women I interviewed:[8]

(1) All the different states the individual experiences – whether depressed, manic, "stable", on or off medication – are all part of one's "real/true" self.[9] Medication thus elicits just one of many versions of the self.
(2) The medication takes control away from the self, and therefore masks the "real/true" self.[10]
(3) The medication corrects a problem, and therefore restores control and brings the individual back to her "real/true" self.

I present examples of each of these views in turn and draw out the common thread I found to underlie all of them – that it is a sense of autonomy (or self-determination) that causes one to feel authentic.

All States Are Authentic

Phoenix, a strong-minded lady who felt herself to have "risen from the ashes", had to deal with a plethora of medical problems as well as bipolar depression. To her, bipolar depression was a clear-cut illness caused by genes and treatable by medication. Yet despite this clear-cut view of her bipolar depression, her view of authenticity was not narrowly defined or a case of either–or but a multifaceted concept which includes a number of different states of being:

Who do you feel is the real Phoenix? Is it when you're in one of your bipolar phases, or now, or does it matter whether you're on medication or not, or is it something else?

Well I think I'm all of those things. Like a cake really when you're making a cake and you have little bits that are one thing and you have some basic flour as a basic person. I think I'm all those things [...] I think like you are Tamara, but you are also a daughter, and I don't know if you have a partner but you're another role and you're also a sister. Everybody is at least three bits.

Phoenix's description compares the different facets of her bipolar disorder with the different facets of everyone's lives, at once owning and normalising this aspect of her experiences. Her bipolar episodes may not be something commonly experienced, but, she explained, they are no more a challenge to her self than any other experiences and relationships are a challenge to ours. A few of the women I interviewed were like Phoenix and felt that that they were their real selves whether on medication or off, or whether depressed or manic or not. However, they also described certain states as feeling slightly *more* authentic than others – a sliding scale of sorts that allows for degrees of authenticity. This more authentic state was the state in which they felt more autonomous. Below, Evelyn describes this view, saying that she felt that all the states she experiences are part of her self, "in the same way that you're the same person when you're tired and when you're not". Medication simply transformed her into a more competent, presentable state, which was helpful for the time-being. Yet she still resented the medication

because I felt *it was changing me in a way out of my control* in a sense. Ideally I'd like to work towards a place where I can be as competent as I am on it, with a version of my genuine unmedicated self that I was happy with. (emphasis added)

At this point, Alexandre Erler might weigh in and state that Evelyn's case shows how "it is not plausible to claim that just because some device helps you acquire certain traits you want to have, it thereby enhances your authenticity" (Erler, 2012: 262). More is needed in order to make such a claim. Evelyn does not go as far as saying that medication makes her *inauthentic*, but indicates that there is a sense in which she feels herself to be relinquishing some control over her thoughts, emotions and behaviours to something external to her self – something with which she feels uncomfortable. In this way, even some women who do not feel *inauthentic* on medication can still grapple with the notion of authenticity and a perceived loss of some of their control to medication.

Medication as a Threat to Authenticity

In contrast with those who felt that medication helped them become more authentic, nearly half of the women I spoke with felt less authentic when on medication. In the following excerpt, Gail is one of the women who articulated exactly why they did not believe that medication enabled authenticity:

Did you feel like a different person when you were on the Chinese medicine? As in did you feel you had a different identity?

I think I felt more like I was gaining control over the situation and I was getting to the meaning of it all. And I think the whole process changed me. But I would not say into a different person but rather back to who I used to be. Kind of finding my true self.

I see. Would you have felt the same on conventional medicine?

No. For the conventional medicine somehow makes me feel helpless, like I do not have any control over the situation and any way how to change things. It is kind of, okay this is the way things are, it is biological and you just need to get it fixed like a broken arm. To me this is associated with no control, no freedom and passivity.

In the above quote, Gail demonstrates a concern similar to that voiced by Leon Kass (2003: 22) in relation to human enhancement:

Human education ordinarily proceeds by speech or symbolic deeds, whose meanings are at least in principle directly accessible to those upon whom they work [. . .] In contrast, biomedical interventions act directly on the human body and mind to bring about their effects on a subject who is not merely passive but who plays no role at all. He can at best *feel* their effects *without understanding their meaning in human terms.*

Both Gail and Kass focus on the individual's passivity as the problematic aspect of psychopharmaceutical medication. Once ingested, its action is beyond conscious control, and it is that element which can cause psychopharmaceuticals to be viewed as a threat to the self. When I questioned Gail as to why she felt differently about Chinese medicine compared with conventional Western medicine for depression, her response appeared to support Kass' claim regarding the difference between education and biomedical intervention:

And how is Chinese medicine different?

You know, I think what I needed was a cognitive engagement with the situation, getting to the roots of things. And when I look back at it, it certainly helped me partially as a medicine at the time of crisis. This aspect of it is the same as conventional medicine – to stabilise the patient. But it also offers you some kind of therapeutic approach and philosophy of life probably. It reminds me a bit of humanistic approach in that it is up to you to change things.

So it's the philosophy that comes with Chinese medicine that gives you that approach?

Yes, I think so.

By offering Gail an opportunity to engage intellectually, this aspect of Chinese medicine is what gave her the chance to play an active role in her recovery. It is not that the Chinese herbs themselves enabled her to return to her true self whereas the conventional medicine would not have. Rather, it is the active role that the individual must take within Chinese medicine that enabled Gail to feel authentic. In this way, even if medication transforms the individual into what she wants to be, its influence on the self in a way which bypasses human agency can, for some, be seen as a threat to authenticity, and for others, a state that is less than ideal. It is the perception that medication undermined their autonomy that prevented them from seeing themselves as authentic when on medication. They considered the thoughts and emotions arising in their minds during that stage to have been influenced by an external force, that is, they were not in control. The implication is that you cannot be your true self if it is not you at the helm.

Wendy, a 28-year-old student, experienced a depression which brought her to the point of physical breakdown, describing a point when she felt unable to leave her house. Having reached an all-time low, she sought medical help and was placed on antidepressants. These seemed to produce a crucial improvement in her mood and knocked her out of the depressed physical cycle she was in. Yet in addition to altering her physical depression and mood, the antidepressants also altered her way of thinking. What others might consider to be a depressed way of thinking was, for her, a sort of creativity and an interesting way of seeing the world. On antidepressants, everything was a "happy way of thinking" – "like constantly being on a high" (in Wendy's words). Rather than welcoming such a change, as one might expect, because this way of thinking was so alien to her, she wanted to come off the medication as soon as possible.

So why did you take yourself off that [medication]?

Wendy: Because it alters the way you think. It completely alters the way you think and behave and everything and that's so disturbing [. . .] The medication wasn't me. Like I say, it just made me completely psycho. It wasn't my normal way of thinking. Okay yes of course that was me, but *it was altered by an outside agent,* so I wouldn't count that as me [. . .] *It's someone else thinking.* (emphasis added)

Carl Elliott, who also views antidepressants as a threat to authenticity, echoes a similar sentiment: "It would be worrying if Prozac altered my personality, even if it gave me a better personality, simply because it isn't *my* personality. This kind of personality change seems to defy an ethics of authenticity" (1998: 182).[11]

Wendy and Elliott's views of the antidepressant self as inauthentic have been voiced in other empirical studies on this issue. As one of Knudsen *et al.*'s interviewees also states, "I really want to live without pills then I can be certain that when I'm happy it's actually me who is happy" (2002: 247). But Wendy goes a step further. It is not simply being on medication that bothers Wendy, but more so the altered phenomenal state she experiences on medication. On antidepressants, Wendy was in a happier state, but it was a state in which she felt inauthentic:

Because I wasn't used to feeling happy about the world anyway so I think I would have ... Well when I was on the medication I felt very uncomfortable with suddenly waking up and being happy and you know. That's just so completely alien that I was probably quite uncomfortable with it.

In fact, it was such an alien feeling that, once her physical function had been restored (at her lowest point, she could not walk for long and could barely write), she stopped taking the medication so that her normal way of thinking – what would be categorised as depression – was restored. Wendy's view might seem odd to those who strive to get rid of depression altogether. Yet as long as she can function, Wendy prefers what others would classify as a mildly depressed state, characterising it as a more creative and interesting way of thinking, regardless of how the rest of the world characterises such a state. What Wendy voices is in fact her own ideal of authenticity – something which Charles Taylor describes in the following way:

There is a certain way of being human that is my way. I am called upon to live my life in this way, and not in imitation of anyone else's life. But this notion gives a new importance to being true to myself. If I am not, I miss the point of my life; I miss what being human is for me. (Taylor, 1991b: 29)

For Wendy, the ideal of authenticity wins over the seemingly positive effects of medication.

Medication as Enabling Authenticity

Wendy's case stands in stark contrast to some of the patients Peter Kramer (1993) describes in *Listening to Prozac* who underwent radical self-transformations on Prozac and came to view their new selves as their authentic selves. Despite having had a very different personality all their lives until they began taking Prozac, their new, happy, more confident self was who they deemed to be their "true" self. Others in Kramer's book used Prozac as a means to shape themselves into who they wish to be – a self that is more in line with their values and how they wish to live. Both of these types of accounts described by Kramer and some of the women I interviewed demonstrate what scholars such as Levy (2011) advocate – that antidepressants can be used as a means of achieving authenticity, whether by moulding the self into what one wants to be (the self-creation view of authenticity) or an aid in returning to, or discovering, one's underlying true self (the self-discovery view of authenticity). How, then, do we reconcile these experiences of antidepressant-generated authenticity with those of individuals such as Wendy, whose radical transformation on Prozac was experienced as *inauthentic*? While all these states may seem markedly different, even contradictory, there is a common perception underlying the different experiences – that is, the degree to which one feels authentic appears to depend upon the extent to which one feels autonomous. If feeling authentic relates to being authentic, then this could have implications for the self-discovery view versus the self-creation view of authenticity. If the emphasis is placed on autonomy rather than on the nature of the change, then whether the transformation occurs via discovering a pre-existing self or by moulding the self is not important. What is important in order for the self to be authentic is that the transformation is autonomously driven. In this way, it is not the direction of the transformation but the fact that it was self-determined that matters.

Let us now turn to Zoe's case. Zoe had always been reluctant to take medication for anything – even paracetamol for headaches. It was not until her third episode of depression when, faced with the option of either taking some time away from university for a period or taking antidepressants in the hope that they would bring her out of depression, she chose to try the antidepressants. They seemed to work. So I asked her when she feels authentic and whether medication poses a challenge to that.

Who do you feel is the real Zoe, if there is a real Zoe?

I don't know. I think the person who feels in control of things and feels positive about things and can take things on and solve problems. That's when I feel most like me. [. . .]

Does being on medication challenge that sort of being your real self if control is a part of it?

Well no. I mean I just think of it as the medication correcting an imbalance, which then allows me to be who I would be if it weren't for that problem. So it's sort of like medication allows me to be me.

Nearly half the women I interviewed felt, as Zoe did, that medication helps them restore or become their authentic self. This view of medication is similar to the illness view, in which medication restores a balance or corrects a defect, thus restoring the individual to her "well" self. As previously mentioned, by reducing inhibitions and symptoms of depression, antidepressants can be seen as enabling authenticity (Petersen, 2011). This view is also reminiscent of that famously recounted by authors such as Kramer, in which individuals can feel that antidepressants restore them to their authentic self – either a "new" self or a return to the "old" self prior to depression (e.g. Grime & Pollock, 2004; Knudsen *et al.*, 2002; Kramer, 1993; Malpass *et al.*, 2009; Ridge, 2008; Ridge *et al.*, 2015). However, it would be naïve to assume that those who hold such a view have a rosy picture of an authenticity guaranteed by a pill. As Gina describes, the authenticity of one's thought processes, emotions and behaviour can still be challenged when they change, even while on medication.

Like none of my behaviour is pathological at the moment. I feel like it's all just me and if I . . . Like I feel like I'm responsible at the moment for all of my behaviour, whereas sometimes I'm not sure. Sometimes I question my behaviour. If my thought processes start to work in a certain way, I get scared and I think, "Is it just because I'm excited or am I getting hypomanic?"

We know that many people taking antidepressants want to understand whether they can attribute their positive moods to being "truly" better or whether their mood is a result of their medication (Bollini *et al.*, 2004; Grime & Pollock, 2004; Haslam *et al.*, 2004; Malpass *et al.*, 2009; Verbeek-Heida & Mathot, 2006). Yet Gina reflects on *what* such attributions could be based. She says that she feels like herself on medication, but that this view is based on the fact that she usually feels in control of her behaviour on the medication. In contrast, she feels more out of control when depressed or manic, and therefore not herself. Recall that the same justification – that is, one based on perceived control – rather than, say, the naturalness or artificiality of the treatment, is used by individuals who do *not* feel authentic on medication. That is, in both cases the circumstances in which individuals feel in control of their mood and behaviour are the circumstances in which they feel truly themselves.

The Importance of Being Authentic

A perceived loss of autonomy and authenticity can have significant consequences for the individual's choice of treatment and whether or not to remain on antidepressants. Recall Gail, a 26-year-old student who viewed her medicine as helping her return to a pre-existing authentic self rather than remaking her self. In her case, we saw the issue of control arise as a necessary element of feeling authentic, but also that this issue was integral to her decision to take Chinese medicine rather than Western medicine to treat her depression.[12]

The importance of self-determination to authenticity demonstrated by those I interviewed supports the link that several other authors (e.g. Betzler, 2009; Dworkin, 1976; Meyers, 1989; Ryan & Deci, 1999) also make between self-determination (or autonomy) and authenticity. However, the way interviewees described the *nature* of the relationship between authenticity and autonomy was slightly different. While the aforementioned authors place authenticity as one of the criteria for judging one's autonomy, those I interviewed used autonomy as a criterion for judging authenticity. That is, autonomy emerged as the most important factor in determining which state was their authentic, or more authentic, self.

I agree that autonomy and authenticity are intimately tied, but posit that, at least when it comes to feeling authentic or autonomous, autonomy *precedes* authenticity – that is, the autonomy condition must be satisfied before one can consider oneself to be authentic. In other words, I support the link, made by several authors so far, between autonomy and authenticity. However, when this link is made, it is usually put that the degree to which an action is autonomous depends on the degree to which it arises from, and accords with, one's authentic self. Or, as Meyers describes, "[a]utonomous conduct expresses the true self" (1987: 619). That is, autonomy depends on authenticity, and authenticity depends on other factors. As an example of some of the other factors put forward as a measure of authenticity, Gerald Dworkin describes authenticity as "the attitude a person takes towards the influences motivating him which determines whether or not they are to be considered 'his'" (1976: 25). In other words, an individual is authentic if he identifies with his feelings. Yet nearly all the women I spoke with identified with the motivation to act and feel happier; it was just that some felt it was not themselves determining their feelings and motivations when on medication. Such women felt it was an external agent causing them to feel better, and this made them feel less authentic despite having a positive attitude towards, and desiring, this feeling. I therefore suggest that, at least when it comes to the relationship between felt authenticity and felt autonomy, it is authenticity that depends on autonomy, rather than the reverse.

I presented similar issues in Chapter 2 regarding the question in individuals' minds as to whether certain behaviours arose from the self or from the illness (illness in this case conceptualised as an external force).

Although it was obvious that the acts in question belonged to the individual, if these acts were viewed as too heavily influenced by an external
force (being depression-as-illness), then in the eyes of these women, they
could not be considered to belong to their true self. As Wendy stated
earlier:

The medication wasn't me [...] Okay yes of course that was me, but *it was altered
by an outside agent*, so I wouldn't count that as me or whatever you want to call it.
(emphasis added)

If we evaluate what these individuals are saying, what it means for the
concept of the authentic self is that it is possible for the mind to give rise to
experiences of self that seem – to another observing self – to feel inauthentic. The reason for this feeling is because not everything arising from the
mind feels self-determined.

The evidence presented in this section which indicates that perceived
autonomy is a requirement for perceived authenticity may be particularly
useful for those who subscribe to the view that what it is to be authentic
should match in some way with how authentic one feels. I do not wish to go
as far as supporting this notion due to discrepancies that can hypothetically
arise between feeling authentic and being authentic (and likewise, between
being autonomous and feeling autonomous). However, the relationship I
describe here at least explains our intuitions concerning our own sense of
authenticity, and how we judge the authenticity of others. Consider the
following scenario. A drug induces Sophie to do ridiculous things that are
completely out of character for her. However, the drug also makes her feel
that she is in control and that her actions express her authentic self. Our
intuitions tell us that although Sophie may *feel* authentic, we would not
consider her to actually *be* authentic because she is being manipulated. If
autonomy is required for authenticity, this explains our intuitions about
Sophie's inauthentic state while on the drug. It is because the seat of
control resides with the drug, not with herself, that we believe her to be
inauthentic in that state. At the same time, we can understand why it is that
Sophie *feels* authentic – because she feels that she is in control.

The account of authenticity I have presented here is that what determines whether an individual feels authentic or not, in whatever mental or
medicated state she is in, is whether she feels self-determined. That is,
perceived self-determination appears to be a precondition for feeling
authentic. Such an account of authenticity may, by now, seem unsurpris-
ing to some readers. Yet the account contrasts with other views, such as at
least one interpretation of a performative approach to authenticity.
Michael Schwalbe recounts the real biographies of Reet and Shine (nick-
names), two African-American men raised in America's south during

racial segregation. Schwalbe recounts how the men both adopt personas in order to survive racial segregation. The men's struggle for authenticity, he contends, is very different to the struggle for authenticity in more privileged groups because it entails attempting to overcome the "insurmountable" hurdles of racial hegemony and subordination. In the story, he shows how "the lives of many men in subordinated groups are characterized by similar struggles to live authentically, without masks worn to please more powerful others" (2009: 140).

Vannini and Williams argue that this means the men's authenticity can only be achieved with a price – that is, the masks worn as protective personas can become self-destructive traps – and that this means "[p]erformative and critical approaches to authenticity such as Schwalbe's show that in everyday life authenticity can be far from 'being in control'" (2009: 9). I beg to differ with this interpretation. Choosing among a very limited array of personas available to African-American men in the segregated south is not true freedom to choose one's authentic self, and therefore not a performance of authenticity. As such, the personas these men adopt in order to survive in difficult circumstances are not authentic personas but simply two of the few "legitimate" personas available to them. While such inauthenticity comes at a price, so does authenticity in this context. In order to adopt an authentic persona and still survive, one would need to have the freedom to do so – something which a highly oppressed group does not have. Although the struggle for authenticity may be hard-won, or never won, given the significant obstacles one would have to surmount in such circumstances, the indication that one has attained authenticity is nevertheless the feeling that one has gained control over one's self. The struggle for authenticity is exceedingly difficult in cases such as that presented by Schwalbe precisely because it is a struggle for control of one's self against far more powerful others.[13] An understanding of authenticity as *authentheo* (being in control), which is supported by this chapter, thus has implications for the way certain accounts (such as Reet and Shine's) are interpreted and helps us understand the significance of the struggle for self-determination by oppressed groups. Such is the importance of authenticity to individuals that the struggle for self-determination is really a struggle for the freedom to be who one truly is.

Implications for Treatment

Earlier, I presented the issues regarding side effects with which many individuals contend when taking medication for unipolar or bipolar depression. As well as having to contend with side effects, a number of individuals feel that taking medication for depression undermines their sense of authenticity by undermining their sense of self-determination and control over their recovery. There is already emerging evidence that patients who exercise greater control over their treatment plans appear to experience better outcomes (Geers *et al.*, 2013), so these issues are not just theoretical but of practical import. For some of the women I spoke with, their diminished sense of authenticity was enough reason to stop, or to want to stop, their medication, or to choose alternatives such as Chinese medicine, herbal remedies or talking therapy. Whether or not one feels authentic on medication therefore seems to be an issue that is important enough to take into account in treatment decisions.[14] Perhaps not surprisingly, taking patient's beliefs and preferences into account helps clinicians understand patient behaviours concerning medication (Schofield *et al.*, 2011) and renders patients more satisfied with their therapeutic relationship and treatment (Anderson *et al.*, 2015). Doing so also appears to benefit treatment outcomes, at least indirectly (Elkin *et al.*, 1999; Hunot *et al.*, 2007; Iacoviello *et al.*, 2007; Kwan *et al.*, 2010).[15]

Aside from the issue of a threat to authenticity associated with medication for some people, there is also some evidence which raises doubt about the effectiveness of antidepressants relative to placebos and talking therapies. Recent meta-analyses suggest that antidepressants are not much more effective than placebos for mild to moderate depression, although they appear to have a greater effect for severe depression (Fournier *et al.*, 2010; Kirsch *et al.*, 2008) and that psychotherapy appears to be just as effective as pharmacotherapy for depression (De Maat *et al.*, 2006; Imel *et al.*, 2008) or perhaps even more effective in some cases (Strawson, 2004). These studies alone give us cause to question whether antidepressants should be prescribed for mild to moderate depression. There are, of course, practical reasons why antidepressants are often the default treatment option for depression – talking therapies may take a longer time to access. But even if the doubt surrounding the effectiveness of antidepressants turns out to be unfounded, the profound effect that some feel antidepressants have on their sense of control and authenticity alone should prompt policymakers to at least make talking therapies more affordable and easier to access so that those who would prefer to use talking therapy rather than medication are not faced with those barriers.

Conclusion

Investigating how the self is affected by psychopharmaceuticals reveals that much depends on how the individual views medication's function in the treatment of depression. If the individual conceptualises a simple biomedical explanation for medication's role in recovery in which it corrects a chemical imbalance and is the sole or most important factor in controlling the individual's mood, then the individual is exonerated from blame for depression, but their ability to control it in the future is undermined. Conversely, if a more complex narrative is used in which medication is not the most important factor, the individual tends to feel she has a greater role in her recovery and in preventing future episodes of depression. However, such individuals did not focus on self-blame but rather on the ways in which they could prevent depression from occurring in the future.

It is also clear that it is not the artificiality or otherwise of medication that threatens a sense of authenticity. Whether medication is perceived as enabling or hindering self-determination, it is the perception of having self-determination that is integral to authenticity. Without feeling self-determination, individuals feel less authentic. Medical practitioners should be aware of the issues that patients have with antidepressants, such as how they can impact on perceptions of authenticity and how important such an issue is to patients, if they are to tailor treatment to the individual and improve patient care.

5   Crossing Your Fingers
Predicting Depression's Role in the Future Self

When I embarked upon this research, I set out to interview women who had been through depression, diagnosis and treatment and were feeling better by the time they volunteered to be interviewed. After the interviewee had recounted her journey into and out of depression, it seemed natural for me to ask, "What next?" to understand what kind of role she envisaged depression would play in her future (if any). Because it seemed like such a natural question to ask, I was surprised to find very little research on how people perceive the role of depression in their future.

There is, of course, much written on evaluating the risk of future depressive episodes/relapse of depression, and significant focus has centred on how certain genetic variations might interact with stressful life events to predispose people to major depression (most notably Caspi *et al.*'s (2003) study).[1] Stressful life events have been well established as a factor in the risk of depression (e.g. Brown *et al.*, 1973; Dohrenwend & Dohrenwend, 1974). Mazure (1998) reviewed studies spanning from 1969 to 1989 and concluded that there is a consistent relationship between stressful life events and the onset of major depression. Paykel and Cooper's (1992) later review concluded that depressive episodes triggered by "stressful life events" (as measured by life events scales) were slightly more likely to have better outcomes than episodes *not* triggered by "stressful life events". Yet there has been comparably little research done on the *significance* people attach to stressful life events. While there has been some life event research which has considered the individual's depression in the context of their life circumstances (e.g. Brown *et al.*, 1985; Monroe & Simons, 1991), there are growing calls for psychiatry to take greater account of the social context of depression, particularly when it comes to nosology (Blazer, 2005; Breggin & Breggin, 1994; Healy, 1997; Horwitz & Wakefield, 2007).[2] This chapter adds to that call by showing that when considering whether or not depression would likely be a part of their future, the women I spoke with looked to their life context and the context in which they believed their episodes arose. I also show the importance of meaning, and consequently a sense of control, as a mediator between the perceived context of depression in an individual's life and the sense that it may be a permanent part of her life not only now but in the future. As a result, this chapter has a dual purpose: first, it extends the theme of perceived control and its importance to perceptions of the self in depression by showing how perceived control is key to how one envisages the role of depression in one's future self, and second, it examines the implications that this finding may have for how depression is categorised, presenting another challenge to the biomedical model of depression.

When interviewees connected their depression to a trigger – something in their lives which they felt precipitated their depression – within their own narratives, they may be said to be categorising their reaction as understandable (or what Horwitz and Wakefield might classify as "normal sadness"). However, as Horwitz and Wakefield (2007) note, some depressions can be disproportionate reactions to events, or persist long after the trigger has disappeared. I did not aim to ascertain whether or not this was the case. As such, despite our shared concern with the issue of categorisation in depression, the trigger versus no-trigger distinction I present here does not adequately map onto the sadness versus depression distinction that Horwitz and Wakefield present. I do, however, support their emphasis on the importance of taking the social context of depression into account in our understanding and treatment of depression in the sense that it is important to women in their perceptions of its future role in their lives.

Perceived Triggers versus Actual Causes

I refer to "perceived triggers" throughout this chapter to denote that which an interviewee felt had catalysed her into a depressive (or manic) episode, as distinct from an actual cause or a perceived cause. I distinguish triggers from causes here because it captures the sense in which it was used by the women I interviewed. There are a number of different theories concerning the aetiology of depression which, if one assumes that there can only be one aetiology underlying depression, are competing theories. Yet the term "trigger" is fairly neutral in relation to aetiology, because while a trigger can be understood as part of a causal pathway, or as an intermediate causal variable, it need not be viewed as *the* primary cause or the most important causal factor. It is perhaps due to this aetiological neutrality that triggers, or the lack thereof, could be discussed by interviewees regardless of their beliefs about depression's cause.

Perceived triggers here are defined solely by the participant's own assessment of the impact of the event on her life and the onset of depression because, unlike other studies that seek to find the causal relationship (if any) between "stressful life events" and depression, I sought to investigate the relationship between an individual's *experience* of depression and her view of its role in her life.[3] My use of the term "trigger" is therefore similar to Bruce McEwen's definition of "stress", which he describes as "an event or events that are interpreted as threatening to an individual and which elicit physiological and behavioral responses" (McEwen, 2000: 173). Such an understanding of the term "trigger" not only distinguishes it from "cause" and captures the sense in which it was invoked in the interviews but also leaves room for different aetiological theories. For instance, in Peter Kramer's view, depression is triggered by stressors in those who are already vulnerable, either due to biological or environmental factors. In his view, "[s]tressful life events, such as child abuse, lay a groundwork for the sorts of deprivation and failure that lead to illness. Humiliating losses trigger episodes. For many sorts of harm, predisposition matters" (Kramer, 2005: 148). Kramer contends that those with a vulnerability to depression perceive events and circumstances differently, which is why the same events and circumstances can result in depression in some individuals but not in others. In contrast, Paul Biegler interprets such life events and circumstances as more than just factors in depression's aetiology or stressors to be avoided (which, on his understanding, is what Kramer reduces them to), but as sites in which meaning can potentially be found. Biegler explains, "[d]epression is a signal that its trigger threatens agential interests on a host of levels, not just as harbingers of disease" (2012: 137). On Biegler's (2012: 137) account, a "trigger" or "stressor" is not just "an unfortunate interpretation of a life event, appearing courtesy of aberrant physiology" but a threat to the individual which, if understood, can lead to increased autonomy. Focusing on triggers rather than causes thus allows room for different interpretations of depression's aetiology such as Kramer's and Biegler's.

It is possible that some women want to find triggers to connect to their episodes, in which case it may be possible to identify anything as having triggered depression or mania. Likewise, some may misremember events, self-deceive or mistakenly attribute events or circumstances as triggers. It may also be that those who do not identify triggers simply do not make any connection between events and circumstances that precede an episode.[4] Thus, it is important to bear in mind that what follows does not reflect differences between those whose episodes were actually triggered and those whose episodes were not triggered (in an epidemiological sense) but between those who believed that there were triggers (which I refer to as the trigger group) and those who did not (which I term the no-trigger group).[5]

Similar circumstances may be occurring in both trigger and no-trigger groups prior to their episodes, but it may simply be that the trigger group makes links between the events and episodes and the no-trigger group does not. The opposite may also be the case in that some of those who believed their depression arose out of nowhere experienced what clinical studies might consider to be "major life events", such as the death of a loved one, but did not believe they experienced a depression in response to it. Their depression may have come years later and seemingly out of nowhere. As a result, although the event may have had a high score on a life events scale such as the Social Readjustment Rating Scale (Holmes & Rahe, 1967), if the individual did not consider it to have much, if any, connection to her depression, I did not classify it as a trigger.

Rebecca is one such case, describing how at first she thought her depression might have been a response to what could be considered a stressful circumstance. Yet she remained unconvinced and, despite counselling and self-examination, was unable to satisfactorily identify anything she thought was a trigger:

[a]nd it was just sort of starting at work where I started having these very low moods, feeling kind of depressed and everything and often having to go to the bathroom to cry and everything. But for a very long time I thought it was just because I was having difficulty settling in at Cambridge or because I was changing, starting a PhD. It was like a major change so for a long time I thought maybe it's just that or the fact that things weren't going so well at work and everything. But then in the summer last year it sort of became gradually more and more clear that that wasn't just it. There was something else wrong . . . But I still haven't been able to find any sort of reason. And also when I have these sort of attacks of bad mood, I mean my counsellor would often ask me what triggered it, what happened before? And usually there was nothing!

This chapter will show how perceiving one's depression as having been triggered by an event or circumstance or not has significant implications for the individual's beliefs concerning her future with depression. This stark contrast between those who perceived triggers and those who did not also poses a challenge to the one-size-fits-all classification of major depression – effectively the biomedical model of depression – as I discuss later in this chapter.

Types of Triggers

As mentioned earlier, relying on the individual's perceptions of what triggered their episodes meant that sometimes what the investigator might consider to be a relatively minor event can have greater significance for the individual or vice versa. For example, Frances did not have any friends or relations killed in the attacks on the United States on 11 September 2001 and was not in the United States at the time, yet she explained that it affected her in a very deep way – so much so that she questions her diagnosis and wonders whether it should in fact be post-traumatic stress disorder rather than bipolar depression.

Among those who experienced triggers, some experienced a raft of what they considered to be triggers, whereas some only experienced one. The following is a list of triggers reported by the women I interviewed. The groups of triggers shown here were formed, as much as possible, in keeping with where the interviewee believed the emphasis should be. For instance, although "difficulty making decisions" could also be considered "work problems" if it was in relation to work, or interpreted as "a fear of failure", such labels were not used for the trigger if the interviewee did not frame it in such a way.

Types of Triggers Reported

Birth of baby
Contraceptive pill
Combination of events all at once
Death
Family problems
Friendship problems
Financial problems
Illicit drug use
Illness
Job interviews
Legal problems for spouse
Making decisions
Medication
Move overseas
Not dealing with stressful circumstances
Physical abuse
Pregnancy
Relationship problems/breakups
Rape
Season change
Sleep deprivation
Work problems
September 11th attacks

The types of triggers reported by those I interviewed show the range of events and circumstances which emerged. The most commonly reported triggers (reported by more than four women, in order of most frequently cited) were relationship problems, family problems (including abusive/ alcoholic/psychotic parents), work-related problems and the death of a family member or friend. These factors were not limited to any particular age group. There were also a few women who experienced several stressful events at around the same time. Overall, just over half of the women I spoke to said that they experienced triggers for most of their depressive or manic episodes.[6]

The variety of triggers included here is a direct result of the approach I decided to take in this research and a feature which differentiates it from other work, such as Brown and Harris' research on life events and depression. In one of their studies, a woman developed depression after an incident which they did not include as an "event" – her disabled son losing his third job in one year:

Our "rules" prevented us from including this event although it was clearly of major significance to her. (We include as "events" only loss of a job to the subject herself or the "chief breadwinner.") (Brown & Harris, 1978: 106)

Rather than deciding on rules regarding what may or may not constitute triggers, using open-ended questions and allowing the individual to judge the significance of an event capture the variety of what could potentially trigger an episode. This technique also shifts the focus away from the trigger itself and onto the focus of this chapter – that is, its significance for the individual. After all, these events do not affect everyone in the same way but are experienced and interpreted uniquely by each individual, and it is this interaction between the event and the individual's internalisation and interpretation of it which may result in depression. It is for this reason that I considered the individual's assessment key in creating this list of triggers.

Perceived Triggers and Their Meanings

That the types of events and circumstances reported as triggers varied so much shows how varied meanings and significance contextual factors can have. Living in a foreign country, for instance, can be a pleasant or exciting experience, or at least one that is not too emotionally difficult. Yet for others, it can be a traumatic experience. Variations were not only found in the types of experiences but in the meanings that one experience might have for different individuals. Here, I emphasise that an experience became a "trigger" when the individual linked it to an episode of depression, and this link was formed as a result of a certain meaning which she ascribed to the experience. This meaning was, in turn, derived from the broader context of the individual's narrative. For example, Frances' response to the 11th September attack on the United States may not make sense to many or may appear to be an over-reaction. Yet to Frances, the attack was a trigger because of the significance it held for her – a significance which derived from her life context. Working as a journalist at the time, and specialising in terrorism and the Middle East, Frances had been talking to those around her about the political issues in the Middle East and for years had warned that such an attack was likely to happen eventually. When it finally did happen, she felt frustrated by how little people seemed to care or understand. In her words, "[n]o-one understands. I'm on my own here".

Below are two more examples which illustrate the range of some of the triggers reported, as described by the women themselves, showing how they were framed, and their significance to each woman's narrative.

So did anything trigger [your depression] you think?

Olivia: I think it was the whole when I was 17 I had to make all the choices about what to do next. It was kind of like I don't want change anymore, you know. I'd just been changed.

When do you think you first started having symptoms of bipolar, in hindsight?

Judy: It's hard to say, really. I mean there were all sorts of things going on actually. I was clearly very depressed and I came from a very difficult ... It was a difficult background, essentially. My parents were pretty abusive, alcoholic and all that kind of thing and I was bullied quite severely at school for about seven years. So that created quite a lot of depression as well. When my parents split up, my father got custody of us and he was a very nasty person, so this clearly created problems. But then at the same time, I had the usual ... You know, there is a lot of medicalising nowadays, you know. So, for instance, I've had the pattern where I'd get absolutely terrible in the winter. Then spring would come out and I'd be like "Wow this is amazing!" But then, everyone feels that to a certain extent, if you know what I mean. And it was only really when I dropped acid a couple of times and ... It was very small experimentation really, but what happened after that, I got a slight personality change.

These quotations illustrate some of the events and circumstances that the women I spoke with reported as triggers, but also the meanings ascribed to these circumstances which made them triggers in the eyes of participants (and which, in turn, prove to be key in the individual's sense of control). For Olivia, facing the prospect of change and the necessity of making choices was what propelled her into depression because of the role it played within her life narrative. She had recently moved to another school, so the instability that another change would create was seen alongside the instability from which she had only recently emerged. For Judy, several events and circumstances constituted triggers to her – each with its own significance – and she draws out her reasons for making these causal inferences. The interviews showed that the "triggers" reported were not triggers for depression in and of themselves – for instance, the chance to make big life decisions could be viewed as a welcome opportunity rather than a cause for stress and depression. Rather, they were triggers because of the roles they played in each individual's life narrative. It is this element of meaning derived from the individual and her life context which provides the connection between triggers and the individual's sense of control, as I elaborate in the next section.

Triggers and Perceiving the Risk of Future Depression

Perceiving a trigger has implications for the way an individual views her depression. When it came to beliefs about one's future with depression, I had expected that those who had experienced depression for a longer period of their lives would be more likely to view depression as something that would probably remain in their lives in the future. Yet this was not the case. Instead, I found an association between perceiving that episodes were usually triggered and believing that depression would be temporary; and conversely, between perceiving that episodes were usually *not* triggered and believing that depression would be chronic. In fact, I found that the only significant difference between the trigger and no-trigger groups was in their distribution across the chronic and temporary categories.[7] Figure 5.1 shows the distribution of those who reported triggers for most of their depressive (or manic) episodes and those who did not, across the belief that their depression is chronic or temporary.[8]

For those who reported that they tended not to experience triggers for their episodes, that fact alone had a special significance. For if depression was seen to be independent of life events or circumstances then, they reasoned, it must have originated within the individual – perhaps with an underlying biological cause that could theoretically be treated with medication. However, these women believed medication to be a treatment, not a cure.

In addition to the inability to get to the heart of the problem, women who said they did not experience triggers for most of their episodes usually found themselves unable to predict when depression would hit, and hence unable to anticipate or prevent it. Thus, not only does the problem seem elusive and incurable (although perhaps manageable by a near constant reliance on medication, if an effective medication is found),

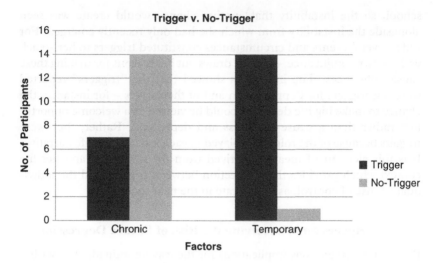

Figure 5.1 The distribution of trigger versus no-trigger across chronic and temporary categories

it is also unpredictable. Some individuals with bipolar disorder experience moods which follow a pattern, such that a depression might usually be preceded by a manic or hypomanic episode. Yet aside from that, these women are usually at the mercy of an unpredictable spectre, haunting even happy periods with the possibility that its next visit might be just around the corner. Ingrid describes what it is like to live with that spectre:

I don't think it's something that you can fight, because you can wake up and it's there. If I saw it coming I could probably do something about it. But I don't. It's just, "Oh that cloud's there again". There's no other way I can describe it really. It's almost like something tormenting you. Like something comes to torment you when you least expect it. So I've really got to make the most of the time when I'm well and just stay positive and hope for the best really. That's all. That's all I *can* do really from how I see things. I don't know if I can fight this. It's just such a strong thing. I've never been able to fight it before. I've had to wait for it to leave me. It's not something you can shake off.

For those who felt they did not experience triggers for most of their episodes, the mystery of their depression's origins, confirmed and compounded by its unpredictability, provides evidence for their view that what they have is chronic. Those who experience triggers have something to latch onto – something to learn and from which to gain insight. For those who do not feel there usually is a trigger, such insight is harder to find, and this impacts on their view of depression. For example, Katie feels that if depression is a problem "in the head" it must be connected to social reasons. Yet her inability to find any such reasons connected to her bouts of depression helps to lead her towards the view of depression as a chronic condition and the exoneration from self-blame it affords:

If it was any other sort of illness, you know, and it happened that number of times and there was no reason why it wouldn't carry on happening, I think most doctors would class it as being something chronic. So it just kind of takes the pressure off a bit, if that makes sense. You know? It's not like a series of successes in that I am no longer depressed and failures when I'm back on the tablets. It's like, you know, maybe this is just one of those things and rather than making the problem twice as hard by feeling like you've stuffed up in some way . . . You know, just a bit more sort of self-acceptance. So maybe that's why the whole thing of chronic sort of appeals, because it sort of takes the pressure off me as the responsibility for whether or not it's gonna happen again. I feel like it's taken away from me. It's like well if it's gonna happen, you know, at a physiological level, there's something that doesn't work quite right with my wiring, you know, and takes the pressure off you for "Maybe if I was more positive in my outlook or something".

Thus, the perception that episodes were usually not triggered could absolve the individual of any responsibility they might feel for their depression but could also lead to less optimism about the risk of relapse. In contrast, those who felt they experienced triggers for most of their episodes were much more hopeful about their chances of overcoming depression. They felt able to predict that their depression is/was temporary due to their ability to understand and thus potentially prevent it from happening again. Of those who believed their condition could be overcome, all but one felt most of their depressive episodes were triggered. Of those who thought their depression would most likely be chronic, most felt that the majority of their episodes were not triggered.

Those for whom depression seemingly arose out of nowhere had more trouble making sense of why it arose in the first place, and hence felt they had very few tools with which to tackle it other than a constant reliance on medication. Depression therefore seemed to them to be a chronic condition rather than something passing or curable. Rebecca describes this feeling succinctly. Despite experiencing only one episode of depression, her inability to ascertain why and where it came from leads to her anxiety that it may have arisen from something permanent within her:

I think it's a mix of some external factors, but a lot of it is just something inside me that I don't know what's going on and I don't think ever will.

You don't think you ever will know?

No, because I think it's such a fine, delicate balance. It's like you can easily tip one way or the other. So I'm feeling better now, but I'm also sort of accepting the thought that this feeling better might not be permanent; that this could happen again later on in life; that I could have these sort of recurrent sort of attacks of depression or whatever you call it.

Why do you feel that way?

I feel that way because when I don't know what started it and I don't know what's making it go away and then I can't guarantee that it won't come back.

Half of those who did not report triggers for most of their episodes wished that they had in fact experienced triggers, as they felt this would have provided a tangible reason for why they became depressed. In the absence of a reason, they were inclined to believe that their depression must have been caused by a "chemical imbalance" in the brain over which they have little, if any, control. Without any control, there is nothing to indicate whether their depression is permanent or temporary. Those who experienced triggers, on the other hand, were more likely to believe that they had played a part in the development of depression. This viewpoint brings depression more within the individual's control and thus within her ability to judge how permanent or temporary it is. Mirowsky and Ross make a similar point regarding control: "Logically, a sense of meaning is necessary for a sense of control. Without knowledge, control is impossible" (2003: 256).

Chloe echoes this idea and explains the connection between the apparent absence of triggers and her perception of bipolar disorder's permanence:

Do you think you could ever be rid of bipolar?

No. No. I think it's here to stay.

Yeah. What makes you think that?

I just think … Everything in my life is perfect, I would say, you know, right now. And I still feel like the mood swings. And I think if I feel like this now, although they're not as severe as they used to be, I can still feel the ups and the downs and I'm just … I just can't see me ever ever being, you know, free of it.

Because you feel like things are as stable as they could be?

Yeah. I think it's not circumstantial. You know, it's not due to my circumstances, my bipolar. I honestly feel that's just a disorder that will never leave. You know, it will never change. I can only find ways of coping with it – managing it.

The importance of this sense of control to being optimistic about over-coming depression seems to support Jean-Paul Sartre's insistence that his philosophy of freedom is a kind of "optimistic toughness". In his lecture, *Existentialism Is a Humanism,* he maintains that realising one's freedom is cause for hope, not despair, since destiny is in one's own hands. Rather than focusing on the responsibility their views placed upon them, the women who perceived triggers and a greater sense of control felt more optimistic about their future. The hope these women expressed, borne from the feeling that they can take action that could prevent depression, supports Sartre's claim that a philosophy that seeks to make people aware of their freedom

can not be taken for a philosophy of quietism, since it defines man in terms of action; nor for a pessimistic description of man – there is no doctrine more optimistic, since man's destiny is within himself; nor for an attempt to discourage man from acting, since it tells him that the only hope is in his acting and that action is the only thing that enables a man to live. (Sartre, 1947: 42)

Of course, the accounts in this chapter cannot go as far as supporting or denying claims concerning the extent of free will that individuals possess. All these accounts can show is that by believing that their depression can be overcome because they feel there is potential to attain some control and take action towards preventing it, these women support Sartre's insistence that existentialism is an optimistic doctrine. A sense of free-dom/control over their situation promotes a sense of hope, showing that the importance that existentialism places on the realisation of one's free-dom indeed seems to be the opposite of pessimism and despair.

Believing in a biomedical model which wrests control away from the individual such that she cannot do otherwise may well be easier or more comforting for the time-being. Yet whether or not the model is an accurate depiction of reality, the determinism (whether it be biological, psychologi-cal or otherwise) that instils individuals with the belief that they simply are the way they are and there is nothing they can do about it is, as Sartre argues, at once reassuring and frightening. The women who did not feel they experienced triggers for most of their episodes may not ascribe speci-fically to a biological determinism, but the feeling they describe – of depression arising apropos of nothing – is a sense that, for them, depression is determined by a force other than themselves. Their pessimism regarding the possibility of overcoming depression is a testament to Sartre's conten-tion that it is not existentialism but determinism that breeds pessimism. Whether these beliefs translate into reality or self-fulfilling prophecies is a matter for another study. All that can be said here is that the phenomenology of depression and control I describe lends support to the characterisation of existentialism as an "optimistic toughness" – that awareness of one's own freedom may well be daunting and less comfortable than determinism, but it ultimately invokes more hope.

So far, I have focused on the story behind the majority view – what the majority of the women were saying and why. But some women did not fit the trend. There were those who believed their depression to be chronic despite experiencing triggers. After analysing their characteristics, the only factor that I noticed was different about this group was that their Beck scores were significantly (about 5 points) higher than those in the "normal" group (i.e. those who believed their condition to be chronic and also reported *not* experiencing triggers for most of their episodes). The Beck Depression Inventory is designed to test how severe one's depression is, so having a higher Beck score means those in that group were "more depressed" than the "normal" group at the time of interview. This could indicate that their mood at the time of interview may have affected how much control they believed they had over depression, thus leading to the view that their depression is chronic despite feeling that they experienced triggers for most of their episodes. This possibility is supported by studies such as Calhoun *et al.* (1974), who found a significant negative correlation between the state of depression in women and the tendency to connect its cause to situations within one's control. Alloy *et al.* (1981) also found that current mood state also altered the degree of control that individuals perceived they had over outcomes.

On the flipside, one woman, Veronica, who believed her depression could eventually be overcome despite stating that her episodes were not triggered, had a Beck score three points higher than those who felt their depression could be overcome and had reported triggers. However, with only one case it would not be meaningful to test whether this difference in Beck scores is significant. Instead, the difference between Veronica and the others in the group who felt their depression could be overcome can be found in her interview:

So do you think you'll have another manic or depressed episode again?

It's a stupid thing to say but I feel I won't! But that's crazy when you think I've had it all my life. But you don't know, do you? It's too good to be true. I don't think it could work like that.

Well why not?

Well if it's something that's sort of in my head. It's very hard to know. And I'm very lucky that I actually don't have psychosis. I had one glimpse of it. Just one night of what it might be like and I wouldn't like it to come around every other night.

So what makes you believe that it might not come back?
You always do. It's a trick. I don't think I ought to. I think I should say, "It very well might, and if it does, I'm here waiting and I'll be fine." You stand like a beast with its back to the storm waiting for it to go, and go it will.

Here, Veronica says she always believes her episodes will not return when they are over, but she is usually proved wrong. She doubts her own belief, revealing another layer – a discrepancy between her current belief and what she thinks she ought to believe. In fact, one might categorise her as belonging to the "chronic" group on the basis of what she thinks she *ought* to believe. This belief may also have a self-fulfilling effect, in that her episodes keep returning because her underlying belief is that they will. Veronica reminds us that beliefs are complex and multi-layered. As a result, categorising beliefs may not be simple, but there are more valuable insights to be gained if we listen carefully to what the individual is saying.

Earlier, I mentioned Paul Biegler's (2012) account of triggers as more than just unfortunate interpretations of life events, but as threats to the individual which can potentially be understood and thereby lead to greater autonomy. Biegler's account of the role of triggers not only echoes those who view depression as a catalyst for change but is also supported by the major theme of this chapter – that to the individual, perceiving triggers carries with it the potential for understanding, and hence the potential for increased control over depression. At first glance, this account may appear to conflict with forms of cognitive behaviour therapy (CBT) that are based on the idea that it is not external events but *interpretations* of those events that are the problem. For instance, approaches to CBT based on Stoicism maintain that negative emotions are usually caused by erroneous perceptions or judgements about situations that may not be accurate (Scarpa & Lorenzi, 2013). Under this philosophy, CBT aims to push individuals to use reasoning and logic to question their thinking about events. Yet the aspect of perceiving triggers which held out hope for the individuals I interviewed was that it signalled to them the potential for an explanation of how they came to be depressed that went beyond a biomedical model that leaves no room for individual control. Thus, it was the mere perception that an event or circumstance played a role in triggering their depression which appeared to determine how they viewed their future with depression, not the content or accuracy of their inter-pretation. The individual's interpretation of the triggering event may or may not be problematic, but what is key here is that a trigger was perceived in the first place. This, it seems, gives the individual something to work with. Once a trigger is identified, its interpretation can either be changed if it is deemed erroneous or used as a catalyst for changing one's life as per the accounts presented in Chapter 2. In either case, there is the potential for meaning, and consequently a sense of control, as long as the individual believed there to have been a trigger.

With perceived control emerging as a key mediator between perceiving triggers for one's depressive episodes, finding meaning in the experience and being more optimistic about the future risk of depression, it is pertinent to ask how this finding relates to research on self-control, locus of control, autobiographical memory, narrative reconstruction, concepts of causation and the categorisation of depression.

Self-Control

One finding from another study which relates to the responses from the majority of women I spoke to comes from Ross and Broh's (2000) study of self-esteem and self-control in academic performance. Ross and Broh found that students with a higher sense of self-control were more likely to believe they could succeed. Academic success can be construed as similar to overcoming depression as the two can be viewed as different types of achievement. Indeed, it could be applied to overcoming other mental illnesses. Loe and Cuttino (2008) also studied university students diagnosed with ADHD and found that for those students, medication was a way of "disciplining behaviour" and gaining a sense of self-control. However, their findings focus on the role of medication and only extend as far as gaining self-control but not overcoming ADHD.

Nonetheless, the importance of personal control in recovery from illness has already been documented by researchers, such as in recovery from heart attacks or stroke (Ewart, 1992; Johnston et al., 1999; Jones et al., 2008; Orbell et al., 2001; Partridge & Johnston, 1989). The contribution of perceived control to an optimistic perspective on recovery is supported by this chapter, and brings with it a challenge to the current categorisation of depression; for if women's perceptions of their control over, and risk of, depression depend more on whether they would categorise their depression as triggered or not than, say, unipolar or bipolar, then there is a case for further investigating this alternative categorisation. The potential significance of an optimistic outlook on recovery is especially important when the condition is mental.

Locus of Control

What I found also bears some resemblance to findings from certain studies conducted on locus of control in self-efficacy and attribution

theory. Albert Bandura, who has conducted extensive work on the relationship between control and self-efficacy beliefs, defines self-efficacy as
the belief as to "how well one can execute courses of action required to
deal with prospective situations" (Bandura, 1982: 122). Since Bandura
introduced the concept of self-efficacy, numerous studies have found that
those with high self-efficacy beliefs show much fewer depressive symptoms (e.g. Bandura, 1997; Cutrona & Troutman, 1986; Maciejewski
et al., 2000; McFarlane *et al.*, 1995). There are two important differences
between these studies and mine. First, I was not concerned with general
self-efficacy beliefs (as the aforementioned studies were) but beliefs of
self-efficacy over depression specifically. Second, I did not measure
whether individuals actually overcame depression or not. Nevertheless,
it would be interesting to see whether beliefs about the ability to control
depression *specifically* also translate into better outcomes.

Attribution theory refers to "how a person explains the cause of his or
her own or another's behavioural outcomes" (Stajkovic & Sommer, 2000:
708). It refers to the perceived causes of events, including psychological
outcomes such as depression (Barber, 1988). Related to attribution theory is the concept of locus of control, which also deals indirectly with the
perceived cause of emotions (Barber, 1988). Developed by Julian B.
Rotter (1966), locus of control refers to an individual's perceived origin
of control of reinforcements, ranging from internality to externality.
According to Altmaier and colleagues, "[i]nternals assume that their
outcomes are primarily determined by their own abilities and efforts,
whereas externals emphasize the importance of external factors, including
luck and chance" (1979: 482). There is a variety of self-report scales by
which locus of control is assessed, the most common being Rotter's
Internal-External Locus of Control Scale (Rotter, 1966).

To apply the concept to this study, one might be tempted to consider
depression as the "outcome" and say that the triggers reported were a
mixture of both "internal" and "external" loci of control. For example,
when an individual stated that she felt the death of a friend triggered an
episode of depression, she may be said to be equating the locus of control
for depression externally if it was seen as the result of chance, whereas for
an individual who believed her depression to have been triggered by having
to make big decisions, the locus of control may be seen as internal to her
self. There was a mixture of loci of control not only within the trigger group
but also within individuals; that is, one individual may have reported
"internal" triggers for some episodes of depression and "external" triggers
for other depressive episodes.

However, it is not accurate to equate triggers with perceived locus of
control of depression because, as explained earlier, the women I

interviewed conceptualised triggers as part of a causal pathway, but not necessarily the cause. For instance, when I asked the interviewee what she believed triggered her depression, she might report a particular event; yet when asked what she believed caused her depression, the most common answer consisted of a complex interplay between biological, psychological and environmental factors. In addition, the Internal-External Locus of Control Scale was not administered to participants because I did not set out to test a concrete hypothesis concerning control. Rather, the issue of perceived control, and perceived triggers, arose unexpectedly.

Taking these factors into consideration means it is not possible to equate the trigger versus no-trigger distinction with the external versus internal locus of control distinction. Rather, my focus is more akin to perceived controllability of depression. Although it is possible for an individual to view both a trigger (such as a friend's death) and no trigger as external loci of control for depression, these women showed that identifying a trigger rendered depression more likely to be understood, and hence increased its controllability. This finding supports the work of authors such as Weiner, Graham and Chandler who emphasise the importance of controllability in causal attributions, rather than the internality/externality of the attributions. In their study, perceived uncontrollability led to feelings of pity regardless of whether the cause was perceived to be internal or external (Weiner *et al.*, 1982).

Furthermore, studying perceptions of controllability, as I did, rather than actual controllability of outcomes, raises the possibility of another angle which could be taken into account in attribution theory. For example, in a study on learned helplessness, Abramson and colleagues (1978) found that uncontrollable outcomes can lead to feelings of helplessness, but that those feelings are more marked in those who believed their helplessness to be due to their own inabilities rather than to environmental factors. What I found, however, implies a different conclusion – that attributing a role for environmental factors (which included uncontrollable events) renders individuals more likely to perceive that their ways of dealing with them play a role in depression, and this renders it more controllable. It may therefore be worth incorporating my approach into some studies of attribution theory to see whether my approach adds complexity to the theory.

At this point, it is worth returning to the significance of controllability rather than internality/externality of causal attributions. Theoretically, a simple environmental causation model for depression – in which the individual becomes depressed in response to events which could be entirely out of her control, such as the death of a loved one or a job loss – circumvents individual control and responsibility to the same extent as the simple biomedical causation model – which states that depression is caused by an imbalance of neurotransmitters. Yet what is striking in the trigger versus no-trigger comparison is that all but one of the women who identified triggers for most of their episodes of depression spoke of their personality and thoughts as playing a pivotal role in the development of depression. By contrast, half of those who did not perceive triggers for most of their episodes espoused the biomedical narrative which relegates individual control to a more passive position. No one espoused a simple environmental causation model in which the individual is equally passive in the development of depression.[9]

This finding implies that although in theory a depression that is supposedly a reaction to external events can be conceptualised as just as external to individual control and responsibility as a supposedly biologically caused depression, in practice this is not necessarily the case. Those who felt they had experienced triggers were more likely to consider themselves to have also played a role (no matter how small) in the development of their depression than those who felt they had *not* experienced triggers. Perhaps it is that events such as the death of a loved one, job loss and so on, no matter how uncontrollable, only affect the individual by virtue of how the individual views and interprets those events. Even if the individual could not control the event itself, she can control how she deals with and processes the event.

This point also complicates attempts to draw too close a parallel to the exogenous versus endogenous distinction (which I discuss in more detail shortly), as it shows that at least when it comes to perceptions, exogenous attributions can also lead to endogenous attributions. This point also has implications for the work on "lay knowledge" about causes of illness, as the literature in this area makes a demarcation between causes seen as external to the individual and causes seen as internal to the individual (e.g. Elder, 1973; Pill & Stott, 1982). What I found suggests that such a demarcation may not be as easy to make as previously thought.

Autobiographical Memory

On another level, the triggers that these women reported might also be viewed as memories which individuals connect with their depressive episodes. Research on autobiographical memory and depression has identified a distinction between "overgeneral" and "specific" memory in those with and without depressive symptoms respectively (e.g. Brewin *et al.*, 1999; Kuyken & Brewin, 1994; Moore *et al.*, 1988; Williams, 1992; Williams *et al.*, 2007). However, I did not find a distinction between the *types* of memories in the trigger and no-trigger groups – both specific and overgeneral memories were present in the trigger group. Instead, I found a distinction between those who associate *some* kind of memory (of a triggering event) with their depression and those who do not associate *any* memory (of a triggering event) with their depression.

The difference between my findings and those of autobiographical memory studies is probably due to differences in methodology. Autobiographical memory experiments have demanded an answer to the question of what events individuals associated with their depression, whereas my investigation did not presuppose that individuals would necessarily associate *any* event with their depression. This raises the possibility that it may be worth rethinking the way the question is raised within autobiographical memory experiments.

Narrative Reconstruction

In studies of the self in chronic illness, narrative reconstruction has become a powerful idea to explain the work done to "repair" the biographical "tear" which can occur as a result of illness. For instance, Bill Cowie (1976) contends that following a heart attack, the individual reconstructs a narrative so that the heart attack does not appear to arise out of nowhere but as a result of prior circumstances or behaviour. From this viewpoint, one might interpret the women in the no-trigger group as having failed to reconstruct their narrative. However, such an analysis fails to capture the way in which perceiving a depressive episode as having arisen out of nowhere is meaningful in itself. It led those women to reconstruct a narrative of sorts in the sense that being unable to "reinterpret events surrounding the onset of illness so that it makes sense in terms of the person's life story" (Radley, 1994: 146) leads to a particular interpretation of their future with depression, which has its own significance.

Exogenous versus Endogenous Depression

In some ways the trigger versus no-trigger distinction resembles the exogenous versus endogenous (or reactive versus endogenous) distinction that was used to classify depression in the past. Essentially, exogenous or reactive depression was thought to be a reaction to stressful life events whereas endogenous depression was thought to have a biological/genetic origin and no associated stressful life events, along with a distinct symptomatology. The distinction also had implications for treatment, with antidepressants and ECT (Electro Convulsive Therapy) developed to address endogenous depression, and psychoanalysis thought to address reactive depression (Walker, 2008).[10] Although the trigger versus no-trigger distinction relies on the individual's own perception of whether the majority of her episodes were reactions to circumstances or life events or not and the exogenous versus endogenous distinction relied on the clinician's assessment, the parallel between the categories is apparent.

First promoted by Emil Kraepelin in 1921, the distinction made its way into the first *DSM* published in 1952 (American Psychiatric Association, 1952). In *DSM-II* published in 1968, the distinction remained but was instead termed neurotic versus psychotic (American Psychiatric Association, 1952). (The term "psychotic" was then used more broadly, with a meaning similar to "organic", and included psychotic depression and bipolar disorder (Boland, 2005).) Textbooks and manuals such as the *DSM* and the *International Classification of Diseases* (*ICD*) continued to use the distinction until 1980, when it was replaced by the classification "major depression" in *DSM-III*. Rick Ingram and colleagues (1999) suggest that the exogenous versus endogenous distinction is reflected in the distinction that is sometimes made between a depressive personality "trait" and depression as a "state" which occurs in reaction to something. The exogenous versus endogenous distinction has since disappeared from clinical manuals such as the *DSM* and the *ICD*, as well as from medical literature (McPherson & Armstrong, 2006). But why did the distinction disappear? The answer appears to be a combination of internal politics among psychiatrists, the influence of the pharmaceutical industry and scientific issues with the distinction.

The shift away from the exogenous versus endogenous distinction was embedded in a larger power shift within psychiatry around the time that *DSM-III* was prepared and produced. Prior to 1976, the psychoanalytic school of psychiatry predominated the American Psychiatric Association (APA) – the organisation responsible for producing the *DSM*. But between around 1976 and 1983 there was a power struggle between psychoanalytic psychiatrists and biological psychiatrists. The latter ended up winning and writing *DSM-III* (McPherson & Armstrong, 2006). Several scholars contend that in order to strengthen their base as a medical profession, psychiatry (at least in the United States) sought to medicalise mental illnesses as much as possible and situate them firmly in the biological realm (Klerman, 1984; McPherson & Armstrong, 2006; Parker, 2005; Wilson, 1993). According to these scholars, part of this process of medicalisation involved stripping classifications of depression of aetiological theories.

Recall that the term "endogenous depression" denotes a depression with a biological origin, and "exogenous depression" that which does not have a biological origin. As *DSM-III* sought to remain aetiologically neutral, these terms had to be abolished (Cole *et al.*, 2008; Sadler *et al.*, 1994; Van Praag,

1990).[11] However, McPherson and Armstrong (2006) believe the move was a subtle but effective way of asserting the dominance of biological psychiatry because it removed the possibility that depression could have an origin that was not biological. That those who advocated aetiological neutrality in the *DSM* also supported the medical model appears to support this point. Further, Fernando (1992), writing just before *DSM-IV* was published, described a trend in psychiatry of emphasising biological aspects of health and illness and ignoring serious social problems within psychiatric practice. Parker (2005) also notes that although "major depression" replaced "exogenous" and "endogenous" depression, its description closely resembles the endogenous symptomatology – including "vegetative and endogeneity symptoms, severe psychomotor disturbance, and worthlessness and guilt ranging up to delusional intensity" (American Psychiatric Association, 1980: 210–211). The decision to discard aetiological classifications such as exogenous and endogenous depression in favour of symptom-based classifications appears to be at least partly attributable to this political shift. Yet what, if anything, was influencing internal politics?

A few commentators cite the emergence of pharmaceuticals for the treatment of unipolar and bipolar depression as having played an important role in shifting psychiatry towards more medicalised models (McPherson & Armstrong, 2006; Pilgrim, 2007; Pilgrim & Bentall, 1999). McPherson and Armstrong hypothesise that the controversy over monoamine oxidase inhibitors (MAOIs) following deaths from hepatotoxicity meant that by the time *DSM-III* was being written, biological psychiatrists wanted to stress that depression could still be treated with drugs like other medical illnesses. Tricyclic antidepressants came to the fore in the 1960s and, according to authors such as Millet (2005), were effective in treating all forms of depression.

The discovery of lithium for the treatment of mania in 1949 also had a major influence on the diagnosis of mental illness. Concerns about its safety made its uptake slow, but by the late 1960s doctors were using it to treat bipolar disorder (then called manic depressive illness) (Kramer, 1993). Its effectiveness in the treatment of mania, but not schizophrenia, brought the distinction between bipolar disorder and other psychiatric categories to the fore. Researchers at the time reasoned that if diagnosis was essential to determining appropriate treatment, then response to treatment should also determine diagnosis. This circular reasoning, and lithium's apparent specificity in the treatment of patients with mania, was interpreted as confirmation of Kraepelin's model of manic depression. The diagnosis of bipolar disorder in the United States increased from that point on (Kramer, 1993). In fact, the *New York Times* reported that the diagnosis of bipolar disorder in American children and teenagers increased 40-fold between 1994 and 2003, which in turn appears to be due at least in part to the fact that medications for bipolar can be three to five times more expensive than those for depression, representing a larger profit for pharmaceutical companies (Carey, 2007). Moreover, Boyce and Hadzi-Pavlovic contend that the use of tricyclic antidepressants was so widespread that by the time *DSM-III-R* was published, depression was already seen as "one disease, one treatment, one outcome". In their words, "prescription trumped description" and made classifications such as "exogenous" and "endogenous" irrelevant (Boyce & Hadzi-Pavlovic, 1996: 18). The new treatment landscape provided biological psychiatrists with the perfect opportunity to reassert their position (McPherson & Armstrong, 2006).

The marketing strategies used by pharmaceutical companies to promote conditions alongside the new drugs supposedly developed for them have also been well documented (see, e.g., Antonuccio *et al.*, 2002; Healy, 1997; Koerner, 2002). Joanna Moncrieff (2006) suggests that the terms "antidepressants" and "antipsychotics" promote the drugs as though they are "magic bullets", placing them at the centre of treatment rather than as merely one form of treatment alongside others. The logic behind the promotion of these medications for depression is the same as that used by psychiatrists who espouse a biomedical model of depression. That is, that depression is a brain disorder requiring treatment with antidepressants. When a patient's mood is lifted, this outcome supposedly vindicates the biological explanation for depression – that it is caused by lower levels of serotonin in the brain. Edward Shorter (1997: vii) remarks:

[i]f there is one central intellectual reality at the end of the twentieth century, it is that the biological approach to psychiatry – treating mental illness as a genetically influenced disorder of brain chemistry – has been a smashing success.

The interests of both pharmaceutical companies and biological psychiatrists have thus gone hand in hand. The pharmaceutical industry also sponsors campaigns such as the UK Royal College of Psychiatrists' "Beat Depression Campaign" (Pilgrim, 2007) and the influence of the pharmaceutical industry (in the form of freebies, promotions, numerous company representatives and drug studies dominating the programme) is ever-present at conferences (Read, 2005).

The pharmaceutical industry is not the only economic influence on psychiatric classification. Since 1983, Medicare and health insurance companies in the United States have required that patients be assigned diagnostic-related groups in order to qualify for medical treatment (Pilgrim, 2007). These external pressures from both pharmaceutical companies and health providers help to reify the categories. But David Pilgrim (2007) reminds us that there are other groups with an interest in reifying the categories, such as relatives of those with psychiatric diagnoses who benefit from feeling that their relative has a "bona fide" medical illness which they feel should immunise them against stigma (although research suggests that the biomedical model of mental illness actually has the opposite effect on stigma (Angermeyer *et al.*, 2011; Read *et al.*, 2006)). Moreover, categorical medical thinking has been present in psychiatry long before drugs became commonly used for these conditions, so it is important not to over-emphasise the influence of the pharmaceutical industry in defining psychiatric categories.

Apart from the politics within psychiatry and the external factors which influenced it, the move away from the exogenous versus endogenous distinction was also partly influenced by difficulties with validating it in certain scientific studies, such as those conducted by Kendell (1976) and Young *et al.* (1986). These studies assessed different aspects of the distinction, not just one. For example, the distribution of scores for depressive symptoms came under scrutiny. It was argued that if there are two types of depression rather than one which only varies by degree, the scores should show a bimodal distribution rather than a unimodal distribution. Hans Eysenck (1970) argued that the results thus far clearly showed that there are two types of depression, whereas Kendell (1976) argued that not many data sets showed a bimodal distribution of scores. Ten years later, Young *et al.* (1986) conducted a similar quantitative study on 788 patients diagnosed with "major depression" and their results also failed to support the exogenous versus endogenous distinction. Instead, their results supported a different distinction – one between anhedonic symptoms (an inability to experience pleasure from things which are usually pleasurable – such as eating, socialising, exercising) and vegetative symptoms (insomnia and loss of appetite).

The aetiological assumptions surrounding the exogenous versus endogenous distinction also came under scrutiny. Endogenous depression, defined as "coming from within", is assumed to be biological in origin, presumably genetic, which is commonly synonymous with "inherited" and which, in turn, is synonymous with a "family history".[12] As such, various studies went about measuring this aetiological theory by measuring the degree to which people judged as presenting endogenous and exogenous symptoms had a family history of depression. For example, a large study was conducted which included 2,942 first-degree relatives of 5,466 people with depression. Despite using four different definitions of endogenous depression, no matter which definition was used, the relatives of those diagnosed with endogenous depression were no more likely to have depression than those in the exogenous group (Kendell & Zealley, 1988). Andreason *et al.* (1986) and McGruffin *et al.* (1988) found similar results. Another study also found that individuals in the endogenous group (classified according to their mental state at the time) were no less likely to have experienced stressful life events than the reactive group in the few months before the onset of depression (Bebbington *et al.*, 1988). Given the debate surrounding the exogenous versus endogenous distinction, it looked as though there was not enough empirical evidence to support it by the time the preparations for *DSM-III* were underway.

In the past, there may have been some evidence to suggest a predominance of endogenous depression in those with bipolar disorder. Kraepelin himself said that "compared to innate predisposition external influences only play a very subordinate part in the causation of manic-depressive insanity" (1899: 127), and a study conducted in 1965 reports that all of their participants with bipolar disorder (of which there were 11) fell into the endogenous category. The endogenous grouping was made as follows: "[o]n the basis of scoring on four out of five symptoms (retardation, diurnal variation, early morning wakening, impaired concentration, and ideas of guilt) patients were classified as endogenous while the rest were classified as neurotic" (Forrest *et al.*, 1965: 251). However, it appears that this finding was not replicated in a larger sample of participants diagnosed with bipolar depression and there does not appear to have been a split between bipolar depression as endogenous and unipolar depression as exogenous. Part of the reason for this might be because the bipolar term seemed to absorb many of the characteristics of endogenous depression anyhow – an impression voiced by some of the women I interviewed. Kendell (1976) and Cole *et al.* (2008) cite the persuasiveness of research which divided unipolar from bipolar depression. Groups diagnosed with bipolar disorder had shorter and more frequent episodes, began experiencing episodes on average 15 years younger than those diagnosed with unipolar depression, the morbidity risk among first-degree relatives was higher than unipolar groups and the conditions "bred true" (first-degree relatives of those in the bipolar group were more likely to be diagnosed with bipolar depression, and first-degree relatives of the unipolar group were more likely to be diagnosed with unipolar depression) (Kendell, 1976). Cole and colleagues (2008: 84) cite genetic studies which, in their words, "firmly establish the taxonomy" of unipolar-bipolar depression.

However, contained within these findings regarding bipolar depression is the risk of circularity. If the criteria for diagnosis of bipolar depression

include a greater frequency of episodes, other first-degree relatives diagnosed with bipolar and so on, then it is no wonder that studies show that
those diagnosed with bipolar disorder are more likely to have these
characteristics. See, for example, Barnett & Smoller, 2009; Craddock &
Sklar, 2009; Farmer *et al.*, 2007; Hayden & Nurnberger, 2005, which
document genetic associations for bipolar disorder. Psychiatrists do ask
patients if they have a family history of unipolar or bipolar depression.[13]
This information could simply allow a clinician to be particularly vigilant
of certain signs and symptoms, or may influence diagnosis either consciously or subconsciously – for example, a psychiatrist who hears a
patient mention triggers for her episodes may be more likely to diagnose
unipolar rather than bipolar depression. The scientific issues with the
exogenous versus endogenous distinction thus centred on the difficulty
with connecting symptom groupings with the presence or absence of a
family history. The distinction between those who experienced "stressful
life events" and those who did not matches the trigger versus no-trigger
distinction more closely, yet there was no scientific consensus for such a
distinction either.[14]

The loss of the exogenous versus endogenous distinction was thus
highly political rather than purely scientific, but its disappearance has
had another effect. In their book, *The Loss of Sadness*, Horwitz and
Wakefield (2007) present how taking sadness out of context has resulted
in an overmedicalisation of normal sadness. They point out that the
symptoms of major depression as listed in the *DSM* – depressed mood,
a lack of interest in activities, change in appetite or weight, insomnia, or
hypersomnia (excessive sleep), a physical slowdown, loss of energy, feelings of worthlessness or guilt, inability to concentrate and make decisions,
recurrent thoughts of death or suicide – are common to both healthy
individuals experiencing normal sadness due to a loss or a stressful event
as well as individuals who experience sadness without any obvious trigger.
Current psychiatric criteria thus do not differentiate normal sadness from
what would have previously been termed endogenous depression. The
fact that such depressive symptoms appear to respond to antidepressants
also fails to prove the biomedical model. There is a great deal of research
which attests to the effect that stress and adversity can have on one's
neurobiology (Harkness & Monroe, 2002: 391). Antidepressants could
therefore be effective regardless of the origin of the individual's
depression.

Although I focused on the *individual's* perception of the triggers (or lack
thereof) for her depression rather than an objective assessment, the
importance of perceived triggers to the individual nevertheless appears
to support the notion that the context of one's depression, or at least the

individual's perception of that context, is in some way significant. By recognising its importance to the individual, the perceived trigger versus no-trigger distinction in a way revives the exogenous versus endogenous distinction. In contrast, focusing on the symptoms and ignoring the context overlooks not only what could be understandable and even appropriate reactions to life events but also the significance of perceiving triggers to how one views one's future with depression. This, in turn, may have implications for the individual's recovery process.

Shifting Categorical Lines

Beyond underlining a difference between lay and professional conceptualisations of the risk of depression as Adelswärd and Sachs (2003) and Hoffman et al. (2003) have done and highlighting what that means for the individual's sense of self, I propose that incorporating subjective assessments of the risk of future depression could be beneficial for our understanding and treatment of depression. As Jens Zinn (2005: 2) states, "[t]he limitations of professional practice that are evident in the failure of much health promotion and the development of alternative therapies especially for chronic illness, can be explained by the failure to recognise and appreciate the importance of subjective and social risk". As I have shown, using a different set of criteria for categorisation places the spotlight onto a phenomenon which may have previously gone unnoticed. For instance, epidemiological studies in aetiology and risk of depression such as Brown and Harris' have historically relied on "objective" measures of life events. Yet the voices of the women I spoke to show that there is something to be gained from including the individual's perceptions in such studies.

Deborah Lupton (1999: 131) believes categorisation to be "the central task of modernity, an attempt to fend off chaos". In fending off chaos, the current approach to categorisation assumes a simple and direct relationship between categories and the entities in the world which they describe. Yet, as several historians of science note, "natural" or "universal" categories do not exist (e.g. Bowker & Star, 2000; Lakoff, 1987; Latour, 1987). As Bob Heyman describes, our classifications "illustrate the current facticity of the risk concept, with risks viewed as natural phenomena which can exist independently of the observer's state of knowledge. This facticity reflects the pivotal and reified status of the risk construct in science-based secular societies" (Heyman, 2004: 299). This classification system has developed according to what we consider to be of practical importance, as outlined earlier.

The distinction I have highlighted in this chapter also demonstrates the contingency of our current mode of categorisation which, as Sarangi and Candlin (2003: 115) note, is inherently "a meaning-making activity, deeply embodied in human experience and understanding". The construction of the risk of depression in terms of a different categorical frame – that is, triggered versus not-triggered – would potentially change how it is understood, and consequently addressed. For if the perception of whether episodes are usually triggered or not influences women's constructions of their future risk of depression, this tells us a number of things: firstly, that even if the medical profession does not take the personal context of depression into account in diagnosis and treatment, it is nevertheless meaningful to individuals; secondly, the meanings that individuals derive from how they perceive their episodes to arise influence the degree of control they feel over depression; thirdly, their perceptions of control and the future risk of depression may, in turn, have a self-fulfilling effect on their actual recovery. If the latter is found to be the case, practitioners might wield this knowledge to either tailor treatment according to what the individual believes would be most appropriate, or they might attempt to shift the individual's understanding of her depression to one which implies a greater degree of personal control, and thus a more optimistic view of recovery.

Women versus Men

It is of course also important to bear in mind that the results could be very different in a study on men. For instance, in their study of gender differences in depression experiences, Danielsson et al. (2009) found that women were more likely to see their own psychological factors as having played a role in the development of their depression whereas men were more likely to believe that depression struck them out of nowhere due to circumstances beyond their control, such as "employer bankruptcy, stock market loss, accusations of sexual harassment or, most commonly, insufferable assignments at work" (Danielsson et al., 2009: 61). This is in stark contrast to the women I interviewed, for whom such triggers made them inclined to view themselves as instrumental in the development of their depression. McMullen (1999) also found that women were inclined to place responsibility for depression on themselves, and Schön (2010) found that women in recovery were more preoccupied with trying to find meaning, whereas men were more preoccupied with symptom management and regaining their independence. Holzinger et al.'s (2011) study of mental illness found that women were more likely to espouse psychosocial understandings of mental illness than men. As the meaning assigned to triggers was integral to the connection between triggers, perceived control and the perceived future with depression in my study, the lack of meaning (or a search for meaning) among men in other studies could mean that the connection found here between perceiving triggers and viewing depression as temporary may not be present among men. It is a question worthy of investigation.

Conclusion

The women I spoke with perceived the risk that depression may be a chronic condition differently according to whether they believed most of their episodes were triggered by an event or circumstance or not. Those who regarded most of their depressive episodes as having been triggered were more likely to see themselves as having also played a role in its development. That is, even though in theory both the concepts of triggers and no triggers can be used to externalise control, in practice those who felt they experienced triggers were more likely to see meaning, or the potential for meaning, behind why they became depressed, and hence to have a higher sense of control over the risk of relapse. Indeed, there are therapists who train their patients to recognise triggers for their depression which they may not have previously recognised in order to enable them to avoid future depressive episodes (Bromet *et al.*, 2011).

It is, of course, possible that this link between perceiving triggers and the perceived risk of future depression may also correspond with a *real* risk of future depression. As Mirowsky and Ross note, "[m]any studies in many sciences find the sense of control associated with lower distress [...] All of the established and emerging social patterns of distress point to the sense of control as a critical link" (Mirowsky & Ross, 2003: 253). Whether a perception of triggers also plays a role in this link is a question that is ripe for further study: that is, whether those who perceive their episodes to have been triggered and believe they would one day overcome their depression do manage to overcome depression, and if the results are different for those who did not perceive triggers. If this turns out to be the case, it could have repercussions for how individuals diagnosed with depression are treated and how depression is classified.

At the very least, the women's voices presented in this chapter provide a further challenge to the biomedical model of depression which reduces depression to an imbalance of neurotransmitters best treated with anti-depressants. For those who experience depression, it is much more than that. Their experience of it has significance for how they view its role in their lives, and this in itself may translate into repercussions for their recovery. The significance of the distinction to which they have given voice may also challenge current psychiatric classification that is based on symptomatology alone – a point which those on the *DSM* and *ICD* working groups may do well to take into account.

In summary, this chapter suggests that if women perceive most of their depressive episodes to have been triggered by something in their lives, there exists the potential to understand why their depression arose and to thereby prevent it, which in turn renders them more likely to envisage a future self without depression. As the women I interviewed perceived their risks of future depression differently according to whether they believed most of their episodes to have been triggered or not, larger-scale epidemiological studies on the relationship between life events and risk of depression could benefit from the inclusion of individuals' perceptions of the role of triggers in the development of their depression.

6   Conclusion

Summary and Contrasts

As I listened to the women I interviewed talk about their experiences of depression, although each story was different, the same relationship began to emerge – an inextricable link between a perception of control and the self. It may have presented itself in different shapes and forms in each interview, but the link was unmistakably there. An account of depression and recovery may be far from ordinary, but despite the unique facets of each account, the link between perceived control and the self is the same thread that runs through the experiences of depression presented in this book.

In Michelle Lafrance's (2007) study of eight women diagnosed with depression in Canada, accounts of depression were presented as either biological flaw or personal flaw. Relatedly, Westerbeek and Mutsaers (2008), who studied ten autobiographies, divide views into "problem-oriented self-views" (in which depression is considered to be separate to the self) and "person-oriented self-views" (in which depression is considered an essential part of the self). They conclude that the use of antidepressants cultivates a problem-oriented self-view, but that the central role of antidepressants in the process of developing one's self-image eventually declines and the problem-oriented self-view is replaced by the person-oriented self-view. In *Speaking of Sadness*, Karp also describes a pharmacological "career" which parallels his notion of a "depression career", in which one at first accepts the biomedical model of depression, only to eventually become disillusioned with antidepressants (Karp, 1996).

While the views of some of those I interviewed indeed take these forms, several are more complex. Moreover, different views, such as the biological flaw view (which I termed the illness view) and personal flaw view (the weakness/emotion view), are not mutually exclusive but more often than not overlap with each other. That is, an individual usually expresses more than one view of depression, and these views do not necessarily contradict each other. The complex array and interplay of narratives invoked is a testament to the complexity of experiences of depression.

One narrative is usually not enough to describe the whole of a depression experience and its relation to the self. What is more, many women are quite reflexive – aware of the moral work of each narrative and its implications for their view of their self.

Beliefs regarding control also prove important in relation to self-labelling. The meanings that the individual ascribes to her diagnosis depend on those beliefs and are the mediating factors between the diagnosis and the effect it has on her. In this respect, a diagnosis seems to (at least initially) be understood in biomedical terms – a testament to the extent to which the biomedical narrative continues to permeate popular discourse on depression despite its lack of scientific support. There is thus an interplay between the diagnosis, the meanings ascribed to the diagnosis by society and the meanings ascribed to the diagnosis by the individual. Yet the almost mythical status of the biomedical model of depression is not without its consequences, as an initial reaction to one's diagnosis in biomedical terms has repercussions for one's sense of self. The biomedical model led some women to re-evaluate whether certain traits were aspects of their selves or aspects of "the illness". This, in turn, also led them to question the degree of control they had over depression, as the biomedical model provides relief from responsibility with one hand and removes the prospect of control over depression with the other.

The relationship between perceived control and the self also manifests itself in the individual's sense of authenticity. That is, having a sense of self-determination appears to be a precondition for a sense of authenticity. This is true for whatever state the individual is in (i.e. whether she feels authentic on medication or off, depressed/manic or not). For instance, there are those who feel less authentic when on medication for depression. When I asked them why they felt that way, they explained that it was because they felt the *medication* was in control of their thoughts, emotions and behaviour, not themselves. In such cases, an external, rather than an internal, force is perceived to be responsible. The implication is that you cannot feel like your true self if you do not believe it is really you at the helm. This means that some feel more authentic when off medication because on medication they are not sure whether it is themselves or the medication that is in control of their mental and emotional state. However, others feel more authentic on medication because they feel more in control of their mind and emotions in that state. In other words, perceived self-determination, rather than the presence or absence of medication, appears to be the key determinant for a sense of authenticity.

Depression is rarely described as one's most authentic state. Wendy is the only one who did so, but made a distinction between depression as the state of being physically unable to function and depression as a way of thinking, with the latter being her authentic state. However, several individuals describe depression as a part of their self, or a "seed" that will always be there. For instance, Rebecca describes how she conceives depression as simultaneously a part of herself and an illness – as something that takes over you in a sense but does not define you.

[...] it's very difficult to separate the depression from yourself and actually say is there any separation at all ... Whenever I had these dark moments I couldn't remember what it was like when I did feel fine. And I know I'd felt fine before and I know that I would probably get through this sort of way down again and come out on the other side, it's just at that moment I didn't remember anything except that I sort of knew that it existed but I couldn't really visualise actually what it was like. So it does feel like it's almost invading you in a sense, but like your cold isn't you, your depression isn't you. It could change you in some way but it's not like this little body snatcher from outer space that goes in and invades every single cell of your body.

In Loe and Cuttino's study of college students diagnosed with ADHD in the United States, the authors note that "[s]tudents use language of the authentic self to discuss what it means to be 'real', juxtaposed against their medicated (sometimes described as temporary, artificial, or even ideal) selves". They say that in this way "medicine can create a sense of inner conflict as the gap widens between perceived 'authentic' and 'ideal' identities" (Loe & Cuttino, 2008: 309). In contrast, Peter Kramer (1993) documented patients who did not report feeling like a different person on Prozac. Rather, they felt like their true selves. One patient said she only felt like herself while on Prozac. This book presents one possible explanation for both of these results – that is, that what determines whether an individual perceives a gap between her "authentic" and "medicated" self or not is her perception of self-determination within those states.

The individual's beliefs regarding control also appear key in determining how she envisages her current and future self. These beliefs are in turn embedded in the individual's understanding of the role that her social context plays (or fails to play) in her depression. Those who consider most of their episodes to have been triggered by events or circumstances in their lives appear more likely to believe that they may one day be free of depression, whereas those who did not are more likely to believe their depression to be chronic. The former feel that a trigger helps them understand why they became depressed, or at least played part of the reason for their depression. This understanding makes them feel they have a greater ability to control their response to triggers, and hence a greater ability to prevent or overcome depression in the future. This finding contrasts with Simone Fullagar's (2009) study of Australian women diagnosed with depression, in which many of the younger women stated that they hoped to stop taking antidepressants sometime in the future, whereas many of the older women had resigned themselves to taking it for the rest of their lives. With a more homogenous sample, I could not make such an age comparison but did investigate whether there was a difference between the two groups in relation to factors such as the number of depressive episodes or length of time on medication. There was no such difference. Instead, the split between those who perceived triggers and those who did not emerged as significant. It is possible that the different countries in which the studies were conducted account for the difference in findings, but it is also possible that Fullagar simply did not ask questions related to perceived triggers.

This book also contrasts with studies which measure the contribution of "life events" to depression. Studies such as those conducted by Brown, Harris and Bifulco which found that the loss of a mother before the age of 17 (by either death or separation) increased the chances of depression later in life, especially when coupled with a "severe life event" such as premarital pregnancy or marital separation/divorce, attempted to make judgements on causation with "objective" measures of life events (Bifulco et al., 1992; Bifulco et al., 1986; Harris et al., 1986). In contrast, I relied on the individuals themselves to decide what life events or circumstances they believed constituted triggers. As a result, what I found relates to the perceptions of causal factors rather than the actual mechanisms behind depression.

At this point, it is worth noting that the relationship between perceiving triggers, feeling a greater sense of control and viewing the future self as one free from depression may itself be shaped by other factors. For instance, those I interviewed consider bipolar depression to be more serious than unipolar depression. This view, combined with the tendency for those diagnosed with bipolar depression to be less likely to report triggers for their episodes than those diagnosed with unipolar depression, may mean that those diagnosed with bipolar depression also feel a lower sense of control and are thus less likely to believe they could one day have depression behind them (over and above simply managing it).

Here, it becomes apparent how difficult it is to separate ideas surrounding diagnosis, triggers and the possibility of overcoming depression. The fact that, at least among the women I spoke with, a greater proportion of those diagnosed with bipolar depression seem to view their condition as chronic compared with those diagnosed with unipolar depression may be a reflection of the severity of bipolar in comparison with unipolar depression, or it may indicate that the diagnosis itself can make a difference to one's outlook on recovery. Again, it is worth noting that those in both unipolar *and* bipolar camps considered bipolar depression to be more serious than unipolar depression in general. It is therefore possible that being diagnosed with unipolar depression may render one more hopeful about the prospect of complete recovery, and such optimism might have the effect of rendering one more likely to perceive triggers for one's episodes of depression. Conversely, a diagnosis of bipolar depression might render one less likely to perceive triggers, and more likely to perceive one's depression as chronic. Or, someone who is simply more optimistic to begin with may be more likely to see her condition as temporary and to also perceive her episodes to have been triggered.

It is also possible that an individual's personality could influence whether she perceives triggers or not, such that some individuals simply need, or are more likely, to attribute their depression to an external event. Take Frances, for example, who attributed one of her episodes of depression to watching the September 11 attacks on the United States on television. This sort of event is not one which is usually included on a life events scale, and although many people witnessed the attacks on television and were affected by them, not many experienced depression as a result. One could conclude that there is either something unique about Frances which caused her to become depressed as a result, or that she is simply more inclined to seek an event that she could link to her depression. The perceived trigger versus no-perceived trigger distinction may actually be a distinction between people who seek an external trigger to which to attribute their depression rather than attributing it to an internal factor. Whatever the case may be, the justification given for feeling that depression could one day be behind them was feeling a potential to understand their depression and thereby control it. Essentially, the message I kept hearing was that in depression, perceptions of control and the self are interlinked. Women's conceptions of the extent of personal control that is possible within their depression may also have implications for how they perceive the role of treatment, which could be taken into account when making treatment decisions.

Implications and Future Directions

While the biomedical model of depression bypasses individual control and responsibility for depression, that is both its blessing and its curse, for an absence of responsibility means an absence of a sense of control. Without a sense of control, the individual feels at the mercy of chemicals – either her own "malfunctioning" chemicals or chemicals supplied by medicine to correct the "malfunction". It may well be that in its haste to assert its place within the medical profession, psychiatry has sought to frame conditions such as depression in medical terms – that is, to diagnose by signs and symptoms, then treat the symptoms. While medication can be effective in treating the symptoms, these interviews show that there are other issues which medication cannot deal with and which may even be *raised* by medication – issues related to self-determination which are rarely addressed in the clinical setting. Yet they are issues with which individuals struggle and that affect how they see their future with the condition.

Pestello and Davis-Berman's (2008) study of internet discussion groups about depression found that many contributors to these discussions suffered from a great deal of anxiety not just from depression but from the use of medication designed to treat it. Another study they conducted, this time consisting of interviews with social work students and practitioners taking psychiatric medication, found that participants felt that taking medication meant they were weak and was a sign of personal failure (Davis-Berman & Pestello, 2005), a feeling also expressed by several of the women I spoke with. Medication is not always an easy answer to depression, even when it works.

We saw how the context in which the individual's depression is perceived to have arisen also plays an important role in how she views depression and its role in her life – especially its role in her future. In fact, it is so important that the distinction between perceiving triggers and not perceiving triggers for depression appears to be more meaningful to how one envisages the future with depression than the clinical distinctions of unipolar and bipolar depression. Epidemiological studies may therefore benefit from including the individual's perception of life events/circumstances and their importance, rather than simply relying on "objective" life event scales.

More than a "loss of sadness", the loss of a distinction between reactive and endogenous depression has meant that all depressions are now treated as though they are endogenous. While the symptoms may be the same or similar, the triggers (or lack thereof) may be quite different, and this in itself is of significance for the individual. The focus on the individual to the neglect of their social context has also made psychiatry's approach to depression at times nonsensical. Take, for instance, a child who is depressed as a result of being raised in a highly abusive family. All the medicine and talking therapy in the world would not solve the crux of the problem, which is the environment in which she lives. In *The Illness Narratives*, Arthur Kleinman presents the stories of two women suffering from chronic illness, one living in communist China and the other in the United States. He shows how the social situations of both these women have contributed to their suffering but argues that despite this "the structure of biomedical care in both cultures tends to preclude the necessary social interventions" (Kleinman, 1988a: 119). Both David Healy (1997) and Judith Kegan Gardiner (1995) believe there is a disconnect between the social forces that contribute to depression and its biomedical treatment – the latter does not directly address the former.

This is not to say that medication and talking therapy are not helpful for depressions which appear to be largely a reaction to social circumstances. Indeed, as some of those I interviewed suggest, they may at least bring the individual to a point where they can begin to take measures to change their environment or make different lifestyle choices, which is difficult to do in the depths of depression. Therapy is also a venue in which one may recognise triggers and develop the skills and motivation to deal with them. However, to ignore the social context in which an individual experiences depression is to ignore something meaningful to the individual. A perception of mitigating factors in the individual's environment means she can make sense of why it occurred. This understanding causes her to feel a degree of control which those whose depressions seemingly arose "out of the nowhere" lack. This feeling of control, in turn, renders her more likely to see depression as temporary rather than permanent. That the perceived absence of mitigating factors has the opposite effect is itself also significant.

Moreover, as Healy (1997) and Rose (2003) remind us, antidepressants hardly ever "cure" the problems they are intended to treat. In fact, the biomedical narrative states that antidepressants restore the "balance" of neurotransmitters, but does not state that the balance is permanently restored. Therefore, according to this narrative, individuals may need to remain on antidepressants indefinitely or risk their neurotransmitters being "off-balance" once again. This aspect of biomedical treatment might be a contributing factor to the views of women who do not consider their depressive episodes to have been triggered; since they cannot identify a social or psychological explanation for depression, the biomedical narrative provides the explanation they can most easily identify with, but one which lends itself to a chronic rather than a temporary view of depression.

If talking therapies such as cognitive behaviour therapy not only help to address the symptoms of depression but also enable the individual to take an active role in her own recovery, then that would at least go some way towards addressing some of the issues raised regarding control. Talking therapies may be especially useful for those who believe their episodes to have been triggered by something in their lives, as an understanding of why depression occurred appears to be the key to having a sense of control and, in turn, the possibility of averting depression in the future. An ability to make sense of one's experience with depression can in itself be therapeutic (Gask et al., 2003). It may be worth investigating the relative effectiveness of talking therapies for those who perceived triggers compared with those who did not.

This book highlights the importance of perceived control as a determinant of how one interprets her diagnosis, whether one feels authentic or not when depressed or on medication, and whether one believes in the possibility of overcoming depression. These beliefs, in turn, may have implications for how depression is diagnosed and treated in practice. Yet unless we conduct further studies, we may not know exactly what those implications are. It may be that talking therapies and/or social interventions, either alone or in addition to medical treatment, may be more beneficial than medical treatment alone for those who feel they experience triggers for their depressive episodes, or those who feel less authentic on medication, compared with those who do not. Differentiating these groups may reveal a more striking difference in the effectiveness of combining interventions than is usually found in studies concerning the effectiveness of treatments for depression.

Given the current dominant message that depression, particularly bipolar depression, is a chronic condition (see numerous medical papers such as Depp *et al.*, 2008; Kilbourne *et al.*, 2007; Simon, 2009; Ward & Wisner, 2007), the number of women who appear to think otherwise is notable. It is also notable that most of the interviewees who feel their depression is something that can be overcome perceived triggers for most of their episodes. The finding is worthy of further investigation in a large quantitative study. Such a study may either support or contest the call to place more emphasis on the individual's perception of the context of her depression. A much larger sample could explore the relationship of perceived triggers to a number of aspects of the experience of depression across a much wider population, including men. Given that ethnicity, culture, gender and class are all implicated in the experience of depression, a larger study would be able to investigate whether these factors also influence the associations recounted in this book – for instance, whether they affect the association between perceived triggers and a belief in the ability to overcome depression.

Although it was beyond the scope of this book to establish whether individuals who consider their depression to be temporary indeed manage to eventually be free of subsequent episodes, such a question could be answered in a longitudinal study. The answer would help to determine to what extent their beliefs are justified. Such a study would need to bear in mind that perception could itself influence outcome in the form of a self-fulfilling prophecy. It may be difficult to disentangle what outcomes are due to a perception of triggers, the actual presence of triggers and the individual's optimism/pessimism.

Another question arising from this book is whether the importance of control plays out similarly in individuals diagnosed with other conditions such as schizophrenia, eating disorders or anxiety. For example, Ilina Singh's (2007) study *Clinical Implications of Ethical Concepts: Moral Self-Understandings in Children Taking Methylphenidate for ADHD* found contrasting interview responses in relation to the issue of authenticity on medication among children. Children in her study indicated that psychopharmaceutical medication does not threaten their sense of authenticity – that their real self is bad at heart despite medication. Since authenticity and perceptions of self-determination are fluid, socially inflected experiences, it is not surprising if studies of different conditions and with different populations yield different results.

It is at least clear from those I interviewed that when it comes to the individual's views of depression, including its diagnosis and recovery, the self and perceived control are intertwined. Further, what the individual believes concerning the degree of control she possesses not only impacts on her view of her self but has potential implications for what she believes to be possible in relation to her future with depression and how depression might best be treated in her particular case. It is yet more evidence that something is lost when the diagnoses of depression, like many other categories of mental illness, focus solely on symptoms to the neglect of contextual factors, or at least the individual's own assessment of what those factors may be. In an era in which the biomedical view of depression dominates and treatments are focused on the individual, these women's voices provide further evidence that even if psychiatry ignores the social context of depression, individuals remain socially embedded and, as such, their context will remain meaningful to them.

Appendix A   Listening and Learning

Gathering Experiences

I used a number of different strategies for finding women for my study – recruiting through a psychiatrist as well as through posters placed in patient waiting rooms, advertisements in newsletters[1] and websites,[2] and word of mouth. As email advertisements in college newsletters proved to be the most effective recruitment strategy, a significant proportion of the women were university students (see Appendix B). As university students may provide different responses to other groups in the population, this factor, as well as the other characteristics of the sample, should be kept in mind with regard to generalisability of the findings. As stated in Chapter 1, I endeavoured to include women with different depression diagnoses and treatments in order to explore a broad range of experiences. By chance, the only diagnoses of depression in the sample were either unipolar or bipolar. None, for example, were diagnosed with postnatal depression, although one of the women diagnosed with bipolar depression had previously been diagnosed with postnatal depression before the diagnosis was changed. However, these categories are not discrete or universally accepted. With debate surrounding the validity of categories and the potential for variation in diagnoses introduced by different clinicians, it was clear to me that the best way forward was to embrace the potential variation and include all diagnoses of depression in principle without attempting a comparative study at the outset. As with the differences noted between other groups within the study, the differences in views of depression or the self noted between unipolar and bipolar groups should also be understood as indicative rather than conclusive.

I deliberately did not select for a particular type of treatment in order to hear from those with different treatment experiences, if they chose their treatment and their reasons for their choice, and what their views are of it in relation to issues of control, responsibility and authenticity. In the end, all but two women received pharmaceutical treatment. For the most part, pharmaceutical treatment consisted of antidepressants. However, several women diagnosed with bipolar depression were prescribed mood stabilisers or antipsychotics, either solely or in addition to antidepressants.

128

The two who did not use pharmaceutical treatment instead chose herbal remedies – one used St John's wort and the other used Chinese herbs – both in conjunction with talking therapy. All but 5 of the 37 women received some kind of talking therapy (although the length of time spent with talking therapy varied). Talking therapies included counselling with a social worker or a psychologist, psychiatric counselling, cognitive behaviour therapy and psychodynamic psychotherapy. Two had also taken part in art therapy.

The in-depth, semi-structured interviews I conducted lasted between one and two hours. They did not necessarily proceed in the order outlined in the Interview Guide (Appendix C) and often moved from topic to topic depending on the flow of the interview in order to make it feel as natural as possible, helping the interviewee to feel at ease. I endeavoured to make questions open-ended as much as possible and paid special attention to the wording in order not to lead the interviewee to certain answers. Further questions were also improvised during the interview, based on the interviewee's answers. The semi-structured interview format also allowed the questions to function as prompts for the women to talk about a particular aspect of their experience, and my questions and comments served to steer the interviewee towards the questions I was investigating. At the same time, the format was flexible enough for the questions to be tailored to the individual and to the flow of the interview itself, allowing me to explore a personal topic in a way that is simultaneously directed yet open to new insights.

Given the results of Fortune et al.'s (2004) study, which found differences between women who were currently depressed and women who were not in their perceptions of how serious and chronic depression would be, I aimed to select, as much as practicable, women who were not currently depressed so that the focus of the analysis would be on other variables. Individuals in a relatively stable condition should also be in a better position to reflect on their experience of depression and treatment. Recruiting individuals at this stage also minimised ethical issues regarding their capacity for informed consent as well as the potential for emotional distress during the interview. These factors informed my decision to conduct interviews sometime after treatment had commenced and the patient judged herself to be feeling better or getting better. I excluded individuals who were "too depressed" (i.e. those with a Beck score of 31 or above, as this is considered "severe depression" according to the Beck scale) in order to have an additional measure that the individuals were, in fact, in a fairly "stable" condition, not just according to their own judgement, but also according to the Beck scale. The threshold was chosen so as to only exclude those at the extreme end of the scale, as excluding more than this would have made it difficult to attain an adequate number of interviewees. Two women were excluded on this basis. Plans and steps were put in place to deal with emotional distress or suicide risk if either emerged during interview.

I aimed to achieve data saturation, and stopped recruitment after a solid pattern of responses had emerged. I anonymised the responses by using pseudonyms. Other identifying details were also removed or changed. Hesitations were not transcribed as they distracted from the content of what the individual was saying, which is where I wished to focus attention. Significant pauses, however, are marked as ... whereas sections in which I have deliberately left out parts of the dialogue are marked as [...].

Understanding the Experiences

Although my study explored depression in context, the context I have looked at is not one of social interactions but an individual's life history, which, as Taylor and Bogdan state, is a qualitative in-depth interview which aims "to capture the salient experiences in a person's life and that person's definitions of those experiences" (1998: 88–89). A life history is especially useful in studying the meanings that individuals associate with their life experiences, and this focus on created meanings also makes it useful for studying themes of identity (Thompson, 2009). In addition to experiences and meanings, I also examined the narratives which women used.

In exploring these biographical narratives, I did not assume they were stable. Rather than seeing the interview as a process of excavating latent information from the individual, I see it as a dialogical process whereby the individual's responses are a product of the unique interaction between the interviewer and the interviewee at that particular point in time, or social productions in which the interviewer and interviewee (or "narrator") collaborate to construct a story and its meaning (Holstein & Gubrium, 1995). The interviewee may present certain responses according to the particular context or what she believes the interviewer wishes to hear – what Garfinkle calls a "texture of relevances" (Garfinkle, 1967: 166–167). Interpretative phenomenology, which influenced my analysis in a number of ways, takes a similar approach to the results of interview analysis, asserting that they are "a co-construction between participant and analyst in that it emerges from the analyst's engagement with the data in the form of the participant's account" (Osborn & Smith, 1998: 67).

With the content of the interviews being the focus of my analysis, I judged a thematic approach to be the most appropriate. It is a flexible approach which simultaneously allows for a rich and detailed account (Braun & Clarke, 2006). Richard Boyatzis (1998: 29) divides thematic coding into three subtypes: (1) theory-driven (otherwise known as a deductive approach, in which the coding frame is created before starting the analysis); (2) prior-data or prior-research-driven (also deductive); and (3) inductive or data-driven (in which themes emerge from the data during analysis) – a process used in grounded theory (Strauss & Corbin, 1990) or interpretative phenomenological analysis (Smith, 1996; Smith, 1999; Smith & Osborn, 2004). Both deductive and inductive approaches have their drawbacks. In deductive approaches (such as content analysis, in which categories are pre-defined and mutually exclusive), the researcher might approach the data with too many preconceptions and rigid interpretations based on prior theories and findings. As Boyatzis notes, in prior-research-driven codes, there is a danger that the labels reflect the researcher's own assumptions and ideas about what is expressed, and do not properly reflect the language and ideas present in the raw data. Moreover, the less flexible the code, the less likely it is to be valid and reliable (Boyatzis, 1998: 33). In inductive approaches (such as grounded theory), the coding process can be too vague and lack transparency.

In order to avoid these pitfalls, I used a combination of deductive and inductive approaches. I first developed an initial coding framework within the macro-code *Views of Depression* based on the main themes to have emerged from the existing literature on the self in depression: (1) depression as part of the self; (2) depression as a catalyst for change/path to the self; and (3) depression as an illness/enemy of the self. These themes were used to ground the coding frame, but in order not to constrain the data, new themes were allowed to emerge during the analysis. I applied the established coding frame flexibly, alongside "data-driven" coding throughout.

While Leventhal's (1997) theory of illness representations provided a good structure for a review of lay knowledge of depression, I avoided using his theory as the basis for the coding frame for several reasons. Firstly, my focus was less on representations of depression per se but rather on representations of depression in relation to the *self*, particularly as they relate to issues of control and responsibility. Thus, combining a data-driven approach with research-driven codes derived from the literature on the *self in depression* rather than Leventhal's illness representations was more appropriate to my research focus. Secondly, as Bury (2001) points out, discussion of a theme such as causation easily turns into a discussion of effects and what actions were, or are, to be taken. As presented in Chapter 2, I observed a merging of Leventhal's themes, and as the analysis progressed, it became apparent that a more tailored approach to the data was required. Thirdly, representations of mental illness can vary widely across cultures. Although this may not seem to be a great concern for this study since it was only undertaken in the United Kingdom, it is worth bearing in mind for those undertaking cross-cultural comparisons, as I have discussed at certain points in earlier chapters. Finally, those in my study at times expressed ideas that did not fit into any pre-existing themes and new themes had to be created. There were also phrases or expressions which were not voiced by participants in previous studies but which nonetheless fit into one of the already established themes. My approach was therefore flexible enough to adjust current themes and create new ones where appropriate.

I wrote a brief summary of an interview directly after most interviews. This step substituted for the first stage of interpretative analysis recommended by Smith (1995) in which initial thoughts and reactions to the interview text are recorded. My summaries were reflections on key issues in the interview, notes of possible emerging themes, or excerpts of quotes and aspects of interviews which stood out. These summaries enabled me to record my immediate thoughts and impressions following the interview, and to take note of any trends or hypotheses which may necessitate modification of the interview guide or further attention in subsequent interviews.

Overall, my emphasis was on identifying emerging themes and patterns. To this end, a detailed qualitative coding scheme was developed, with the codes then grouped under more general codes. While prior research informed the development of some of the codes, coding was only one tool within the overall interpretative approach which sought to develop, rather than impose, a theory onto the data. I first entered the 37 transcripts into the hermeneutic unit "Depression" into my coding software. For the second stage of analysis, I initially coded transcripts according to the themes derived from the literature, to which data-driven codes were then added. Codes encompassed sentences or paragraphs which referred to the same issue or idea, and their titles were conceptual, aiming to capture the ideas represented in the text. I subdivided some overarching themes according to variations in the way themes were addressed – for example, the code "diagnosis" designated the way participants first reacted to their diagnosis. I then subdivided the code into "diagnosis – relief", "diagnosis – doubt", "diagnosis – meant I would get help" and so on in order to capture more specific issues within the larger theme. The coding process was iterative, creating a total of 96 codes. In keeping with the third stage of interpretative phenomenological analysis, the themes were grouped under seven cluster labels, or macro-codes. For the integration of cases, I checked the themes I had identified in later transcripts against earlier transcripts to ensure consistency, ensuring that themes had not been overlooked and that new themes did in fact reflect genuinely new concepts and were not simply different manifestations of old themes.

I compared codes within transcripts to those in other transcripts, as in the technique of "constant comparison", in order to develop macro-codes that connect codes across transcripts (Strauss & Corbin, 1990). The first macro-code was *views of depression*. This consists of the themes derived from the literature as well as new themes derived from the data. This macro-code was included due to its obvious relevance to issues of the self in depression and in order to investigate any relationships these descriptions had with other factors of interest as well as with each other.

The second macro-code was *diagnosis*, which I chose because diagnosis is widely thought to play an important role in shaping the individual's illness identity (Brown, 1995; Hall, 1996; Hayne, 2003; Keil, 1992; Vellenga & Christenson, 1994; Warner *et al.*, 1989). For instance, Bjorklund (1996: 1329) believes the diagnosis determines "present and future life expectations". This macro-code is also distinct from Leventhal's "identity" term because it was concerned not with the label which individuals ascribed to their depression but rather with how they felt about that label (the diagnosis), their initial feelings towards it, how they interpreted the meaning of the diagnosis for their life and how/whether they believe it affected how others view them.

The third macro-code was the *future* (i.e. the role individuals believed depression would play in their future). I designated this code because it seemed important not only for images of one's future self but also for the roles and choices one makes in the present. Within this category, I developed codes for whether individuals believed their condition to be chronic or temporary/curable, and whether or not they identified events/circumstances which they believed had triggered certain episodes. Data-driven coding was a particular advantage here, as the relationship between codes that I observed during analysis of this theme had not been envisaged previously. This macro-code also had the advantage of embracing the overlapping nature of themes as they occurred within narratives rather than treating the questions "how long will it last?" (time-line); "how will it affect me?" (consequences); "can it be controlled or cured?" (cure/control) and even "what caused it?" (cause) as discrete entities. By maintaining a broad and open approach rather than attempting to compartmentalise individuals' responses according to Leventhal's theory, relationships between themes were allowed to emerge and become encapsulated in different terms. For instance, although what an individual believed triggered her depressive episode might be construed as a "cause", the interviews showed that the two concepts were subtly distinguished. Furthermore, I found the issue of cure/control to be integral to the question of how long the individual believed depression would last and how it would affect her.

The fourth macro-code incorporated issues related to *medication* and the self. Existing literature had already highlighted medication, particularly antidepressants, as posing a potential threat to authenticity, or at least problematised the notion of authenticity itself (e.g. Kramer, 1993; Singh, 2005), and it was an element I wished to further investigate.

The fifth and sixth macro-codes, *causes* and *recovery* respectively, were included for their potential relevance to and influence on other macro-codes. Again, a flexible approach allowed for recognition of the overlapping nature of the codes. *Causes*, for instance, related to the individual's views of depression as well as to their ideas regarding their future with depression, yet the interviews testified to a qualitative distinction between them. *Recovery* covered elements that the individual felt had helped in her recovery process. This was not restricted to elements such as "counselling" or "friends and family" but also included codes such as "responsibility" when the individual stated that she felt taking responsibility for her depression had been key in her recovery. *Medication* could have been placed under this macro-code, but given that medication loomed large in issues of authenticity within interviews, I decided that it deserved a category in its own right.

The final macro-code was a *miscellaneous* group of codes that did not fit into the other categories but which nevertheless were of potential interest or relevance to my investigation. Some of the codes referred to the actual experience of being depressed or manic – attempts at describing what such a state feels like – and others refer to feelings associated with having had depression, such as guilt, failure, gain/loss of creativity and stigma – which have been a focus of research on depression in the recent past (e.g. Chafetz *et al.*, 1992; Kearns & Taylor, 1989; Penn & Martin, 1998; Raingruber, 2002; Rosenfield, 1997; Vellenga & Christenson, 1994). The first four macro-codes correspond to the main chapters.

Once I had transcribed and coded the interviews, I created excel spreadsheets and converted them into bar graphs in order to help identify patterns within themes of interest. Although the focus was on the ideas expressed by the women, this method for identifying patterns proved helpful in identifying how widespread the ideas were, what kind of individuals expressed them or on what the ideas depended. This, in turn, helped to ascertain possible reasons for why interviewees expressed certain ideas. I ran chi-square ($\chi 2$) tests for association in the categorical data and Mann–Whitney U-tests for differences between groups for ordinal variables in order to have an indication of the validity of the results. However, given the small size of the sample, I decided not to include the quantitative elements in this book.

Appendix B Women Interviewed

Number	Pseudonym	Age	Diagnosis	Occupation
1	Annette	35	Bipolar	Unemployed
2	Charlotte	53	Bipolar	Unemployed
3	Debbie	19	Bipolar	Student
4	Felicity	50	Bipolar	Unemployed
5	Frances	44	Bipolar	Retired
6	Gina	31	Bipolar	Student
7	Hazel	28	Bipolar	Student
8	Imogen	23	Bipolar	Student
9	Ingrid	43	Bipolar	Unemployed
10	Layla	24	Bipolar	Publishing
11	Phoenix	65	Bipolar	Retired
12	Theresa	25	Bipolar	Student
13	Veronica	61	Bipolar	Volunteer for mental health charity
14	Judy	35	Bipolar	Psychologist
15	Belinda	30	Bipolar	Student
16	Chloe	26	Bipolar	Contract management
17	Anne	28	Unipolar	Student
18	Barbara	22	Unipolar	Student
19	Bridget	39	Unipolar	Doctor
20	Diana	32	Unipolar	Student
21	Ellie	28	Unipolar	Student
22	Evelyn	22	Unipolar	Student
23	Gail	26	Unipolar	Student
24	Heather	20	Unipolar	Student
25	Jane	53	Unipolar	Social worker
26	Karen	27	Unipolar	Student
27	Miriam	27	Unipolar	Student
28	Nancy	50	Unipolar	Self-employed (business)
29	Olivia	19	Unipolar	Student
30	Penny	22	Unipolar	Childcare worker
31	Rebecca	31	Unipolar	Student
32	Stacey	47	Unipolar	Administrative assistant
33	Ursula	32	Unipolar	Student and civil servant
34	Wendy	28	Unipolar	Student
35	Zoe	21	Unipolar	Student
36	Katie	28	Unipolar	Healthcare worker
37	Vanessa	20	Unipolar	Student

Appendix C   Interview Guide

(Used to prompt further discussion and improvised questions.)

Depression history
- How do you feel now?
- How did your depression start?
- Could you please draw a timeline of your depression, talking me through your mood and events over time?
- What made you go to the doctor?
- When did you first start to think that you might be depressed?
- What did you think was wrong before you were diagnosed?
- How did you feel about going to the doctor/counsellor? What made you feel that way?
- Did you expect the diagnosis?

Treatment/model of depression
- How did you feel about the treatment suggested?
- If you were to describe depression to a friend, how would you describe it?
- If you were to describe it to a doctor, how would you describe it?
- Which description do you think is more accurate to how you feel about it?
- Do you feel it is part of who you are, an illness or something else?
- What makes you see it that way?/What do you think has influenced the way you see it?
- Does taking a pill fit into the way you see depression?
- Do you feel like a different person when you're on medication?
- Do you want to decrease your drug dose or come off it completely? Why/why not?

The Self
- Has your idea of depression changed over the years?
- What do you think changed the way you see it?
- Describe what it feels like to be depressed.

- How did you feel about yourself when you came off antidepressants?
- Has depression changed you as a person? How?
- Is there a real you? Who is the real you? When do you see yourself as most yourself?

Responsibility
- What do you think caused your depression?
- Do you think genes have anything to do with it?
- Did anyone else in your family have it? Did you feel it was inevitable that you would get it?
- What do you think were the main things that helped you improve?
- Out of those, which do you think made the biggest difference?
- Do you feel in control of your recovery?
- Could you imagine life without depression? What would it be like?
- If you could press a button that would get rid of your depression forever, would you press it? Why/why not?
- What kind of role do you see depression as having in your life in the future?

Miscellaneous
- How would you feel if you were diagnosed with depression/bipolar disorder instead?
- Do you worry about stigma?
- Have you read any autobiographies?
- What made you decide to volunteer for this study?

Notes

1   The Self and Related Concepts

1. The Beck Depression Inventory is one of the most frequently used methods for measuring the severity of depression. It consists of 21 multiple-choice questions which ask about feelings of hopelessness, guilt, irritability, punishment and physical signs such as tiredness, lack of interest in sex and weight loss (Beck & Alford, 2009). The conventional cut-off score for depression is 10. Scores above this are considered to indicate depressive symptomatology (Forkmann *et al.*, 2009). This concept of a cut-off involves a binary classification of depression rather than a dimensional one for treatment and management purposes – a categorical frame which is the subject of much debate, (e.g. Blazer, 2005; Cuthbert, 2005; Menninger, 1963; Parker, 2006; Widiger & Sankis, 2000).
2. Fogelson (1982) argues that as Radin (1920) was the first ethnographer to conduct a systematic study into life histories in his cultural research, that should make him the first anthropological researcher of the self.
3. For example, he contends that "I" causes us to believe that there is a unified and coherent location for the behaviour of the speaker.
4. I do not espouse the Cartesian definition, which separates the mind from the body, with the mind as the sole locus of the self.
5. Note that this difference between men and women could be the result of socialisation rather than ingrained or pre-existing biological differences.
6. I shall use the terms "autonomy" and "self-determination" synonymously.

2   The View from Inside: The Variety of Views of Depression

1. The different reasons provided here resonate with the work of Mildred Blaxter (1990) and Irving Kenneth Zola (1973), who discuss the work that categorising something as an illness does for individuals.
2. The idea has also been described by Norman Daniels but has been criticised by several bioethicists.
3. It is possible that at first depression is viewed by some as all of the self before being viewed as just part of the self. Perhaps such a view would have been expressed if I had interviewed women while they were depressed rather than when they were feeling better.
4. It could also be argued that Wendy's own behaviour, or even her depressive tendency, influenced her social environment to some extent.

5. An example of such a view can be found in Wisdom *et al.* (2008: 492), who cite one interviewee as stating:

> The depression I experience never feels like an illness. To me, it's a bad attitude, a deficiency of willpower, and something I brought upon myself. It is a weakness I'm ashamed of ... Depression is who I am, not what I have, because that's a simpler explanation than trying to understand how both distinctions might be true.

Rather than categorising this as a "depression as weakness" view, the authors present it as an example of individuals who tired of trying to differentiate between their "self" and the "illness".

6. Family history here is widely defined, consisting of at least one member of the immediate or extended family who was said to have had unipolar or bipolar depression.

7. Although genetics and family history were often perceived to be closely linked, some women recognised that a family history does not necessarily imply a genetic inheritance but may imply a social inheritance with its impact on family life, especially if they were raised by someone with depression/bipolar. It is also worth noting that diseases or disorders can be caused by genetic factors that are not necessarily inherited.

8. Whether depression should be considered a chronic illness is, of course, a point of contention. Nevertheless, Williams' interpretation of the individual's account of the causes of an illness and the function of such an account is equally applicable to depression.

9. In contrast, South Asian women in Britain appear to embrace the label "depression" and to strongly associate it with somatic symptoms (Fenton & Sadiq-Sangster, 1996). (Burr and Chapman (2004) challenge this, finding that South Asian women freely described their emotional pain and how this connected to their physical symptoms.) In another cultural comparison, Renata Kokanovic and colleagues (2008) found that instead of couching depression in illness terms, East African refugees in Australia framed it in terms of familial and socio-political difficulties. "Depression" was also described in collective rather than individualistic terms. Kokanovic and colleagues (2008) suggest that the differences between Anglo-Australian and East African refugee accounts do not stem from a different experience of suffering but a difference in categorising and interpreting it. Kokanovic *et al.*'s (2010) study of depression in East Timorese and Vietnamese refugees in Australia also found a resistance to the view of depression as an illness.

3   Going for Help: The Impact of Diagnosis on the Self

1. In practical terms, the diagnosis usually decides what type of treatment the individual will receive. If the diagnosis is unipolar depression, the individual is normally prescribed antidepressants. If the diagnosis is bipolar depression, the individual is normally prescribed a mood stabiliser or antipsychotic either solely or in addition to antidepressants. Both those diagnosed with unipolar and those diagnosed with bipolar depression may receive some form of talking therapy.

2. Studies such as Estroff, 1981; Garfinkle, 1956; Goffman, 1961; Karp, 1994; Pilgrim & Rogers, 1993; and Scheff, 1966 have explored the symbolic meaning of a diagnosis for the patient. More recent studies have specifically identified patients' reactions to receiving a diagnosis of mental illness, with some patients feeling relief (Dinos *et al.*, 2004; Pitt *et al.*, 2009; Proudfoot *et al.*, 2009; Rose & Thornicroft, 2010), some feeling stigmatised by the diagnosis (Dickerson *et al.*, 2002; Dinos *et al.*, 2004; Fink & Tasman, 1992; Gallagher *et al.*, 2010; Knight *et al.*, 2003; Pitt *et al.*, 2009; Proudfoot *et al.*, 2009; Rose & Thornicroft, 2010; Sartorius, 2007; Vellenga & Christenson, 1994), some rejecting their diagnosis (Bradfield, 2003; Gallagher *et al.*, 2010; Proudfoot *et al.*, 2009; Rose & Thornicroft, 2010), and others feeling shocked (Proudfoot *et al.*, 2009), scared (Gallagher *et al.*, 2010), disempowered or despairing about their future (Gallagher *et al.*, 2010; Pitt *et al.*, 2009; Proudfoot *et al.*, 2009). Hayne (2003) found that on the one hand patients felt the diagnosis legitimised particular traits, but on the other hand de-legitimised their self. Karp (1994) and Proudfoot *et al.* (2009) documented how a diagnosis often caused individuals to re-evaluate their sense of self.
3. While such a process seems to be a reasonable causal explanation of reactive forms of depression, and the biomedical model an explanation for depression which seems to arise out of nowhere, I cannot draw any conclusions about causal models here.
4. Lafrance and Stoppard, along with Fullagar, also identify pressure to be a "good woman" at the heart of why the women in their studies became depressed.
5. Shaw (2002) problematises the notion of lay beliefs on the basis of the difficulty in separating professional from lay discourse – the latter being so infused by the former in Western society. However, Kokanovic *et al.* (2008) show that lay views of depression are constantly in conflict with the medical view. The preceding chapter certainly reflected this conflict, and that the issue of self-determination is behind much of it. Viewed in light of this current chapter, we could say that at least initial reactions to one's diagnosis tend to assume that the label entails a biomedical model, but this view is then questioned, comes into conflict, is combined, or replaced, with other views of depression.
6. Note, however, that the National Alliance on Mental Illness is in the United States, where the biomedical paradigm is even more dominant.
7. Mechanic (1995) believes that neurasthenia is depression, although patients and doctors deny that it is.
8. Framing emotional distress as more of a social, rather than clinical, issue – an understandable reaction to difficult life situations – may also be more common among ethnic minorities in Western societies (Karasz, 2005; 1995). This has implications for diagnosis, because if individuals do not present the doctor with what he or she could interpret as "symptoms", they may be less likely to be diagnosed (Helman, 1994). In Britain, an ethnic minority such as Black Caribbean women may engage in a different discourse about emotional distress, leading them to conceptualise and describe their complaints differently to their Western counterparts in a medical consultation. Faced with a more social explanation and description than what they are used to, a GP may then decide not to categorise the complaints as "depression" and to view them as

understandable responses to stress instead (Edge *et al.*, 2004). Yet Black Caribbean women may not judge their GP's decision not to diagnose depression negatively, as they may not wish to be labelled with depression (Edge *et al.*, 2004). This resistance to the depression label, however, is predicated on a belief that what they are experiencing is not befitting of a biomedical label (Edge & Rogers, 2005). Black Caribbean women's resistance to the biomedical label appears to precede their diagnosis, and probably contributes to their lower rates of diagnosis.

In contrast, East Timorese and Vietnamese refugees in Australia may present to the GP with embodied forms of emotional distress (Kokanovic *et al.*, 2010), such as medically unexplained aches and pains (Wileman *et al.*, 2002), or frequently making appointments for minor symptoms (Bellón *et al.*, 1999), which the GP may then infer as indicative of depression. They may also present a more practical and social narrative of their distress to a clinician who nevertheless diagnoses them with depression, resulting in a clash between "horrendous life experience" and biomedical narratives which the GP may attempt to work around (Kokanovic *et al.*, 2010). In such a scenario, the same Western biomedical concept of depression is presented to the patient, but would probably be met with even more resistance than acceptance in comparison with those whom I interviewed due not only to the different constructions of distress among these communities compared with my sample, but also to the increased negative connotations of the diagnosis of a mental illness within these communities (Kokanovic *et al.*, 2010).

4   Taking the Medicine: The Impact of Medication on the Self

1. Although treatment for some also involved some form of counselling or psychotherapy, this was always prior to, following, or in conjunction with a form of medication (whether antidepressants, antipsychotics, mood stabilisers, herbal remedies or Chinese medicine). All those I interviewed therefore received some form of medication, whether prescription or complementary. Although herbal remedies and Chinese medicine are considered complementary medicines and are not subject to the same clinical standards as prescription medicine, in my view they have similar issues associated with them as with prescription medicine for the purposes of this chapter.

2. All but one of the 16 women I interviewed who had been diagnosed with bipolar disorder were being treated by a psychiatrist. The one exception was Debbie, who was treated by a psychologist. Of the 21 women diagnosed with unipolar depression, five were being treated by a psychiatrist at the time of interview, one saw a psychologist and the rest had seen GPs.

3. St John's wort (Hypericum perforatum) is a plant with a yellow flower which contains an ingredient called hyperforin. Hyperforin is thought to have an antidepressant effect by raising the level of serotonin in the brain (Werneke, 2007). There is disagreement within the scientific literature as to the effectiveness of St John's wort, with some suggesting it is only as effective as placebo for treating moderate to major depression but more effective for the treatment of mild depression (e.g. Lecrubier *et al.*, 2002; Linde *et al.*, 2005; National

Center for Complementary and Alternative Medicine, 2007), and others suggesting it is at least as effective as prescription antidepressants even for moderate to major depression (e.g. Kasper & Dienel, 2002; Linde *et al.*, 1996; Szegedi *et al.*, 2005; Williams *et al.*, 2000).

There are a number of different Chinese herbs used to treat depression, and they are thought to work by bringing the body's energy (called "qi") back into balance (National Alliance on Mental Illness, 2009). An example of one such herb is Banxia Houpu Decoction. Its medicinal formula consists of pinellia ternata, poria cocos, magnolia officinalis, perilla frutescens and zingiber officinale.

4. There are also risks associated with taking St John's wort in conjunction with other medication – something which is especially difficult to control for given that only 33 per cent of people who use alternative therapies mention this to their doctor (Mehta *et al.*, 2008). For example, St John's wort interacts with the immunosuppressant cyclosporin, which can lead to transplant rejection (Brinker, 2001; Ernst, 2000).

5. This sentiment has also been expressed in a number of studies (Byrne *et al.*, 2006; Grime & Pollock, 2003; Hansen & Kessing, 2007; Knudsen *et al.*, 2003; Malpass *et al.*, 2009; Maxwell, 2005; Schofield *et al.*, 2011).

6. Not all psychiatrists subscribe to the biomedical view that psychiatric medication works by correcting chemical imbalances. Joanna Moncrieff, for example, suggests that psychiatric medication works by creating a different mental state which suppresses the symptoms of the condition as well as other mental and emotional faculties (2009).

7. Views similar to those described by Nancy and Barbara have also been described by people in other studies who view antidepressants as enabling the individual to deal with issues, and as a tool in recovery rather than a cure (Bollini *et al.*, 2004; Givens *et al.*, 2006; Grime & Pollock, 2004; Holt, 2007; Knudsen *et al.*, 2003; Malpass *et al.*, 2009; Stevenson & Knudsen, 2008; Verbeek-Heida & Mathot, 2006).

8. A few women were unsure who their "real" self is, and as such, a relationship between antidepressants and authenticity was not apparent in those cases. The cases discussed in this chapter are therefore not exhaustive of the variety of views on authenticity (or lack thereof) in general among interviewees but are focused specifically on those who *do* believe they have a "real" self and could articulate which state they believed that to be and why.

9. It is worth noting that in most cases, I introduced the construction of "the real self" in interviews, so by asking interviewees how they felt about it I also potentially introduced something they may not have previously thought about, or had thought about in completely different terms. Talking about authenticity in this way during interviews also means there is a risk that something is lost in translation between the "real self" that interviewees referred to and the "authentic self" that is discussed here. However, my interview technique was to ask several follow-up questions in order to understand the interviewee's notion of the "real self" as much as possible in order to minimise this risk.

10. Several studies on patients' beliefs about antidepressants have also identified a view that by reducing symptoms of depression, antidepressants enable the

individual to take control of his or her life, as well as the view that antidepressants can also be seen as undermining control (Bollini *et al.*, 2004; Givens *et al.*, 2006; Grime & Pollock, 2004; Holt, 2007; Knudsen *et al.*, 2003; Verbeek-Heida & Mathot, 2006). The proportion of women who regarded antidepressants as a challenge to agency was roughly half of my sample, but in studies such as that by Fosgerau and Davidson (2014), the proportion was much greater. Separately, prior studies have identified individuals who feel less authentic on antidepressants (Garfield *et al.*, 2003; Karp, 1993; Knudsen *et al.*, 2002; Maxwell, 2005; Nolan & Badger, 2005; Schofield *et al.*, 2011), and individuals who feel more authentic on antidepressants (e.g. Grime & Pollock, 2004; Knudsen *et al.*, 2002; Kramer, 1993; Ridge, 2008). The perspectives of those I interviewed show how these seemingly disparate views connect.

11. Although Wendy does not explicitly mention her *personality* being changed by medication as Carl Elliott discusses, the elements which she says were changed – her thought and behaviour – are elements which, at least according to the *Cambridge Dictionary* online (Personality, 2016), are thought to express one's personality.

12. We know, of course, that there are other factors which affect treatment decisions. For example, Erdal *et al.*'s (2011) study in Norway found that immigrants and refugees, especially those of non-Western origin, supported more self-help treatments for depression than did native Norwegians, who were more in favour of medical and professional treatments. Black Caribbean women in the United Kingdom, for instance, are quite averse to using antidepressants (Gabe & Thorogood, 1986); their emphasis on the importance of being strong and in control contributing to their belief that their depression (if they even accept the label) is not medically treatable (Edge *et al.*, 2004). Gabe and Thorogood (1986) document that black working-class women also cite other resources – such as support from their daughters, religion and their jobs – as reasons for not needing to use medication or to minimise their reliance on it as much as possible. In contrast, white working-class women in Gabe and Thorogood's study who were long-term users of psychiatric medication cited fewer resources than other white women and did not experience the same benefit from them as black women. Resources such as family, jobs and leisure were not considered a good substitute for medication. Medication might therefore be viewed as more enabling than undermining autonomy by white working-class women, at least in comparison to black women.

13. At this point, it is worth noting the tension between conceptions of the self as asocial and conceptions of the self as socially embedded. While I do not support the completely asocial representations of the self, it seems that if the culture in which we live plays too great a role in delineating how we can express ourselves, it could impinge on our authenticity. The question then is, "How much social embeddedness can we have before the self becomes inauthentic?" A great many authors have devoted time to resolving this tension and the debate is beyond the scope of this chapter. However, those interested in this issue could begin with Christman (2004); Mackenzie & Stoljar (2000); Meyers (1989).

14. There may have been a number of individuals who may never have considered the issue of authenticity until I prompted them to reflect on it. Clearly, perceived authenticity would not need to be taken into account in such cases, and sensitivity may need to be exercised in order to strike a balance between giving a patient the opportunity to raise the issue, and making something into an issue that it would not otherwise have been. An open question such as "How do you feel about taking antidepressants?" Or, "Do you have any concerns?" might suffice.

15. American Psychiatric Association (2010) guidelines encourage practitioners to take patient preference regarding treatment into account.

5   Crossing Your Fingers: Predicting Depression's Role in the Future Self

1. There has been no consensus to date on the success of replication of gene–environment interaction studies, and a meta-analysis found no evidence that the proposed interaction is associated with an increased risk of depression (Risch et al., 2009).

2. These authors note the contribution of economic and social factors to depression. The buffering hypothesis, for example, states that strong social support networks reduce the risk of depression following a stressful life event (Aneshensel & Stone, 1982; Cohen & Wills, 1985). Although it is not a simple or direct relationship, it is among the elements which might explain why many people do not become clinically depressed following a stressful life event.

3. I asked interviewees, "Do you think anything triggered your depression?" or "Do you think that most of the time your episodes were triggered by something?" and if the answer was no, then no trigger was recorded. These questions were only introduced into the interview schedule when a trend began to emerge after several interviews. In all of the initial interviews, the issue of triggers arose unsolicited from the interviewee. The question was not asked if the answer was obvious from the individual's interview. There is theoretically no reason to believe that simply prompting an individual to think about whether her episodes were triggered or not encourages her to respond one way or another. Further, the results show that in practice, interviewees were just as likely to respond in the negative as the affirmative.

4. Morris states that "[p]ain in effect spends its existence moving in-between the extremes of absolute meaninglessness and full meaning" (Morris, 1991: 35). In a similar sense, the views expressed by the women I spoke with may not be static and, in making sense of depression (as a form of mental pain), they may also move from these extremes of meaninglessness and full meaning. It would be interesting to see if this is the case in a longitudinal study.

5. This is not to say that my investigation is unique in examining what individuals perceive to have triggered their depression. Ridge (2008), for example, also found that while the biomedical model of depression is quite prevalent in Western culture, there are nevertheless some who believe that stressful circumstances or events in their lives triggered their depression.

6. One interviewee was excluded from the statistical analysis because she felt she had experienced triggers for half of her episodes and no triggers for the other half. In

terms of diagnostic sub-categories and triggers, there was a slight correlation between perceiving triggers and being diagnosed with unipolar depression – most of those in the trigger group were diagnosed with unipolar depression, and most in the no-trigger group were diagnosed with bipolar depression.

7. Despite charting the distribution of perceived triggers versus no perceived triggers across other factors such as diagnosis, views of depression, family history and feelings of authenticity on medication, the difference in distribution between those who experienced triggers and those who did not was not significant among other factors.

8. It is worth noting that a similar investigation undertaken in another ethnic group or region could result in very different distribution of people in these categories. For instance, Khan *et al.* (2007) reviewed depression studies among different populations in the United Kingdom and found that certain groups were more inclined to cite stressful life events as playing explanatory roles in their depression. These groups were South Asian women (Burr & Chapman, 2004), people from Shropshire (Grime & Pollock, 2004), a randomly selected population from urban GP practices (Kadam *et al.*, 2001) and patients from GP practices in Greater Manchester (Rogers *et al.*, 2001). Likewise, Kokanovic *et al.*'s studies found that refugee communities in Australia did not subscribe to the biomedical model but described their problems in terms of life stresses and social difficulties (Kokanovic *et al.*, 2008; Kokanovic *et al.*, 2010). It is thus possible that if my study were to be conducted in these communities, a much greater proportion of interviewees would describe their depression as having been triggered. The nature of life events cited in these studies – such as material disadvantage and racism – was also different to the types of triggers cited by the women I interviewed.

Age may also affect the number of people in each category. One indication of this is that in a study of 65 primary care patients in England, most people sought to fully recover rather than to simply manage their depression (similar to the "temporary" group in my study) and this was especially the case for the younger participants (Schofield *et al.*, 2011). Older participants, on the other hand, had modified their expectations over time and sought to simply manage their condition (which I would have grouped in the "chronic" category). In contrast, in my study, the average age of individuals in both "temporary" and "chronic" groups was the same (32 years old). The difference in results may be a reflection of the wider variety of ages in Schofield *et al.*'s study (as well as the subtle difference between *seeking* to fully recover and *believing* that full recovery is possible. My study asked the latter whereas Schofield *et al.* asked the former.)

9. It is worth remembering that women in a different country may have generated different responses. For instance, Asian Americans, who embrace a more holistic view, might consider life events to be outside the realm of personal responsibility and not as stigmatising as personal failure or interpersonal causal factors, as found by Wong *et al.* (2010). Likewise, Gask *et al.*'s (2011) study of British Pakistani women found that many in the sample felt their depression would not subside because it was tied to family problems which they viewed as inescapable. The implications for beliefs about their future with depression

may thus be very different for a "trigger" group among these populations. The distinction between those who view their depression as chronic and those who view it as temporary may then instead be between those who believe their depression to be due to some sort of personal failure or interpersonal cause, and those who do not.

10. An alternative distinction – between "reactive" and "autonomous" depression – was propounded by Gillespie in 1929. Unlike the term "endogenous", "autonomous" does not have the same a aetiological assumptions – whether genetic, biological or otherwise – but simply indicates that after the first episode of depression, further bouts arise or continue of their own accord regardless of external events. "Reactive", on the other hand, indicates that the patient's mood is responsive to the external events (Boyce & Hadzi-Pavlovic, 1996). Nevertheless, it was primarily the exogenous versus endogenous distinction that was used and investigated seriously among psychiatrists.

11. Critics of the current "major depression" classification question the value of a diagnosis which says nothing about the individual's prognosis or likely response to different types of treatment – which aetiology plays an important role in predicting (Van Praag, 1990).

12. I will not enter into the precise difficulties of progressing from one step to the other here; suffice to say that "coming from within the individual" need not necessarily mean "coming from their biology", and that a biological origin, and indeed a genetic one, need not necessarily be evidenced by a family history.

13. Personal communication with Dr Furhan Iqbal on 28th September 2009.

14. In 1992, Paykel and Cooper reviewed 14 studies and concluded that depressions triggered by "stressful life events" (as measured by life events scales) were slightly more likely to have better outcomes (Paykel & Cooper, 1992). Mazure (1998) also reviewed studies spanning from 1969 to 1989 and concluded that there is a consistent relationship between stressful life events and the onset of major depression. However, the degree of influence that stressful events have on depression is contested because the correlation between stressful events and depression has tended to be low (Rabkin, 1993; Rabkin & Streuning, 1976). Brown (1981) and Monroe and Depue (1991) point out that it may be more appropriate to view the relationship inversely. They provide an analogy to lung cancer – that is, most people who smoke do not develop lung cancer, but of those with lung cancer, nearly all cases are related to smoking.

Appendix A Listening and Learning

1. These consisted of newsletters for patient support groups and college newsletters.

2. Websites consisted of online support groups, a local news website and Enter Trials. A website for the study was created in order to instantly link potential participants to information about the study.

References

Abramson, L. Y., Seligman, M. E., & Teasdale, J. D. (1978). Learned Helplessness in Humans: Critique and Reformulation. *Journal of Abnormal Psychology*, 87(1), 49–74.

Adelswärd, V., & Sachs, L. (2003). The Messenger's Dilemmas – Giving and Getting Information in Genealogical Mapping for Hereditary Cancer. *Health, Risk & Society*, 5(2), 125–138.

Alloy, L. B., Abramson, L. Y., & Viscusi, D. (1981). Induced Mood and the Illusion of Control. *Journal of Personality and Social Psychology Bulletin*, 41(6), 1129–1140.

Altmaier, E. M., Leary, M. R., Forsyth, D. R., & Ansel, J. C. (1979). Attribution Therapy: Effects of Locus of Control and Timing of Treatment. *Journal of Counseling Psychology*, 26(6), 481–486.

American Psychiatric Association (Ed.). (1952). *Diagnostic and Statistical Manual of Mental Disorders: DSM-I*. Washington, DC: American Psychiatric Association.

American Psychiatric Association (Ed.). (1980). *Diagnostic and Statistical Manual of Mental Disorders: DSM-III* (3rd edn.). Washington, DC: American Psychiatric Association.

American Psychiatric Association. (2010). *Practice Guideline for the Treatment of Patients with Major Depressive Disorder* (3rd edn.). Arlington, VA: American Psychiatric Association (APA).

Anderson, C., Kirkpatrick, S., Ridge, D., Kokanovic, R., & Tanner, C. (2015). Starting Antidepressant Use: A Qualitative Synthesis of UK and Australian Data. *BMJ Open*, 5(12), e008636.

Andreasen, N. C., Scheftner, W. A., Reich, T., & Hirschfeld, R. M. (1986). The Validation of the Concept of Endogenous Depression. *Archives of General Psychiatry*, 43(3), 246–255.

Aneshensel, C. S., & Stone, J. D. (1982). Stress and Depression: A Test of the Buffering Model of Social Support. *Archives of General Psychiatry*, 39(12), 1392–1396.

Angermeyer, M. C., Holzinger, A., Carta, M. G., & Schomerus, G. (2011). Biogenetic Explanations and Public Acceptance of Mental Illness: Systematic Review of Population Studies. *British Journal of Psychiatry*, 199(6), 367–372.

Angst, J., Gamma, A., Gastpar, M., Lépine, J.-P., Mendlewicz, J., & Tylee, A. (2002). Gender Differences in Depression. *European Archives of Psychiatry and Clinical Neuroscience*, 252(5), 201–209.

Anonymous. (1989). First Person Account: How I've Managed Chronic Mental Illness. *Schizophrenia Bulletin, 15*(4), 635–640.

Antonuccio, D. O., Burns, D. D., & Danton, W. G. (2002). Antidepressants: A Triumph of Marketing over Science. *Prevention and Treatment, 5*(1), 25.

Arehart-Treichel, J. (2002). Bipolar Disorder Guidelines Revised to Reflect Treatment Advances. *Psychiatric News, 37*(1), 12.

Aristotle. (2001). On the Soul (J. A. Smith, Trans.). Blacksburg, VA: Virginia Tech.

Aronowitz, R. A. (1998). *Making Sense of Illness: Science, Society, and Disease.* Cambridge: Cambridge University Press.

Ashmore, R. D., & Jussim, L. (1997). Introduction: Toward a Second Century of the Scientific Analysis of Self and Identity. In R. D. Ashmore & L. Jussim (Eds.), *Self and Identity: Fundamental Issues.* Oxford: Oxford University Press.

Badger, F., & Nolan, P. (2006). Concordance with Antidepressant Medication in Primary Care. *Nursing Standard, 20*(52), 35–40.

Ball, M., & Orford, J. (2002). Meaningful Patterns of Activity Amongst the Long-Term Inner City Unemployed: A Qualitative Study. *Journal of Community & Applied Social Psychology, 12*(6), 377–396.

Bandura, A. (1982). Self-Efficacy Mechanism in Human Agency. *American Psychologist, 37*(2), 122–147.

Bandura, A. (1997). *Self-Efficacy: The Exercise of Control.* New York: W. H. Freeman.

Barber, L. C. (1988). *Self-Efficacy for Preferred Therapy as a Function of Emotional Locus of Control and Personal Relevance.* PhD thesis, Texas: Texas Tech University.

Barnes, C., & Mitchell, P. (2005). Considerations in the Management of Bipolar Disorder in Women. *Australian New Zealand Journal of Psychiatry, 39*(8), 662–673.

Barnett, J. H., & Smoller, J. W. (2009). The Genetics of Bipolar Disorder. *Neuroscience, 164*(1), 331–343.

Baumeister, R. F. (1987). How the Self Became a Problem: A Psychological Review of Historical Research. *Journal of Personality and Social Psychology, 52*(1), 163–176.

Baumeister, R. F. (1999). The Nature and Structure of the Self: An Overview. In R. F. Baumeister (Ed.), *The Self in Social Psychology* (pp. 1–20). Philadelphia: Psychology Press.

Baxter, M. (1990). *Health and Lifestyles.* London: Routledge.

Beane, J. A., & Lipka, R. P. (1980). Self-Concept and Self-Esteem: A Construct Differentiation. *Child Study Journal, 10*(1), 1–6.

Bebbington, P. E., Brugha, T., MacCarthy, B., Potter, J., Sturt, E., Wykes, T., Katz, R., & McGruffin, P. (1988). The Camberwell Collaborative Depression Study: Depressed Probands: Adversity and the Form of Depression. *British Journal of Psychiatry, 152*(6), 754–765.

Beck, A. T., & Alford, B. A. (2009). *Depression: Causes and Treatment.* Philadelphia: University of Pennsylvania Press.

Becker, E. (1973). *The Denial of Death.* New York: Free Press.

Beike, D. R., & Landoll, S. L. (2000). Striving for a Consistent Life Story: Cognitive Reactions to Autobiographical Memories. *Social Cognition, 18*(3), 292–318.

Bell, N. J. (2009). Making Connections: Considering the Dynamics of Narrative Stability from a Relational Approach. *Narrative Inquiry, 19*(2), 280–305.

Bellón, J., Delgado, A., Luna, J., & Lardelli, P. (1999). Psychosocial and Health Belief Variables Associated with Frequent Attendance in Primary Care. *Psychological Medicine, 29*(06), 1347–1357.

Bennett, J. (2013). How I Beat Depression. Retrieved 19 March 2016, from www.howibeatdepression.com/how-jk-rowling-beat-depression/.

Benney, M., Riesman, D., & Star, S. A. (2003). Age and Sex in the Interview. In N. Fielding (Ed.), *Interviewing* (pp. 34–47). London: Sage.

Bentall, R. (2016, 19 February 2016). All in the Brain? Retrieved 29 March 2016, from https://blogs.canterbury.ac.uk/discursive/all-in-the-brain/.

Berkowitz, M. W. (1982). Self-Control Development and Relation to Prosocial Behavior: A Response to Peterson. *Merrill-Palmer Quarterly, 28*(2), 223–236.

Bertaux, D. (1981). Introduction. In D. Bertaux (Ed.), *Biography and Society: The Life History Approach in the Social Sciences* (pp. 1–15). Beverly Hills, CA: Sage.

Bertaux, D., & Kohli, M. (2009). The Life Story Approach: A Continental View. In B. Harrison (Ed.), *Life Story Research* (Vol. 1, pp. 42–65). London: Sage.

Betzler, M. (2009). Authenticity and Self-Governance. In M. Salmela & V. E. Mayer (Eds.), *Emotions, Ethics and Authenticity* (Vol. 5). Amsterdam: John Benjamins Pub. Co.

Bhugra, D., & Cochrane, R. (Eds.). (2001). *Psychiatry in Multi-Cultural Britain.* London: Gaskell Publishers.

Biegler, P. (2012). *The Ethical Treatment of Depression: Autonomy through Psychotherapy.* Cambridge, MA: MIT Press.

Bifulco, A., Harris, T., & Brown, G. W. (1992). Mourning or Early Inadequate Care? Reexamining the Relationship of Maternal Loss in Childhood with Adult Depression and Anxiety. *Development and Psychopathology, 4*(3), 433–449.

Bifulco, A. T., Brown, G. W., & Harris, T. O. (1986). Childhood Loss of Parent, Lack of Adequate Parental Care and Adult Depression: A Replication. *Journal of Affective Disorders, 12*(2), 115–128.

Bjorklund, R. (1996). Psychiatric Labels: Still Hard to Shake. *Psychiatric Services, 47*(12), 1329–1330.

Blackburn, S. (2008). *Personal Identity* Vol. Oxford Reference Online. *The Oxford Dictionary of Philosophy* Retrieved 27 January 2010, from www.oxfordreference.com/views/ENTRY.html?subview=Main&entry=t98.e2362.

Blazer, D. G. (2005). *The Age of Melancholy: "Major Depression" and Its Social Origins.* New York: Routledge.

Bleuler, E. (1950). *Dementia Praecox or the Group of Schizophrenias.* New York: International Universities Press.

Blumer, H. (1969). *Symbolic Interactionism: Perspective and Method.* Berkeley: University of California Press.

Blyth, D. A., & Traeger, C. M. (1983). The Self-Concept and Self-Esteem of Early Adolescents. *Theory Into Practice, 22*(2), 91–96.

Boland, R. (2005). Depression in Medical Illness (Secondary Depression). In D. J. Stein, D. J. Kupfer & A. F. Schatzberg (Eds.), *The American Psychiatric Publishing Textbook of Mood Disorders* (pp. 639–652). Washington, DC: American Psychiatric Publishing.

Bollini, P., Tibaldi, G., Testa, C., & Munizza, C. (2004). Understanding Treatment Adherence in Affective Disorders: A Qualitative Study. *Journal of Psychiatric and Mental Health Nursing, 11*(6), 668–674.

Boorse, C. (1977). Health as a Theoretical Concept. *Philosophy of Science, 44*(4), 542–573.

Bowker, G. C., & Star, S. L. (2000). *Sorting Things Out: Classification and Its Consequences.* Cambridge, MA: MIT.

Boyatzis, R. E. (1998). *Transforming Qualitative Information: Thematic Analysis and Code Development.* Thousand Oaks, CA: Sage Publications.

Boyce, P., & Hadzi-Pavlovic, D. (1996). Issues in Classification: I. Some Historical Aspects. In G. Parker & D. Hadzi-Pavlovic (Eds.), *Melancholia: A Disorder of Movement and Mood.* Cambridge: Cambridge University Press.

Bradfield, B. C. (2003). *The Phenomenology of Psychiatric Diagnosis: An Exploration of the Experience of Intersubjectivity.* Master's thesis, Rhodes University.

Braun, V., & Clarke, V. (2006). Using Thematic Analysis in Psychology. *Qualitative Research in Psychology, 3*(2), 77–101.

Breggin, P. R., & Breggin, G. R. (1994). *Talking Back to Prozac: What Doctors Won't Tell You about Today's Most Controversial Drug.* New York: St. Martin's Press.

Breier, A., Schreiber, J. L., Dyer, J., & Pickar, D. (1991). National Institute of Mental Health Longitudinal Study of Chronic Schizophrenia. Prognosis and Predictors of Outcome. *Archives of General Psychiatry, 48*(3), 239–246.

Brewin, C. R., Reynolds, M., & Tata, P. (1999). Autobiographical Memory Processes and the Course of Depression. *Journal of Abnormal Psychology, 108*(3), 511–517.

Brinker, F. J. (2001). *Herb Contraindications and Drug Interactions* (3rd edn.). Sandy, OR: Eclectic Medical Publications.

Brody, H. (1994). "My Story Is Broken; Can You Help Me Fix It?": Medical Ethics and the Joint Construction of Narrative. *Literature and Medicine, 13*(1), 79–92.

Bromet, E., Andrade, L. H., Hwang, I., Sampson, N. A., Alonso, J., de Girolamo, G., de Graaf, R., Demyttenaere, K., Hu, C., Iwata, N., Karam, A. N., Kaur, J., Kostyuchenko, S., Lépine, J.-P., Levinson, D., Matschinger, H., Mora, M. E. M., Browne, M. O., Posada-Villa, J., Viana, M. C., Williams, D. R., & Kessler, R. C. (2011). Cross-National Epidemiology of DSM-IV Major Depressive Episode. *BMC Medicine, 9*(1), 90–106.

Brooks, N. A., & Matson, R. R. (1987). Managing Multiple Sclerosis. *Research in the Sociology of Health Care, 6*, 73–106.

Brown, G. W. (1981). Life Events, Psychiatric Disorder and Physical Illness. *Journal of Psychosomatic Research, 25*(5), 461–473.

Brown, G. W., Craig, T. K., & Harris, T. O. (1985). Depression: Distress or Disease? Some Epidemiological Considerations. *The British Journal of Psychiatry, 147*, 612–622.

Brown, G. W., & Harris, T. (1978). *Social Origins of Depression: A Study of Psychiatric Disorder in Women.* London: Tavistock Publications.

Brown, G. W., Harris, T. O., & Peto, J. (1973). Life Events and Psychiatric Disorders. *Psychological Medicine, 3*(2), 159–176.

Brown, J. S., Casey, S. J., Bishop, A. J., Prytys, M., Whittinger, N., & Weinman, J. (2011). How Black African and White British Women Perceive Depression and Help-Seeking: A Pilot Vignette Study. *International Journal of Social Psychiatry*, 57(4), 362–374.

Brown, L. (1993). *The New Shorter Oxford English Dictionary* (Vol. 2). Oxford: Oxford University Press.

Brown, P. (1995). Naming and Framing: The Social Construction of Diagnosis and Illness. *Journal of Health and Social Behavior, Extra Issue: Forty Years of Medical Sociology: The State of the Art and Directions for the Future*, 34–52.

Bruner, J. S. (1986). *Actual Minds, Possible Worlds*. Cambridge, MA: Harvard University Press.

Buber, M. (1958). *I and Thou*. New York: Scribner.

Buckner, J. P., & Fivush, R. (1998). Gender and Self in Children's Autobiographical Narratives. *Applied Cognitive Psychology*, 12(4), 407–429.

Burke, P. J. (1991). Identity Processes and Social Stress. *American Sociological Review*, 56(6), 836–849.

Burr, J., & Chapman, T. (2004). Contextualising Experiences of Depression in Women from South Asian Communities: A Discursive Approach. *Sociology of Health & Illness*, 26(4), 433–452.

Burr, V. (2003). *Social Constructionism* (2nd edn.). Hove, England: Routledge.

Burroughs, H., Lovell, K., Morley, M., Baldwin, R., Burns, A., & Chew-Graham, C. (2006). "Justifiable Depression": How Primary Care Professionals and Patients View Late-Life Depression? A Qualitative Study. *Family Practice*, 23(3), 369–377.

Burt, V., & Rasgon, N. (2004). Special Considerations in Treating Bipolar Disorder in Women. *Bipolar Disorder*, 6(1), 2–13.

Bury, M. (1982). Chronic Illness as Biographical Disruption. *Sociology of Health and Illness*, 4(2), 167–182.

Bury, M. (2001). Illness Narratives: Fact or Fiction? *Sociology of Health and Illness*, 23(3), 263–285.

Butler, S., & Rosenblum, B. (1991). *Cancer in Two Voices*. San Francisco: Spinsters Book Co.

Byrne, N., Regan, C., & Livingston, G. (2006). Adherence to Treatment in Mood Disorders. *Current Opinion in Psychiatry*, 19(1), 44–49.

Calhoun, L. G., Cheney, T., & Dawes, A. S. (1974). Locus of Control, Self-Reported Depression, and Perceived Causes of Depression. *Journal of Consulting and Clinical Psychology*, 42(5), 736.

Calkins, M. W. (1900). Psychology as a Science of Selves. *Philosophical Review*, 9(5), 490–501.

Carey, B. (2007). Bipolar Diagnoses Soaring. *New York Times*. Retrieved 4 September 2009, from www.nytimes.com/2007/09/04/health/04psych.html? scp=1&sq=Bipolar%20diagnosis%20soaring&st=cse.

Carricaburu, D., & Pierret, J. (1995). From Biographical Disruption to Biographical Reinforcement: The Case of HIV-Positive Men. *Sociology of Health and Illness*, 17(1), 65.

Carver, C. S., & Scheier, M. F. (2000). Autonomy and Self-Regulation. *Psychological Inquiry*, 11(4), 284–291.

Caspi, A., Sugden, K., Moffitt, T. E., Taylor, A., Craig, I. W., Harrington, H., McClay, J., Mill, J., Martin, J., Braithwaite, A., & Poulton, R. (2003). Influence of Life Stress on Depression: Moderation by a Polymorphism in the 5-HTT Gene. *Science, 301*(5631), 386–389.

Chafetz, L., Risch, N., Furlong, C., & Underwood, P. (1992). Psychosocial Rehabilitation with the Severely and Persistently Mentally Ill. In H. Wilson & C. Kneisl (Eds.), *Psychiatric Nursing* (pp. 420–438). Menlo Park, CA: Addison-Wesley.

Charmaz, K. (1983). Loss of Self: A Fundamental Form of Suffering in the Chronically Ill. *Sociology of Health & Illness, 5*(2), 168–195.

Charmaz, K. (1991). *Good Days, Bad Days: The Self in Chronic Illness and Time.* New Brunswick, NJ: Rutgers University Press.

Chew-Graham, C. A., May, C. R., Cole, H., & Hedley, S. (2000). The Burden of Depression in Primary Care: A Qualitative Investigation of General Practitioners' Constructs of Depressed People in the Inner City. *International Journal of Psychiatry in Clinical Practice, 6*(4), 137–141.

Christman, J. (2004). Relational Autonomy, Liberal Individualism, and the Social Constitution of Selves. *Philosophical Studies, 117*(1), 143–164.

Cobb, A. K., & Hamera, E. (1986). Illness Experience in a Chronic Disease–ALS. *Social Science & Medicine, 23*(7), 641–650.

Cohen, S., & Wills, T. A. (1985). Stress, Social Support, and the Buffering Hypothesis. *Psychological Bulletin, 98*(2), 310–357.

Cole, J., McGruffin, P., & Farmer, A. E. (2008). The Classification of Depression: Are We Still Confused? *The British Journal of Psychiatry, 192*(2), 83–85.

Comaroff, J., & Maguire, P. (1981). Ambiguity and the Search for Meaning: Childhood Leukaemia in the Modern Clinical Context. *Social Science & Medicine. Part B: Medical Anthropology, 15B*(2), 115–123.

Conway, M. A. (1997). *Recovered Memories and False Memories.* Oxford: Oxford University Press.

Conway, M. A., & Haque, S. (1999). Overshadowing the Reminiscence Bump: Memories of a Struggle for Independence. *Journal of Adult Development, 6*(1), 35–44.

Conway, M. A., & Pleydell-Pearce, C. W. (2000). The Construction of Autobiographical Memories in the Self-Memory System. *Psychological Review, 107*(2), 261–288.

Conway, M. A., & Rubin, D. C. (1993). The Structure of Autobiographical Memory. In A. E. Collins, S. E. Gathercole, M. A. Conway & P. E. M. Morris (Eds.), *Theories of Memory* (pp. 103–137). Hove, England: Erlbaum.

Conway, M. A., & Tacchi, P. C. (1996). Motivated Confabulation. *Neurocase, 2*(4), 325–339.

Cooley, C. H. (1902). *Human Nature and the Social Order.* New York: Scribner's.

Corbin, J. M., & Strauss, A. (1987). Accompaniments of Chronic Illness: Changes in Body, Self, Biography, and Biographical Time. *Research in the Sociology of Health Care, 6*(3), 249–282.

Cousins, S. D. (1989). Culture and Self-Perception in Japan and the United States. *Journal of Personality and Social Psychology, 56*(1), 124–131.

Cowie, B. (1976). The Cardiac Patient's Perception of His Heart Attack. *Social Science and Medicine, 10*(2), 87–96.

Craddock, N., & Sklar, P. (2009). Genetics of Bipolar Disorder: Successful Start to a Long Journey. *Trends in Genetics, 25*(2), 99–105.

Crossley, M. L. (2000). *Introducing Narrative Psychology: Self, Trauma, and the Construction of Meaning.* Buckingham, England: Open University Press.

Cuthbert, B. N. (2005). Dimensional Models of Psychopathology: Research Agenda and Clinical Utility. *Journal of Abnormal Psychology, 114*(4), 565–569.

Cutrona, C. E., & Troutman, B. R. (1986). Social Support, Infant Temperament, and Parenting Self-Efficacy: A Mediational Model of Postpartum Depression. *Child Development, 57*(6), 1507–1518.

Czuchta, D. M., & Johnson, B. A. (1998). Reconstructing a Sense of Self in Patients with Chronic Mental Illness. *Perspectives in Psychiatric Care, 34*(3), 31–36.

Damon, W., & Hart, D. (1982). The Development of Self-Understanding from Infancy through Adolescence. *Child Development, 53*(4), 841–864.

Damon, W., & Hart, D. (1986). Stability and Change in Children's Self-Understanding. *Social Cognition, 4*(2), 102–118.

Danielsson, U., Bengs, C., Lehti, A., Hammarström, A., & Johansson, E. E. (2009). Struck by Lightning or Slowly Suffocating – Gendered Trajectories into Depression. *BMC Family Practice, 10*(1), 1–11.

Danielsson, U., & Johansson, E. E. (2005). Beyond Weeping and Crying: A Gender Analysis of Expressions of Depression. *Scandinavian Journal of Primary Health Care, 23*(3), 171–177.

Danielsson, U. E., Bengs, C., Samuelsson, E., & Johansson, E. E. (2010). "My Greatest Dream Is to Be Normal": The Impact of Gender on the Depression Narratives of Young Swedish Men and Women. *Qualitative Health Research, 20*(10), 1–13.

Davidson, L., & Strauss, J. S. (1992). Sense of Self in Recovery from Severe Mental Illness. *The British Journal of Medical Psychology, 65*(2), 131–145.

Davis-Berman, J., & Pestello, F. G. (2005). Taking Psychiatric Medication: Listening to Our Clients. *Social Work in Mental Health, 4*(1), 17–31.

De Maat, S., Dekker, J., Schoevers, R., & De Jonghe, F. (2006). Relative Efficacy of Psychotherapy and Pharmacotherapy in the Treatment of Depression: A Meta-Analysis. *Psychotherapy Research, 16*(5), 566–578.

de Swaan, A. (1990). *The Management of Normality.* London: Routledge.

Deci, E. L., & Ryan, R. M. (1991). A Motivational Approach to Self: Integration in Personality. In R. Dienstbier (Ed.), *Nebraska Symposium on Motivation: Vol. 38. Perspectives on Motivation* (Vol. 38, pp. 237–288). Lincoln: University of Nebraska Press.

Deci, E. L., & Ryan, R. M. (1995). Human Autonomy: The Basis for True Self-Esteem. In M. Kernis (Ed.), *Efficacy, Agency, and Self-Esteem* (pp. 31–49). New York: Plenum Press.

Deegan, P. (1989). *A Letter to My Friend Who Is Giving Up.* Paper presented at the Connecticut Conference on Supported Employment, Cromwell, CT.

Dennett, D. C. (1992). The Self as a Center of Narrative Gravity. In F. Kessel, P. Cole & D. Johnson (Eds.), *Self and Consciousness: Multiple Perspectives.* Hillsdale, NJ: Erlbaum.

Denzin, N. K. (1989). *Interpretive Biography.* Newbury Park, CA: Sage.

Denzin, N. K. (1989). *Interpretive Interactionism.* Newbury Park, CA: Sage.

Depp, C. A., Moore, D. J., Patterson, T. L., Lebowitz, B. D., & Jeste, D. V. (2008). Psychosocial Interventions and Medication Adherence in Bipolar Disorder. *Dialogues in Clinical Neuroscience, 10*(2), 239–247.

Dickerson, F. B., Sommerville, J., Origoni, A. E., Ringel, N. B., & Parente, F. (2002). Experiences of Stigma among Outpatients with Schizophrenia. *Schizophrenia Bulletin, 28*(1), 143–155.

Dinos, S., Stevens, S., Serfaty, M., Weich, S., & King, M. (2004). Stigma: The Feelings and Experiences of 46 People with Mental Illness: Qualitative Study. *The British Journal of Psychiatry, 184*(2), 176–181.

Dohrenwend, B. P., & Dohrenwend, B. S. (1974). Social and Cultural Influences on Psychopathology. *Annual Review of Psychology, 25*(1), 417–452.

Dowrick, C. (2009). *Beyond Depression: A New Approach to Understanding and Management* (2nd edn.). Oxford: Oxford University Press.

Dumit, J. (2003). Is It Me or My Brain? Depression and Neuroscientific Facts. *Journal of Medical Humanities, 24*(1–2), 35–47.

Dworkin, G. (1976). Autonomy and Behavior Control. *Hastings Center Report, 6*(1), 23–28.

Edge, D., Baker, D., & Rogers, A. (2004). Perinatal Depression among Black Caribbean Women. *Health & Social Care in the Community, 12*(5), 430–438.

Edge, D., & Rogers, A. (2005). Dealing with It: Black Caribbean Women's Response to Adversity and Psychological Distress Associated with Pregnancy, Childbirth, and Early Motherhood. *Social Science and Medicine, 61*(1), 15–25.

Eisenberg, L. (1977). Disease and Illness Distinctions between Professional and Popular Ideas of Sickness. *Culture, Medicine and Psychiatry, 1*(1), 9–23.

Elder, R. G. (1973). Social Class and Lay Explanations of the Etiology of Arthritis. *Journal of Health and Social Behavior, 14*(1), 28–38.

Elkin, I., Yamaguchi, J., Arnkoff, D., Glass, C., Sotsky, S., & Krupnick, J. (1999). "Patient-Treatment Fit" and Early Engagement in Therapy. *Psychotherapy Research, 9*(4), 437–451.

Elliott, C. (1998). The Tyranny of Happiness: Ethics and Cosmetic Psychopharmacology. In E. Parens (Ed.), *Enhancing Human Traits. Ethical and Social Implications.* Washington, DC: Georgetown University Press.

Emslie, C., Ridge, D., Ziebland, S., & Hunt, K. (2007). Exploring Men's and Women's Experiences of Depression and Engagement with Health Professionals: More Similarities Than Differences? A Qualitative Interview Study. *BMC Family Practice, 8*(1), 1–10.

Emslie, C., Ridge, D. T., Ziebland, S., & Hunt, K. (2006). Men's Accounts of Depression: Reconstructing or Resisting Hegemonic Masculinity? *Social Science and Medicine, 62*(9), 2246–2257.

Epstein, S. (1973). The Self-Concept Revisited: Or a Theory of a Theory. *American Psychologist, 28*(5), 404–414.

Epstein, S. (1980). The Self-Concept: A Review and the Proposal of an Integrated Theory of Personality. In E. Staub (Ed.), *Personality: Basic Aspects and Current Research*. Englewood Cliffs, NJ: Prentice Hall.

Erdal, K., Singh, N., & Tardif, A. (2011). Attitudes about Depression and Its Treatment among Mental Health Professionals, Lay Persons and Immigrants and Refugees in Norway. *Journal of Affective Disorders, 133*(3), 481–488.

Erickson, R. J. (1995). The Importance of Authenticity for Self and Society. *Symbolic Interaction, 18*(2), 121–144.

Erler, A. (2012). One Man's Authenticity Is Another Man's Betrayal. *Journal of Applied Philosophy, 29*(3), 257–265.

Ernst, E. (2000). Herb-Drug Interactions: Potentially Important but Woefully under-Researched. *European Journal of Clinical Pharmacology, 56*(8), 523–524.

Essom, C. R., & Nemeroff, C. B. (1996). Treatment of Depression in Adulthood. In K. I. Shulman, M. Tohen & S. P. Kutcher (Eds.), *Mood Disorders across the Life Span* (pp. 251–264). New York: Wiley.

Estroff, S. E. (1981). *Making It Crazy: An Ethnography of Psychiatric Clients in an American Community*. Berkeley and Los Angeles: University of California Press.

Estroff, S. E., Lachicotte, W. S., Illingworth, L. C., & Johnston, A. (1991). Everybody's Got a Little Mental Illness: Accounts of Illness and Self among People with Severe, Persistent Mental Illnesses. *Medical Anthropology Quarterly, 5*(4), 331–369.

Everyday Health. (2010). Common Misconceptions about Bipolar Disorder. Retrieved 10 March 2010, from www.everydayhealth.com/health-report/bipolar-depression/bipolar-disorder-misconceptions.aspx.

Ewart, C. (1992). The Role of Physical Self Efficacy in the Recovery from a Heart Attack. In R. Schwarzer (Ed.), *Self-Efficacy: Thought Control of Action* (Vol. 1, pp. 287–305). Philadelphia: Taylor & Francis.

Eysenck, H. J. (1970). The Classification of Depressive Illness. *British Journal of Psychiatry, 117*(538), 241–250.

Ezzy, D. (2001). *Narrating Unemployment*. Burlington: Ashgate.

Fabrega, H., & Manning, P. K. (1972). Disease, Illness and Deviant Careers. In R. A. Scott & J. D. Douglas (Eds.), *Theoretical Perspectives on Deviance*. New York: Basic Books.

Farmer, A., Elkin, A., & McGuffin, P. (2007). The Genetics of Bipolar Affective Disorder. *Current Opinion in Psychiatry, 20*(1), 8–12.

Fenton, S., & Sadiq-Sangster, A. (1996). Culture, Relativism and the Expression of Mental Distress: South Asian Women in Britain. *Sociology of Health & Illness, 18*(1), 66–85.

Fernando, S. (1992). Psychiatry. *OpenMind, 58*, 8–9.

Fine, M., & Asch, A. (1988). Disability Beyond Stigma: Social Interaction, Discrimination, and Activism. *Journal of Social Issues, 44*(1), 3–21.

Fink, P. J., & Tasman, A. (Eds.). (1992). *Stigma and Mental Illness*. Washington, DC; London: American Psychiatric Press.

Fitzgerald, J. M. (1988). Vivid Memories and the Reminiscence Phenomenon: The Role of a Self Narrative. *Human Development, 31*(5), 261–273.

Fitzgerald, J. M. (1996). Intersecting Meanings of Reminiscence in Adult Development and Aging. In D. C. Rubin (Ed.), *Remembering Our Past:*

Studies in Autobiographical Memory (pp. 360–383). Cambridge: Cambridge University Press.

Fogelson, R. T. (1982). Person, Self, and Identity: Some Anthropological Retrospects, Circumspects, and Prospects. In B. Lee (Ed.), *Psychosocial Theories of the Self* (pp. 67–109). New York: Plenum.

Forkmann, T., Vehren, T., Boecker, M., Norra, C., Wirtz, M., & Gauggel, S. (2009). Sensitivity and Specificity of the Beck Depression Inventory in Cardiologic Inpatients: How Useful Is the Conventional Cut-Off Score? *Journal of Psychosomatic Research, 67*(4), 347–352.

Forrest, A. D., Fraser, R. H., & Priest, R. G. (1965). Environmental Factors in Depressive Illness. *British Journal of Psychiatry, 111*(472), 243–253.

Fortune, G., Barrowclough, C., & Lobban, F. (2004). Illness Representations in Depression. *British Journal of Clinical Psychology, 43*(4), 347–364.

Fosgerau, C. F., & Davidsen, A. S. (2014). Patients' Perspectives on Antidepressant Treatment in Consultations with Physicians. *Qualitative Health Research, 24*(5), 641–653.

Foucault, M. (1998). *The History of Sexuality Vol. 1: The Will to Knowledge.* London: Penguin.

Fournier, J. C., DeRubeis, R. J., Hollon, S. D., Dimidjian, S., Amsterdam, J. D., Shelton, R. C., & Fawcett, J. (2010). Antidepressant Drug Effects and Depression Severity: A Patient-Level Meta-Analysis. *Journal of the American Medical Association, 303*(1), 47–53.

Fox, N. J. (1993). *Postmodernism, Sociology and Health.* Buckingham: Open University Press.

Francis, L. E. (1997). Ideology and Interpersonal Emotion Management: Redefining Identity in Two Support Groups. *Social Psychology Quarterly, 60*(2), 153–171.

Frank, A. W. (1991). *At the Will of the Body: Reflections on Illness.* Boston, MA: Houghton Mifflin.

Frankl, V. (1959). *Man's Search for Meaning.* Boston, MA: Beacon Press.

Frankl, V. E. (1959). *From Death-Camp to Existentialism: A Psychiatrist's Path to a New Therapy.* Boston, MA: Beacon Press.

Freeman, M., & Gelenberg, A. (2005). Bipolar Disorder in Women: Reproductive Events and Treatment Considerations. *Acta Psychiatrica Scandinavica, 112*(2), 88–96.

Freud, S. (1958). Psychoanalytic Notes on an Autobiographical Account of a Case of Paranoia (J. Strachey, Trans.). In J. Strachey (Ed.), *The Standard Edition of the Complete Psychological Works of Sigmund Freud* (Vol. 22, pp. 3–82). London: Hogarth Press.

Fulford, K. W. M. (2001). "What Is (Mental) Disease?": An Open Letter to Christopher Boorse. *Journal of Medical Ethics, 27*(2), 80–85.

Fullagar, S. (2009). Negotiating the Neurochemical Self: Anti-Depressant Consumption in Women's Recovery from Depression. *An Interdisciplinary Journal for the Social Study of Health, Illness and Medicine, 13*(4), 389–403.

Gabe, J., & Thorogood, N. (1986). Prescribed Drug Use and the Management of Everyday Life: The Experiences of Black and White Working Class Women. *Sociological Review, 34*(4), 737–772.

Gallagher, A., Arber, A., Chaplin, R., & Quirk, A. (2010). Service Users' Experience of Receiving Bad News about Their Mental Health. *Journal of Mental Health*, *19*(1), 34–42.

Gardiner, J. K. (1995). Can Ms. Prozac Talk Back? Feminism, Drugs, and Social Constructionism. *Feminist Studies*, *21*(3), 501–517.

Garfield, S., Smith, F., & Francis, S. A. (2003). The Paradoxical Role of Antidepressant Medication-Returning to Normal Functioning While Losing the Sense of Being Normal. *Journal of Mental Health*, *12*(5), 521–535.

Garfinkle, H. (1956). Conditions of Successful Degradation Ceremonies. *American Journal of Sociology*, *61*(5), 420–424.

Garfinkle, H. (1967). *Studies in Ethnomethodology*. Englewood Cliffs, NJ: Prentice-Hall.

Gask, L., Aseem, S., Waquas, A., & Waheed, W. (2011). Isolation, Feeling "Stuck" and Loss of Control: Understanding Persistence of Depression in British Pakistani Women. *Journal of Affective Disorders*, *128*(1–2), 49–55.

Gask, L., Rogers, A., Oliver, D., May, C., & Roland, M. (2003). Qualitative Study of Patients' Perceptions of the Quality of Care for Depression in General Practice. *The British Journal of General Practice*, *53*(489), 278–283.

Gecas, V. (1982). The Self-Concept. *Annual Review of Sociology*, *8*, 1–33.

Geers, A. L., Rose, J. P., Fowler, S. L., Rasinski, H. M., Brown, J. A., & Helfer, S. G. (2013). Why Does Choice Enhance Treatment Effectiveness? Using Placebo Treatments to Demonstrate the Role of Personal Control. *Journal of Personality and Social Psychology*, *105*(4), 549–566.

Geertz, C. (1973). *The Interpretation of Cultures: Selected Essays*. New York: Basic Books.

Geertz, C. (1979). From the Native's Point of View: On the Nature of Anthropological Understanding. In P. Rabinow & W. Sullivan (Eds.), *Interpretive Social Science: A Reader*. California: University of California Press.

Geertz, C. (1983). *Local Knowledge: Further Essays in Interpretive Anthropology*. New York: Basic Books.

Georgakopoulou, A. (2006). Thinking Big with Small Stories in Narrative and Identity Analysis. *Narrative Inquiry*, *16*(1), 122–129.

Gergen, K. J. (1977). The Social Construction of Self-Knowledge. In T. Mischel (Ed.), *The Self: Psychological and Biological Issues*. Oxford: Blackwell.

Gerhardt, U. (1989). *Ideas about Illness: An Intellectual and Political History of Medical Sociology*. London: Macmillan.

Giddens, A. (1991). *Modernity and Self-Identity: Self and Society in the Late Modern Age*. Stanford, CA: Stanford University Press.

Gilligan, C. (1982). *In a Different Voice: Psychological Theory and Women's Development*. Cambridge, MA: Harvard University Press.

Giorgi, A., & Giorgi, B. (2008). Phenomenological Psychology. In C. Willig & W. S. Rogers (Eds.), *The Sage Handbook of Qualitative Research in Psychology*. London: Sage.

Givens, J. L., Datto, C. J., Ruckdeschel, K., Knott, K., Zubritsky, C., Oslin, D. W., Nyshadham, S., Vanguri, P., & Barg, F. K. (2006). Older Patients' Aversion to Antidepressants. *Journal of General Internal Medicine*, *21*(2), 146–151.

Glaser, B. G., & Strauss, A. L. (1967). *The Discovery of Grounded Theory*. Chicago: Aldine.

Goffman, E. (1961). *Asylums*. Harmondsworth: Penguin.

Goffman, E. (1971). *The Presentation of Self in Everyday Life*. Hammondsworth: Penguin.

Goodman, L. E. (1992). *Avicenna*. London: Routledge.

Goodwin, R., & Gotlib, I. (2004). Gender Differences in Depression: The Role of Personality Factors. *Psychiatry Research, 126*(2), 135–142.

Gordon, S. L. (1989). Institutional and Impulsive Orientations in Selectively Appropriating Emotions to Self. In D. D. Franks & E. D. McCarthy (Eds.), *The Sociology of Emotions: Original Essays and Research Papers* (pp. 115–135). Greenwich, CT: JAI Press.

Graham, H. (1986). *The Human Face of Psychology*. Milton Keynes: Open University Press.

Grawe, K. (2004). *Psychological Therapy*. Toronto: Hogrefe & Huber.

Greenwald, A. G., Bellezza, F. S., & Banaji, M. R. (1988). Is Self-Esteem a Central Ingredient of the Self-Concept? *Personality and Social Psychology Bulletin, 14*(1), 34–45.

Grime, J., & Pollock, K. (2003). Patients' Ambivalence about Taking Antidepressants: A Qualitative Study. *Pharmaceutical Journal, 271*(7270), 516–519.

Grime, J., & Pollock, K. (2004). Information versus Experience: A Comparison of an Information Leaflet on Antidepressants with Lay Experience of Treatment. *Patient Education and Counseling, 54*(3), 361–368.

Gubrium, J., & Holstein, J. A. (1995). Biographical Work and New Ethnography. In T. Josselson & A. Lieblich (Eds.), *Interpreting Experience: The Narrative Study of Lives* (pp. 45–58). Newbury Park, CA: Sage.

Gubrium, J. F., & Holstein, J. A. (1998). Narrative Practice and the Coherence of Personal Stories. *Sociological Quarterly, 39*(1), 163–187.

Gubrium, J. F., Holstein, J. A., & Buckholdt, D. R. (1994). *Constructing the Life Course*. Dix Hills, NY: General Hall.

Guignon, C. (2004). *On Being Authentic*. London: Routledge.

Habermas, T., & Bluck, S. (2000). Articles – Getting a Life: The Emergence of the Life Story in Adolescence. *Psychological Bulletin, 126*(5), 748–769.

Hall, B. A. (1990). The Struggle of the Diagnosed Terminally Ill Person to Maintain Hope. *Nursing Science Quarterly, 3*(4), 177–184.

Hall, B. A. (1996). The Psychiatric Model: A Critical Analysis of Its Undermining Effects on Nursing in Chronic Mental Illness. *Advances in Nursing Science, 18*(3), 16–26.

Hallowell, A. I. (1955). *Culture and Experience*. Philadelphia: University of Pennsylvania Press.

Hansen, H. V., & Kessing, L. V. (2007). Adherence to Antidepressant Treatment. *Expert Review of Neurotherapeutics, 7*(1), 57–62.

Harkness, K. L., & Monroe, S. M. (2002). Childhood Adversity and the Endogenous versus Nonendogenous Distinction in Women with Major Depression. *American Journal of Psychiatry, 159*(3), 387–393.

Harré, R. (1985). The Language Game of Self-Ascription: A Note. In K. J. Gergen & K. E. Davis (Eds.), *The Social Construction of the Person*. New York: Springer-Veral.

Harré, R. (1987). The Social Construction of Selves. In K. Yardley & T. Honess (Eds.), *Self and Identity* (pp. 41–52). New York: John Wiley & Sons.

Harré, R. (1989). Language Games and the Texts of Identity. In J. Shotter & K. J. Gergen (Eds.), *Texts of Identity*. London: Sage.

Harris, T., Brown, G. W., & Bifulco, A. (1986). Loss of Parent in Childhood and Adult Psychiatric Disorder: The Role of Lack of Adequate Parental Care. *Psychological Medicine, 16*(3), 641–659.

Harrow, M., & Jobe, T. H. (2010). How Frequent Is Chronic Multiyear Delusional Activity and Recovery in Schizophrenia: A 20-Year Multi–Follow-Up. *Schizophrenia Bulletin, 36*(1), 192–204.

Harter, S. (1983). Competence as a Dimension of Self-Evaluation: Toward a Comprehensive Model of Self-Worth. In R. Leahy (Ed.), *The Development of the Self*. New York: Academic Press.

Harter, S. (1997). The Personal Self in Social Context: Barriers to Authenticity. In R. D. Ashmore & L. Jussim (Eds.), *Self and Identity: Fundamental Issues*. Oxford: Oxford University Press.

Harter, S. (2005). Authenticity. In C. R. Snyder & S. J. Lopez (Eds.), *Handbook of Positive Psychology* (pp. 382–394). London: Oxford University Press.

Hartmann, C. E. (2002). Personal Accounts: Life as Death: Hope Regained with ECT. *Psychiatric Services, 53*(4), 413–414.

Haslam, C., Brown, S., Atkinson, S., & Haslam, R. (2004). Patients' Experiences of Medication for Anxiety and Depression: Effects on Working Life. *Family Practice, 21*(2), 204–212.

Hawkins, A. H. (1990). A Change of Heart: The Paradigm of Regeneration in Medical and Religious Narrative. *Perspectives in Biology and Medicine, 33*(4), 547–559.

Hawkins, A. H. (1993). *Reconstructing Illness: Studies in Pathography*. West Lafayette, IN: Purdue University Press.

Hayden, E. P., & Nurnberger, J. I. J. (2005). Molecular Genetics of Bipolar Disorder. *Genes, Brain and Behavior, 5*(1), 85–95.

Hayne, Y. M. (2003). Experiencing Psychiatric Diagnosis: Client Perspectives on Being Named Mentally Ill. *Journal of Psychiatric & Mental Health Nursing, 10*(6), 722–729.

Healy, D. (1997). *The Anti-Depressant Era*. Harvard: Harvard University Press.

Heidegger, M. (1962). *Being and Time* (J. Macquarrie & E. Robinson, Trans.). New York: Basic Books.

Helman, C. G. (1988). Psyche, Soma and Society: The Social Construction of Psychosomatic Disorders. In M. Lock & D. R. Gordon (Eds.), *Biomedicine Examined*. Dordrecht, Boston and London: Kluwer Academic Publishers.

Helman, C. G. (1994). Doctor-Patient Interactions. In C. G. Helman (Ed.), *Culture, Health and Illness* (pp. 101–145). Oxford: Butterworth Heinemann.

Herzlich, C. (1973). *Health and Illness: A Social Psychological Analysis* (D. Graham, Trans.). London: Academic Press.

Heyman, B. (2004). Risk and Mental Health. *Health, Risk and Society*, 6(4), 297–301.

Higgins, E. T. (1987). Self-Discrepancy: A Theory Relating Self and Affect. *Psychological Review*, 94(3), 319–340.

Higgins, P. C. (1992). *Making Disability: Exploring the Social Transformation of Human Variation*. Springfield, IL: C.C. Thomas.

Hoffmann, M., Linell, P., Lindh-Åstrand, L., & Kjellgren, K. (2003). Risk Talk: Rhetorical Strategies in Consultations on Hormone Replacement Therapy. *Health, Risk & Society*, 5(2), 139–154.

Hogg, M. A., & Cooper, J. (2003). *The Sage Handbook of Social Psychology*. London: Sage.

Holmes, T. H., & Rahe, R. H. (1967). The Social Readjustment Rating Scale. *Journal of Psychosomatic Research*, 11(2), 213–218.

Holstein, J. A., & Gubrium, J. F. (1995). *The Active Interview*. Thousand Oaks, CA: Sage Publications.

Holt, M. (2007). Agency and Dependency within Treatment: Drug Treatment Clients Negotiating Methadone and Antidepressants. *Social Science & Medicine*, 64(9), 1937–1947.

Holzinger, A., Floris, F., Schomerus, G., Carta, M., & Angermeyer, M. (2011). Gender Differences in Public Beliefs and Attitudes about Mental Disorder in Western Countries: A Systematic Review of Population Studies. *Epidemiology and Psychiatric Sciences*, 1(1), 1–13.

Horwitz, A. V., & Wakefield, J. C. (2007). *The Loss of Sadness: How Psychiatry Transformed Normal Sorrow into Depressive Disorder*. Oxford: Oxford University Press.

Hughes, J. C., & Ramplin, S. (2012). Clinical and Ethical Judgement. In C. Cowley (Ed.), *Reconceiving Medical Ethics* (Vol. Continuum Studies in Philosophy). London: Continuum.

Hume, D. (2007 [1739]). *A Treatise of Human Nature – a Critical Edition*. Oxford: Clarendon Press.

Hunot, V. M., Horne, R., Leese, M. N., & Churchill, R. C. (2007). A Cohort Study of Adherence to Antidepressants in Primary Care: The Influence of Antidepressant Concerns and Treatment Preferences. *Primary Care Companion to the Journal of Clinical Psychiatry*, 9(2), 91–99.

Hydén, L.-C. (1995). The Rhetoric of Recovery and Change. *Culture, Medicine and Psychiatry*, 19(1), 73–90.

Hydén, L.-C. (1997). Illness and Narrative. *Sociology of Health & Illness*, 19(1), 48–69.

Iacoviello, B. M., McCarthy, K. S., Barrett, M. S., Rynn, M., Gallop, R., & Barber, J. P. (2007). Treatment Preferences Affect the Therapeutic Alliance: Implications for Randomized Controlled Trials. *Journal of Consulting and Clinical Psychology*, 75(1), 194–198.

Imel, Z. E., Malterer, M. B., McKay, K. M., & Wampold, B. E. (2008). A Meta-Analysis of Psychotherapy and Medication in Unipolar Depression and Dysthymia. *Journal of Affective Disorders*, 110(3), 197–206.

Ingram, R. E., Scott, W., & Siegle, G. (1999). Depression: Social and Cognitive Aspects. In T. Millon, P. H. Blaney & R. D. Davis (Eds.), *Oxford Textbook of Psychopathology* (pp. 203–226). Oxford: Oxford University Press.

Issakainen, M. (2014). Young People Negotiating the Stigma around Their Depression. *Young, 22*(2), 171–184.

James, W. (1890). *Principles of Psychology*. New York: Holt.

Jaspers, K. (1971). *Philosophy of Existence*. Philadelphia: University of Pennsylvania Press.

Jensen, L. A., & Allen, M. N. (1994). A Synthesis of Qualitative Research on Wellness-Illness. *Qualitative Health Research, 4*(4), 349–369.

Jobe, T. H., & Harrow, M. (2010). Schizophrenia Course, Long-Term Outcome, Recovery, and Prognosis. *Current Directions in Psychological Science, 19*(4), 220–225.

Johnston, M., Morrison, V., Macwalter, R., & Partridge, C. (1999). Perceived Control, Coping and Recovery from Disability Following Stroke. *Psychology and Health., 14*(2), 181–192.

Jones, F., Mandy, A., & Partridge, C. (2008). Reasons for Recovery after Stroke: A Perspective Based on Personal Experience. *Disability and Rehabilitation, 30*(7), 507–516.

Jorm, A. F., Medway, J., Christensen, H., Korten, A. E., Jacomb, P. A., & Rodgers, B. (2000). Public Beliefs about the Helpfulness of Interventions for Depression: Effects on Actions Taken When Experiencing Anxiety and Depression Symptoms. *Australian and New Zealand Journal of Psychiatry, 34*(4), 619–626.

Kadam, U. T., Croft, P., McLeod, J., & Hutchinson, M. (2001). A Qualitative Study of Patients' Views on Anxiety and Depression. *British Journal of General Practice, 51*(466), 375–380.

Kant, I. (2004 [1788]). Critique of Practical Reason (T. K. Abbott, Trans.) (2004 edn.). Mineola, NY: Dover.

Karasz, A. (2005). Cultural Differences in Conceptual Models of Depression. *Social Science & Medicine, 60*(7), 1625–1635.

Karp, D. A. (1993). Taking Anti-Depressant Medications: Resistance, Trial Commitment, Conversion, Disenchantment. *Qualitative Sociology, 16*(4), 337–359.

Karp, D. A. (1994). Living with Depression: Illness and Identity Turning Points. *Qualitative Health Research, 4*(1), 6–30.

Karp, D. A. (1996). *Speaking of Sadness: Depression, Disconnection, and the Meanings of Illness*. Oxford: Oxford University Press.

Karp, D. A. (2006). *Is It Me or My Meds?: Living with Antidepressants*. Cambridge, MA: Harvard University Press.

Kasper, S., & Dienel, A. (2002). Cluster Analysis of Symptoms During Antidepressant Treatment with Hypericum Extract in Mildly to Moderately Depressed Out-Patients. A Meta-Analysis of Data from Three Randomized, Placebo-Controlled Trials. *Psychopharmacology (Berl), 164*(3), 301–308.

Kass, L. (2003). Ageless Bodies, Happy Souls. *The New Atlantis, 1*(Spring), 9–28.

Kasser, T., & Ryan, R. M. (1993). A Dark Side of the American Dream: Correlates of Financial Success as a Central Life Aspiration. *Journal of Personality and Social Psychology, 65*(2), 410–422.

Kasser, T., & Ryan, R. M. (1996). Further Examining the American Dream: Differential Correlates of Intrinsic and Extrinsic Goals. *Personality and Social Psychology Bulletin, 22*(3), 280–287.

Kaufman, J. M., & Johnson, C. (2004). Stigmatized Individuals and the Process of Identity. *The Sociological Quarterly, 45*(4), 807–833.

Kearns, R. A., & Taylor, S. M. (1989). Daily Life Experiences of People with Chronic Disabilities in Hamilton, Canada. *Canada's Mental Health, 37*(4), 1–4.

Keil, J. (1992). The Mountain of My Mental Illness. *Journal of the California Alliance for the Mentally Ill, 3*(2), 5–6.

Keitner, G. I., Ryan, C. E., & Solomon, D. A. (2009). Commentary. *British Medical Journal, 12*(2), 48.

Kendell, R. E. (1976). The Classification of Depression: A Review of Contemporary Confusion. *British Journal of Psychiatry, 129*(1), 15–28.

Kendell, R. E., & Zealley, A. K. (1988). *Companion to Psychiatric Studies.* Edinburgh: Churchill Livingstone.

Kennett, J., & Matthews, S. (2002). Identity, Control and Responsibility: The Case of Dissociative Identity Disorder. *Philosophical Psychology, 15*(4), 509–526.

Kessing, L. V., Hansen, H. V., Demyttenaere, K., & Bech, P. (2005). Depressive and Bipolar Disorders: Patients' Attitudes and Beliefs Towards Depression and Antidepressants. *Psychological Medicine, 35*(8), 1205–1213.

Kessler, R. (2003). Epidemiology of Women and Depression. *Journal of Affective Disorders, 74*(1), 5–13.

Khan, N., Bower, P., & Rogers, A. (2007). Guided Self-Help in Primary Care Mental Health: Meta-Synthesis of Qualitative Studies of Patient Experience. *The British Journal of Psychiatry, 191*(3), 206–211.

Kierkegaard, S., Thomte, R., & Anderson, A. (1980). *The Concept of Anxiety: A Simple Psychologically Orienting Deliberation on the Dogmatic Issue of Hereditary Sin.* Princeton, NJ: Princeton University Press.

Kilbourne, A., Post, E., Bauer, M., Zeber, J., Copeland, L., Good, C., & Pincus, H. (2007). Therapeutic Drug and Cardiovascular Disease Risk Monitoring in Patients with Bipolar Disorder. *Journal of Affective Disorders, 102*(1), 145–151.

Kim, M. T. (2002). Measuring Depression in Korean Americans: Development of the Kim Depression Scale for Korean Americans. *Journal of Transcultural Nursing, 13*(2), 109–117.

Kirsch, I., Deacon, B. J., Huedo-Medina, T. B., Scoboria, A., Moore, T. J., & Johnson, B. T. (2008). Initial Severity and Antidepressant Benefits: A Meta-Analysis of Data Submitted to the Food and Drug Administration. *PLOS Medicine, 5*(2), e45.

Kleinman, A. (1988a). *The Illness Narratives: Suffering, Health, and the Human Condition.* New York: Basic Books.

Kleinman, A. (1988b). *Rethinking Psychiatry: From Cultural Category to Personal Experience.* New York: Free Press.

Klerman, G. L. (1984). The Advantages of DSM-III. *American Journal of Psychiatry, 141*(4), 539–542.

Knight, M. T. D., Wykes, T., & Hayward, P. (2003). "People Don't Understand": An Investigation of Stigma in Schizophrenia Using Interpretative Phenomenological Analysis (IPA). *Journal of Mental Health, 12*(3), 209–222.

Knudsen, P., Hansen, E. H., & Eskildsen, K. (2003). Leading Ordinary Lives: A Qualitative Study of Younger Women's Perceived Functions of Antidepressants. *Pharmacy World & Science, 25*(4), 162–167.

Knudsen, P., Hansen, E. H., Traulsen, J. M., & Eskildsen, K. (2002). Changes in Self-Concept While Using SSRI Antidepressants. *Qualitative Health Research, 12*(7), 932–944.

Koerner, B. I. (30 July 2002). First, You Market the Disease ... Then You Push the Pills to Treat It. *The Guardian*, 8–9.

Kohut, H. (1977). *The Restoration of the Self*. New York: International Universities Press.

Kokanovic, R., Bendelow, G., & Philip, B. (2013). Depression: The Ambivalence of Diagnosis. *Sociology of Health and Illness, 35*(3), 377–390.

Kokanovic, R., Dowrick, C., Butler, E., Herrman, H., & Gunn, J. (2008). Lay Accounts of Depression Amongst Anglo-Australian Residents and East African Refugees. *Social Science & Medicine, 66*(2), 454–466.

Kokanovic, R., May, C., Dowrick, C., Furler, J., Newton, D., & Gunn, J. (2010). Negotiations of Distress between East Timorese and Vietnamese Refugees and Their Family Doctors in Melbourne. *Sociology of Health and Illness, 32*(4), 511–527.

Kondo, D. K. (1990). *Crafting Selves: Power, Gender, and Discourses of Identity in a Japanese Workplace*. Chicago: University of Chicago Press.

Kraepelin, E. (1899). *A Textbook for Students and Physicians* (H. Metoui & A. Ayed, Trans.). Canton: Watson Publishing International.

Kraepelin, E. (1904). *Clinical Psychiatry* (A. R. Diefendorf, Trans. 6th edn.). New York: Macmillan.

Kramer, P. D. (1993). *Listening to Prozac*. New York: Viking.

Kramer, P. D. (2005). *Against Depression*. New York: Viking.

Kueher, C. (2003). Gender Differences in Unipolar Depression: An Update of Epidemiological Findings and Possible Explanations. *Acta Psychiatrica Scandinavica, 108*(3), 163–174.

Kuyken, W., & Brewin, C. R. (1994). Intrusive Memories of Childhood Abuse During Depressive Episodes. *Behaviour Research and Therapy, 32*(5), 525–528.

Kuyken, W., Brewin, C. R., Power, M., & Furnham, A. (1992). Causal Beliefs about Depression in Depressed Patients, Clinical Psychologists and Lay Persons. *British Journal of Medical Psychology, 65*(3), 257–268.

Kvale, S. (1996). *Interviews: An Introduction to Qualitative Research Interviewing*. Thousand Oaks, CA: Sage Publications.

Kwan, B. M., Dimidjian, S., & Rizvi, S. L. (2010). Treatment Preference, Engagement, and Clinical Improvement in Pharmacotherapy versus Psychotherapy for Depression. *Behaviour Research and Therapy, 48*(8), 799–804.

Lafrance, M. N. (2007). A Bitter Pill: A Discursive Analysis of Women's Medicalized Accounts of Depression. *Journal of Health Psychology, 12*(1), 127–140.

Lafrance, M. N., & Stoppard, J. M. (2007). Re-Storying Women's Depression: A Material-Discursive Approach. In C. Brown & T. Augusta-Scott (Eds.), *Narrative Therapy: Making Meaning, Making Lives*. Thousand Oaks, CA: Sage.

Laing, R. D. (1959). *The Divided Self.* London: Tavistock.

Laing, R. D. (1961). *Self and Others.* London: Tavistock.

Laing, R. D., & Esterson, A. (1970). *Sanity, Madness, and the Family.* Harmondsworth: Penguin.

Lakoff, G. (1987). *Women, Fire, and Dangerous Things: What Categories Reveal about the Mind.* Chicago: University of Chicago Press.

Latour, B. (1987). *Science in Action: How to Follow Scientists and Engineers through Society.* Cambridge, MA: Harvard University Press.

Leary, M. R., & Tangney, J. P. (2003). *Handbook of Self and Identity.* New York: Guilford Press.

Lecrubier, Y., Clerc, G., Didi, R., & Kieser, M. (2002). Efficacy of St. John's Wort Extract WS 5570 in Major Depression: A Double-Blind, Placebo-Controlled Trial. *American Journal of Psychiatry, 159*(8), 1361–1366.

Ledermann, E. K. (1984). *Mental Health and Human Conscience: The True and the False Self.* Amersham, England: Avebury.

Leibenluft, E. (1996). Women with Bipolar Illness: Clinical and Research Issues. *American Journal of Psychiatry, 153*(2), 163–173.

Leibenluft, E. (1997). Issues in the Treatment of Women with Bipolar Illness. *Journal of Clinical Psychiatry, 58* (Suppl 15), 5–11.

Lester, H., & Gask, L. (2009). The Service User Perspective. In L. Gask, H. Lester, T. Kendrick & R. Peveler (Eds.), *Primary Care Mental Health.* London: RCPsych Publications.

Leventhal, H., Benyamini, Y., Brownlee, S., Diefenbach, M., Leventhal, E. A., Patrick-Miller, L., & Robitaille, C. (1997). Illness Representations: Theoretical Foundations. In K. J. Petrie & J. Weinman (Eds.), *Perceptions of Health and Illness: Current Research and Applications* (pp. 19–45). Amsterdam: Harwood Academic Press.

Lévi-Strauss, C. (1966). *The Savage Mind.* Chicago: University of Chicago Press.

Levy, N. (2011). Enhancing Authenticity. *Journal of Applied Philosophy, 28*(3), 308–318.

Lienhardt, G. (1985). *Self: Public, Private: Some African Representations.* Cambridge: Cambridge University Press.

Linde, K., Berner, M., Egger, M., & Mulrow, C. (2005). St John's Wort for Depression. *The British Journal of Psychiatry, 186*(2), 99–107.

Linde, K., Berner, M., & Kriston, L. (2008). Cochrane Database Systematic Review. *Art. No.: CD000448, Iss. 4,* 7–15.

Linde, K., Ramirez, G., Mulrow, C. D., Pauls, A., Weidenhammer, W., & Melchart, D. (1996). St John's Wort for Depression – an Overview and Meta-Analysis of Randomised Clinical Trials. *British Medical Journal, 313*(7052), 253–258.

Linville, P. W., & Carlston, D. E. (1994). Social Cognition Perspective on Self. In P. G. Devine, D. L. Hamilton & T. M. Ostrom (Eds.), *Social Cognition: Contributions to Classic Issues in Social Psychology* (pp. 143–193). New York: Springer-Verlag.

Locke, J. (1959). *An Essay Concerning Human Understanding.* New York: Dover Publications.

Loe, M., & Cuttino, L. (2008). Grappling with the Medicated Self: The Case of ADHD College Students. *Symbolic Interaction, 31*(3), 303–323.

Luo, L., Wang, J. N., Kong, L. D., Jiang, Q. G., & Tan, R. X. (2000). Antidepressant Effects of Banxia Houpu Decoction, a Traditional Chinese Medicinal Empirical Formula. *Journal of Ethnopharmacology, 73*(1–2), 277–281.

Lupton, D. (1999). *Risk*. London: Routledge.

Maciejewski, P. K., Prigerson, H. G., & Mazure, C. M. (2000). Self-Efficacy as a Mediator between Stressful Life Events and Depressive Symptoms. Differences Based on History of Prior Depression. *The British Journal of Psychiatry, 176*(4), 373–378.

Mackenzie, C., & Atkins, K. (2008). *Practical Identity and Narrative Agency*. New York: Routledge.

Mackenzie, C., & Stoljar, N. (2000). *Relational Autonomy: Feminist Perspectives on Autonomy, Agency, and the Social Self*. Oxford: Oxford University Press.

Malpass, A., Shaw, A., Sharp, D., Walter, F., Feder, G., Ridd, M., & Kessler, D. (2009). "Medication Career" or "Moral Career"? The Two Sides of Managing Antidepressants: A Meta-Ethnography of Patients' Experience of Antidepressants. *Social Science & Medicine, 68*(1), 154–168.

Markus, H. (1977). Self-Schemata and Processing Information about the Self. *Journal of Personality and Social Psychology, 35*(2), 63–78.

Markus, H., & Kunda, Z. (1986). Stability and Malleability of the Self-Concept. *Journal of Personality and Social Psychology, 51*(4), 858–866.

Markus, H., & Nurius, P. (1986). Possible Selves. *American Psychologist, 41*(9), 954–969.

Markus, H. R., & Kitayama, S. (1991). Culture and the Self: Implications for Cognition, Emotion, and Motivation. *Psychological Review, 98*(2), 224.

Marsella, A. J. (1980). Depressive Experience and Disorder across Cultures. In H. Triadis & J. Draguns (Eds.), *Handbook of Cross-Cultural Psychology* (Vol. 6, pp. 237–289). Boston: Allyn and Bacon.

Maslow, A. H. (1976). *The Farther Reaches of Human Nature*. Hammondsworth: Penguin.

Mauthner, N. S. (2002). *The Darkest Days of My Life: Stories of Postpartum Depression*. Cambridge, MA: Harvard University Press.

Maxwell, M. (2005). Women's and Doctors' Accounts of Their Experiences of Depression in Primary Care: The Influence of Social and Moral Reasoning on Patients' and Doctors' Decisions. *Chronic Illness, 1*(1), 61–71.

May, R., & Yalom, I. D. (1989). Existential Psychotherapy. In R. J. Corsini & W. Danny (Eds.), *Current Psychotherapies* (4th edn., pp. 363–404). Itasca, IL: Peacock.

Mazure, C. M. (1998). Life Stressors as Risk Factors in Depression. *Clinical Psychology: Science and Practice, 5*(3), 291–313.

McAdams, D. P. (1982). Experiences of Intimacy and Power: Relationships between Social Motives and Autobiographical Memory. *Journal of Personality and Social Psychology, 42*(2), 292–302.

McAdams, D. P. (1985). *Power, Intimacy, and the Life Story: Personological Inquiries into Identity*. New York: Guilford Press.

McAdams, D. P. (2001). The Psychology of Life Stories. *Review of General Psychology, 5*(2), 100–122.

McAdams, D. P. (2006). The Problem of Narrative Coherence. *Journal of Constructivist Psychology, 19*(2), 109–125.

McAdams, D. P., Diamond, A., de Aubin, E., & Mansfield, E. (1997). Stories of Commitment: The Psychosocial Construction of Generative Lives. *Journal of Personality and Social Psychology, 72*(3), 678–694.

McCall, G. J., & Simmons, J. L. (1966). *Identities and Interactions.* New York: Free Press.

McEwen, B. S. (2000). The Neurobiology of Stress: From Serendipity to Clinical Relevance. *Brain Research, 886*(1–2), 172–189.

McFarlane, A. H., Bellissimo, A., & Norman, G. R. (1995). The Role of Family and Peers in Social Self-Efficacy: Links to Depression in Adolescence. *The American Journal of Orthopsychiatry, 65*(3), 402–410.

McGrath, E. E., Keita, G. P. E., Strickland, B. R., & Russo, N. F. E. (1990). *Women and Depression: Risk Factors and Treatment Issues.* Washington, DC: American Psychological Association.

McGruffin, P., Katz, R., & Bebbington, P. E. (1988). The Camberwell Collaborative Depression Study: Depression and Adversity in the Relatives of Depressed Probands. *British Journal of Psychiatry, 152*(6), 775–782.

McKenzie-Mohr, S., & Lafrance, M. N. (2011). Telling Stories without the Words: "Tightrope Talk" in Women's Accounts of Coming to Live Well after Rape or Depression. *Feminism and Psychology, 21*(1), 49–73.

McLean, G. (1991). *Restoring the Image: A Grounded Theory Investigation of the Experience and Meaning of Acute Myeloid Leukemia.* Unpublished Master's thesis, Cardiff: University of Wales.

McMullen, L. M. (1999). Metaphors in the Talk of "Depressed" Women in Psychotherapy. *Canadian Psychology, 40*(2), 102–111.

McPherson, S., & Armstrong, D. (2006). Social Determinants of Diagnostic Labels in Depression. *Social Science and Medicine, 62*(1), 50–58.

McPherson, S., & Armstrong, D. (2009). Negotiating "Depression" in Primary Care: A Qualitative Study. *Social Science & Medicine, 69*(8), 1137–1143.

Mead, G. H. (1934). *Mind, Self and Society from the Standpoint of a Social Behaviorist.* Chicago: University of Chicago Press.

Mechanic, D. (1995). Sociological Dimensions of Illness Behavior. *Social Science and Medicine, 41*(9), 1207–1216.

Mehta, D. H., Gardiner, P. M., Phillips, R. S., & McCarthy, E. P. (2008). Herbal and Dietary Supplement Disclosure to Health Care Providers by Individuals with Chronic Conditions. *The Journal of Alternative and Complementary Medicine, 14*(10), 1263–1269.

Melbourne MediBrain Centre. (2009). Bipolar Disorder. Retrieved 10 March 2010, from www.medibrain.com.au/bipolar-disorder.htm.

Menninger, K. (1963). *The Vital Balance: The Life Process in Mental Health and Illness.* New York: Viking Press.

Merriam-Webster Online Dictionary. (2010). Merriam-Webster Online Dictionary. Retrieved 1 June 2010, from www.merriam-webster.com/diction ary/self.

Meyers, D. (1989). *Self, Society, and Personal Choice*. New York: Columbia University Press.

Meyers, D. T. (1987). Personal Autonomy and the Paradox of Feminine Socialization. *The Journal of Philosophy, 84*(11), 619–628.

Mijuskovic, B. (1979). *Loneliness in Philosophy, Psychology and Literature*. Assen, Netherlands: Van Gorcum.

Millet, B. (2005). What Are the Core Symptoms of Depression? *Medicographia, 27*(3), 266.

Mirowsky, J., & Ross, C. E. (2003). *Social Causes of Psychological Distress*. New York: Aldine de Gruyter.

Moncrieff, J. (2006). The Politics of Psychiatric Drug Treatment. In D. Double (Ed.), *Critical Psychiatry: The Limits of Madness*. Basingtoke: Palgrave.

Moncrieff, J. (2009). *The Myth of the Chemical Cure: A Critique of Psychiatric Drug Treatment*. Hampshire: Palgrave Macmillan.

Monroe, S. M., & Depue, R. A. (1991). Life Stress and Depression. In J. Becker & A. Kleinman (Eds.), *Psychosocial Aspects of Depression* (pp. 101–130). Hillsdale, NJ: Erlbaum.

Monroe, S. M., & Simons, A. D. (1991). Diathesis-Stress Theories in the Context of Life Stress Research: Implications for the Depressive Disorders. *Psychological Bulletin, 110*(3), 406–425.

Moore, R. G., Watts, F. N., & Williams, J. M. (1988). The Specificity of Personal Memories in Depression. *The British Journal of Clinical Psychology, 27*(3), 275–276.

Morris, D. B. (1991). *The Culture of Pain*. Berkeley: University of California Press.

Morse, J. M., & Johnson, J. L. (1991). *The Illness Experience: Dimensions of Suffering*. Newbury Park, CA: Sage Publications.

Murray, C. J., & Lopez, A. D. (1996). Evidence-Based Health Policy–Lessons from the Global Burden of Disease Study. *Science, 274*(5288), 740.

National Alliance on Mental Illness. (2009). Acupuncture. Retrieved 28 July 2010, from http://nccam.nih.gov/health/acupuncture/.

National Center for Complementary and Alternative Medicine. (2007). St. John's Wort and Depression. Retrieved 28 July 2010, from http://nccam.nih.gov/health/stjohnswort/sjw-and-depression.htm.

Nehamas, A. (1999). *Virtues of Authenticity*. Princeton, NJ: Princeton University Press.

Nicolson, P. (1998). *Post-Natal Depression: Psychology, Science, and the Transition to Motherhood*. New York: Routledge.

Nolan, P., & Badger, F. (2005). Aspects of the Relationship between Doctors and Depressed Patients That Enhance Satisfaction with Primary Care. *Journal of Psychiatric and Mental Health Nursing, 12*(2), 146–153.

O'Brien, R., Hunt, K., & Hart, G. (2005). "It's Caveman Stuff, But That Is to a Certain Extent How Guys Still Operate": Men's Accounts of Masculinity and Help Seeking. *Social Science and Medicine, 61*(3), 503–516.

O'Connor, W., Nazroo, J. Y., Bhui, K., & National Centre for Social, R. (2002). *Ethnic Differences in the Context and Experience of Psychiatric Illness: A Qualitative Study*. London: The Stationary Office.

Ogden, J., Boden, J., Caird, R., Chor, C., Flynn, M., Hunt, M., Khan, K., MacLurg, K., Swade, S., & Thapar, V. (1999). "You're Depressed"; "No I'm Not": GPs' and Patients' Different Models of Depression. *British Journal of General Practice, 49*(439), 123–124.

Orbell, S., Johnston, M., Rowley, D., Davey, P., & Epsley, A. (2001). Self-Efficacy and Goal Importance in the Prediction of Physical Disability in People Following Hospitalisation: A Prospective Study. *British Journal of Health Psychology, 6*(1), 25–40.

Osborn, M., & Smith, J. A. (1998). The Personal Experience of Chronic Benign Lower Back Pain: An Interpretative Phenomenological Analysis. *British Journal of Health Psychology, 3*(1), 65–84.

Parker, G. (2005). Beyond Major Depression. *Psychological Medicine, 35*(4), 467–474.

Parker, G. (2006). The DSM Classification of Depressive Disorders: Debating Its Utility. *The Canadian Journal of Psychiatry, 51*(14), 871–873.

Parsons, T. (1951). *The Social System*. Glencoe, IL: Free Press.

Parsons, T. (1972). Definitions of Health and Illness in Light of American Values and Social Structure. In E. G. Jaco (Ed.), *Patients, Physicians and Illness* (pp. 107–127). New York: Free Press.

Partridge, C., & Johnston, M. (1989). Perceived Control of Recovery from Physical Disability: Measurement and Prediction. *The British Journal of Clinical Psychology, 28*(1), 53–59.

Patel, V. (1995). Explanatory Models of Mental Illness in Sub-Saharan Africa. *Social Science & Medicine, 40*(9), 1291–1298.

Paul, K. I., & Moser, K. (2006). Incongruence as an Explanation for the Negative Mental Health Effects of Unemployment: Meta-Analytic Evidence. *Journal of Occupational and Organizational Psychology, 79*(4), 595–621.

Paykel, E. S., & Cooper, Z. (1992). Life Events and Social Stress. In E. S. Paykel (Ed.), *Handbook of Affective Disorders* (Vol. 2nd edn.). New York: Guilford Press.

Penn, D. L., & Martin, J. (1998). The Stigma of Severe Mental Illness: Some Potential Solutions for a Recalcitrant Problem. *Psychiatric Quarterly, 69*(3), 235–247.

Personality. (2016) Cambridge Advanced Learner's Dictionary & Thesaurus. Retrieved 25 August, 2016 from http://dictionary.cambridge.org/dictionary /english/personality (Vols. 2016). Online: Cambridge University Press.

Pestello, F. G., & Davis-Berman, J. (2008). Taking Anti-Depressant Medication: A Qualitative Examination of Internet Postings. *Journal of Mental Health, 17*(4), 349–360.

Petersen, A. (2011). Authentic Self-Realization and Depression. *International Sociology, 26*(1), 5–24.

Petkova, B. (1995). New Views on the Self: Evil Women – Witchcraft or PMS? *Psychological Review, 2*(1), 16–19.

Piccinelli, M., & Wilkinson, G. (2000). Gender Differences in Depression. *The British Journal of Psychiatry, 177*(6), 486–492.

Pilgrim, D. (2007). The Survival of Psychiatric Diagnosis. *Social Science and Medicine, 65*(3), 536–547.

Pilgrim, D., & Bentall, R. (1999). The Medicalisation of Misery: A Critical Realist Analysis of the Concept of Depression. *Journal of Mental Health, 8*(3), 261–274.

Pilgrim, D., & Rogers, A. (1993). *A Sociology of Mental Health and Illness.* Buckingham and Philadelphia: Open University Press.

Pill, R., & Stott, N. C. H. (1982). Concepts of Illness Causation and Responsibility: Some Preliminary Data from a Sample of Working Class Mothers. *Social Science & Medicine, 16*(1), 43–52.

Pitt, L., Kilbride, M., Welford, M., Nothard, S., & Morrison, A. P. (2009). Impact of a Diagnosis of Psychosis: User-Led Qualitative Study. *Psychiatric Bulletin, 33*(11), 419–423.

Polkinghorne, D. (1988). *Narrative Knowing and the Human Sciences.* Albany: State University of New York Press.

Potter, J., & Wetherell, M. S. (1987). *Discourse and Social Psychology: Beyond Attitudes and Behavior.* London: Sage.

Pound, P., Gompertz, P., & Ebrahim, S. (1998). Illness in the Context of Older Age: The Case of Stroke. *Sociology of Health and Illness, 20*(4), 489–506.

Power, M., & Dalgleish, T. (1996). *Cognition and Emotion: From Order to Disorder.* London: Psychology Press.

Proudfoot, J. G., Parker, G. B., Benoit, M., Manicavasagar, V., Smith, M., & Gayed, A. (2009). What Happens after Diagnosis? Understanding the Experiences of Patients with Newly-Diagnosed Bipolar Disorder. *Health Expectations, 12*(2), 120–129.

Rabkin, J. G. (1993). Stress and Psychiatric Disorders. In L. Goldberger & S. Breznitz (Eds.), *Handbook of Stress: Theoretical and Clinical Aspects* (2nd edn., pp. 477–495). New York: Free Press.

Rabkin, J. G., & Streuning, E. L. (1976). Life Events, Stress and Illness. *Science, 194*(4269), 1013–1020.

Radin, P. (1920). *The Autobiography of a Winnebago Indian.* Berkeley, CA: University of California Press.

Radley, A. (1994). *Making Sense of Illness: The Social Psychology of Health and Disease.* London: Sage Publications Ltd.

Radley, A., & Green, R. (1985). Styles of Adjustment to Coronary Graft Surgery. *Social Science and Medicine, 20*(5), 461–472.

Radley, A., & Green, R. (1987). Illness as Adjustment: A Methodology and Conceptual Framework. *Sociology of Health & Illness, 9*(2), 179–207.

Raingruber, B. (2002). Client and Provider Perspectives Regarding the Stigma of and Nonstigmatizing Interventions for Depression. *Archives of Psychiatric Nursing, 16*(5), 201–207.

Rank, O. (1989). *Art and Artist: Creative Urge and Personality Development* (C. Atkinson, Trans.). New York: Norton.

Read, J. (2005). The Bio-Bio-Bio Model of Madness. *The Psychologist, 18*(10), 596–597.

Read, J., Haslam, N., Sayce, L., & Davies, E. (2006). Prejudice and Schizophrenia: A Review of the "Mental Illness Is an Illness Like Any Other" Approach. *Acta Psychiatrica Scandinavica, 114*(5), 303–318.

Register, C. (1987). *Living with Chronic Illness: Days of Patience and Passion*. New York: Free Press.

Reynolds, J. R., & Turner, R. J. (2008). Major Life Events: Their Personal Meaning, Resolution, and Mental Health Significance. *Journal of Health and Social Behavior, 49*(2), 223–237.

Richardson, J. C., Ong, B. N., & Sim, J. (2006). Is Chronic Widespread Pain Biographically Disruptive? *Social Science and Medicine, 63*(6), 1573–1585.

Ridge, D. (2008). *Recovery from Depression Using the Narrative Approach: A Guide for Doctors, Complementary Therapists, and Mental Health Professionals*. London and Philadelphia: Jessica Kingsley Publishers.

Ridge, D., Kokanovic, R., Broom, A., Kirkpatrick, S., Anderson, C., & Tanner, C. (2015). "My Dirty Little Habit": Patient Constructions of Antidepressant Use and the "Crisis" of Legitimacy. *Social Science and Medicine, 146*, 53–61.

Riessman, C. K. (1993). *Narrative Analysis*. Newbury Park, CA: Sage.

Risch, N., Merikangas, K. R., Herrell, R., Lehner, T., Griem, A., Liang, K. Y., Eaves, L., Hoh, J., Kovacs, M., & Ott, J. (2009). Interaction between the Serotonin Transporter Gene (5-HTTLPR), Stressful Life Events, and Risk of Depression: A Meta-Analysis. *Journal of the American Medical Association, 301*(23), 2462–2471.

Robinson, L. (1974). *Liaison Nursing: Psychological Approach to Patient Care*. Philadelphia: F.A. Davis.

Rogers, A., May, C., & Oliver, D. (2001). Experiencing Depression, Experiencing the Depressed: The Separate Worlds of Patients and Doctors. *Journal of Mental Health, 10*(3), 317–333.

Rogge, B. (2011). Mental Health, Positive Psychology and the Sociology of the Self. In D. Pilgrim, A. Rogers & B. Pescosolido (Eds.), *The Sage Handbook of Mental Health and Illness*. Los Angeles: Sage.

Romano, D. M., McCay, E., Goering, P., Boydell, K., & Zipursky, R. (2010). Reshaping an Enduring Sense of Self: The Process of Recovery from a First Episode of Schizophrenia. *Early Intervention in Psychiatry, 4*(3), 243–250.

Rose, D., & Thornicroft, G. (2010). Service User Perspectives on the Impact of a Mental Illness Diagnosis. *Epidemiologia e Psichiatria Sociale, 19*(2), 140–147.

Rose, N. (2003). Neurochemical Selves. *Society, 41*(1), 46–59.

Rose, N. (2007). *The Politics of Life Itself: Biomedicine, Power and Subjectivity in the Twenty-First Century*. London: Routledge.

Rosenberg, M. (1979). *Conceiving the Self*. New York: Basic Books.

Rosenfield, S. (1997). Labeling Mental Illness: The Effects of Received Services and Perceived Stigma on Life Satisfaction. *American Sociological Review, 2*(4), 660–672.

Ross, C., & Broh, B. (2000). The Roles of Self-Esteem and the Sense of Personal Control in the Academic Process. *Sociology of Education, 73*(4), 270–284.

Rossler, W., Lauber, C., Angst, J., Haker, H., Gamma, A., & Eich, D. (2007). The Use of Complementary and Alternative Medicine in the General Population: Results from a Longitudinal Community Study. *Psychological Medicine, 37*(1), 73–84.

Rotter, J. B. (1966). Generalized Expectancies for Internal versus External Control of Reinforcement. *Psychological Monographs, 80*(1), 1–28.

Russell, J. A. (1991). Culture and the Categorization of Emotions. *Psychological Bulletin, 110*(3), 426–450.

Ryan, R. M., & Deci, E. L. (1999). Approaching and Avoiding Self-Determination: Comparing Cybernetic and Organismic Paradigms of Motivation. In J. R. S. Wyer (Ed.), *Advances in Social Cognition* (Vol. 12, pp. 193–215). Mahwah, NJ: Lawrence Erlbaum Associates, Inc.

Sadler, J. Z., Hulgus, Y. F., & Agich, G. J. (1994). On Values in Recent American Psychiatric Classification. *Journal of Medicine and Philosophy, 19*(3), 261–277.

Salmela, M. (2005). What Is Emotional Authenticity? *Journal for the Theory of Social Behaviour, 35*(3), 209–230.

Sarangi, S., & Candlin, C. (2003). Categorization and Explanation of Risk: A Discourse Analytical Perspective. *Health, Risk & Society, 5*(2), 115–124.

Sartorius, N. (2007). Stigma and Mental Health. *The Lancet, 370*(9590), 810–811.

Sartre, J.-P. (1947). *Existentialism* (B. Frechtman, Trans.). New York: Philosophical Library.

Sartre, J.-P. (1956). *Being and Nothingness.* New York: Philosophical Library.

Sartre, J.-P. (2007 [1947]). *Existentialism and Humanism* (P. Mairet, Trans. new edn.). London: Methuen.

Scarpa, A., & Lorenzi, J. (2013). Cognitive-Behavioral Therapy with Children and Adolescents: History and Principles. In A. Scarpa, S. W. White & T. Attwood (Eds.), *CBT for Children and Adolescents with High-Functioning Autism Spectrum Disorders* (pp. 3–26). New York and London: The Guilford Press.

Schafer, R. (1992). *Retelling a Life: Narration and Dialogue in Psychoanalysis.* New York: Basic Books.

Scheff, T. (1966). *Being Mentally Ill: A Sociological Theory.* Chicago: Aldine.

Scheibe, K. E. (1985). Historical Perspectives on the Presented Self. In B. R. Schlenker (Ed.), *The Self and Social Life* (pp. 33–64). New York: McGraw-Hill.

Scheper-Hughes, N. (1990). Three Propositions for a Critically Applied Medical Anthropology. *Social Science & Medicine, 30*(2), 189–197.

Schlenker, B. R., & Weigold, M. F. (1992). Interpersonal Processes Involving Impression Regulation and Management. *Annual Review of Psychology, 43*(1), 133–168.

Schneider, J. W., & Conrad, P. (1983). *Having Epilepsy: The Experience and Control of Illness.* Philadelphia: Temple University Press.

Schofield, P., Crosland, A., Waheed, W., Aseem, S., Gask, L., Wallace, A., Dickens, A., & Tylee, A. (2011). Patients' Views of Antidepressants: From First Experiences to Becoming Expert. *British Journal of General Practice, 61*(585), 142–148.

Schön, U.-K. (2010). Recovery from Severe Mental Illness, a Gender Perspective. *Scandinavian Journal of Caring Sciences, 24*(3), 557–564.

Schwalbe, M. L. (1993). Goffman against Postmodernism: Emotion and the Reality of the Self. *Symbolic Interaction, 16*(4), 333–350.

Schwalbe, M. L. (2009). We Wear the Mask: Subordinated Masculinity and the Persona Trap. In P. Vannini & J. P. Williams (Eds.), *Authenticity in Culture, Self and Society* (pp. 139–152). Farnham, England; Burlington, VT: Ashgate.

Sells, D. J., Stayner, D. A., & Davidson, L. (2004). Recovering the Self in Schizophrenia: An Integrative Review of Qualitative Studies. *Psychiatric Quarterly*, 75(1), 87–97.

Shaw, I. (2002). How Lay Are Lay Beliefs? *Health*, 6(3), 287–299.

Shorter, E. (1997). *A History of Psychiatry: From the Era of the Asylum to the Age of Prozac*. New York: John Wiley & Sons.

Siegel, B. S. (1990). *Love, Medicine & Miracles: Lessons Learned about Self-Healing from a Surgeon's Experience with Exceptional Patients: With a New Introduction by the Author*. New York: Perennial Library.

Simon, G. (2009). Practical Lessons from Effectiveness Trials of Care Management and Psychoeducation for Bipolar Disorder. *Journal of Clinical Psychiatry*, 70(8), 28.

Singer, J. A., & Salovey, P. (1993). *The Remembered Self: Emotion and Memory in Personality*. New York: Maxwell Macmillan.

Singh, I. (2002). Bad Boys, Good Mothers, and the "Miracle" of Ritalin. *Science in Context*, 15(4), 577–603.

Singh, I. (2005). Will the "Real Boy" Please Behave: Dosing Dilemmas for Parents of Boys with ADHD. *American Journal of Bioethics*, 5(3), 34–47.

Singh, I. (2007). Clinical Implications of Ethical Concepts: Moral Self-Understandings in Children Taking Methylphenidate for ADHD. *Clinical Child Psychology and Psychiatry*, 12(2), 167–182.

Smith, J., Flowers, P., & Osborn, M. (1997). Interpretative Phenomenological Analysis and the Psychology of Health and Illness. In L. Yardley (Ed.), *Material Discourses of Health and Illness* (pp. 68–92). London: Routledge.

Smith, J. A. (1995). Semi-Structured Interviewing and Qualitative Analysis. In J. A. Smith, R. Harré & L. V. Langenhove (Eds.), *Rethinking Methods in Psychology*. London: Sage.

Smith, J. A. (1996). Beyond the Divide between Cognition and Discourse: Using Interpretative Phenomenological Analysis in Health Psychology. *Psychology & Health*, 11(2), 261.

Smith, J. A. (1997). Developing Theory from Case Studies: Self-Reconstruction and the Transition to Motherhood. In N. Hayes (Ed.), *Doing Qualitative Analysis in Psychology*. Hove: Psychology Press.

Smith, J. A. (1999). Identity Development During the Transition to Motherhood: An Interpretative Phenomenological Analysis. *Journal of Reproductive and Infant Psychology*, 17(3), 281.

Smith, J. A., & Osborn, M. (2004). Interpretative Phenomenological Analysis. In G. Breakwell (Ed.), *Doing Social Psychology* (pp. 229–254). Oxford: Blackwell.

Spijker, J., Graaf, R., Bijl, R. V., Beekman, A. T., Ormel, J., & Nolen, W. A. (2004). Functional Disability and Depression in the General Population. Results from the Netherlands Mental Health Survey and Incidence Study (Nemesis). *Acta Psychiatrica Scandinavica*, 110(3), 208–214.

Spiro, M. E. (1993). Is the Western Conception of the Self "Peculiar" within the Context of the World Cultures? *Ethos*, 21(2), 107–153.

Stajkovic, A. D., & Sommer, S. M. (2000). Self-Efficacy and Causal Attributions: Direct and Reciprocal Links. *Journal of Applied Social Psychology*, 30(4), 707–737.

Steffens, D. C., Skoog, I., Norton, M. C., Hart, A. D., Tschanz, J. T., Plassman, B. L., Wyse, B. W., Welsh-Bohmer, K. A., & Breitner, J. C. S. (2000). Prevalence of Depression and Its Treatment in an Elderly Population. *Archives of General Psychiatry, 57*(6), 301–307.

Stevenson, F., & Knudsen, P. (2008). Discourses of Agency and the Search for the Authentic Self: The Case of Mood-Modifying Medicines. *Social Science & Medicine, 66*(1), 170–181.

Stoppard, J. M. (2000). *Understanding Depression: Feminist Social Constructionist Approaches.* London: Routledge.

Strauss, A. L., & Corbin, J. M. (1990). *Basics of Qualitative Research: Grounded Theory Procedures and Techniques.* Newbury Park, CA.: Sage Publications.

Strawson, G. (2004). Against Narrativity. *Ratio, 17*(4), 428–452.

Stryker, S. (1980). *Symbolic Interactionism: A Social Structural Version.* Menlo Park, CA: Benjamin/Cummings Pub. Co.

Stryker, S. (1987). Identity Theory: Developments and Extensions. In K. Yardley & T. Honess (Eds.), *Self and Identity: Psychosocial Perspectives* (pp. 89–103). New York: Wiley.

Stryker, S., & Burke, P. J. (2000). The Past, Present, and Future of an Identity Theory. *Social Psychology Quarterly, 63*(4), 284.

Sullivan, H. S. (1940). *Conceptions of Modern Psychiatry.* New York: Norton.

Svenaeus, F. (2007). Do Antidepressants Affect the Self? A Phenomenological Approach. *Medicine, Health Care and Philosophy, 10*(2), 153–166.

Szegedi, A., Kohnen, R., Dienel, A., & Kieser, M. (2005). Acute Treatment of Moderate to Severe Depression with Hypericum Extract WS 5570 (St John's Wort): Randomised Controlled Double Blind Non-Inferiority Trial versus Paroxetine. *British Medical Journal, 330*(7490), 503–508.

Taussig, M. T. (1980). Reification and the Consciousness of the Patient. *Social Science and Medicine, 14B*(1), 3–13.

Taylor, C. (1989). *Sources of the Self: The Making of the Modern Identity.* Cambridge: Cambridge University Press.

Taylor, C. (1991a). *The Ethics of Authenticity.* Cambridge, MA: Harvard University Press.

Taylor, C. (1991b). *The Malaise of Modernity.* Concord, Canada: Anansi Press.

Taylor, M. A. (1992). Are Schizophrenia and Affective Disorder Related? A Selective Literature Review *American Journal of Psychiatry, 149*(1), 22–32.

Taylor, S. J., & Bogdan, R. (1998). *Introduction to Qualitative Research Methods: A Guidebook and Resource* (3rd edn.). New York: John Wiley & Sons.

Thomas-MacLean, R., & Stoppard, J. M. (2004). Physicians' Constructions of Depression: Inside/Outside the Boundaries of Medicalization. *Health, 8*(3), 275–293.

Thompson, C. P. (1998). *Autobiographical Memory: Theoretical and Applied Perspectives.* Mahwah, NJ: L. Erlbaum.

Thompson, P. (2009). Pioneering the Life Story Method. In B. Harrison (Ed.), *Life Story Research* (pp. 38–41). London: Sage.

Thompson, T. (1995). *The Beast: A Reckoning with Depression.* New York: G. P. Putnam's Sons.

Thwaites, R., Dagnan, D., Huey, D., & Addis, M. E. (2004). The Reasons for Depression Questionnaire (RFD): UK Standardization for Clinical and Non Clinical Populations. *Psychology and Psychotherapy: Theory, Research and Practice, 77*(3), 363–374.

Tillich, P. (1952). *The Courage to Be.* New Haven: Yale University Press.

Tillich, P. (1960). Existentialism, Psychotherapy, and the Nature of Man. *Pastoral Psychology, 11*(5), 10–18.

Toombs, S. K. (1988). Illness and the Paradigm of Lived Body. *Theoretical Medicine, 9*(2), 201–226.

Torpy, J. M. (2009). Bipolar Disorder. *The Journal of the American Medical Association, 301*(5), 564.

Triandis, H. C., McCusker, C., Betancourt, H., Iwao, S., Leung, K., Salazar, J. M., Setiadi, B., Sinha, J. B. P., Touzard, H., & Zaleski, Z. (1993). An Etic-Emic Analysis of Individualism and Collectivism. *Journal of Cross-Cultural Psychology, 24*(3), 366–383.

Trilling, L. (1971). *Sincerity and Authenticity.* New York: Harcourt Brace Jovanovich.

Tully, L. A., Parker, G. B., Wilhelm, K., & Malhi, G. S. (2006). Why Am I Depressed?: An Investigation of Whether Patients' Beliefs about Depression Concur with Their Diagnostic Subtype. *The Journal of Nervous and Mental Disease, 194*(7), 543–546.

Turner, R. H., & Schutte, J. (1981). The True Self Method for Studying the Self-Conception. *Symbolic Interaction, 4*(1), 1–20.

Üstün, T. B., Ayuso-Mateos, J. L., Chatterji, S., Mathers, C., & Murray, C. J. (2004). Global Burden of Depressive Disorders in the Year 2000. *British Journal of Psychiatry, 184*(5), 386–392.

Valenstein, E. S. (1998). *Blaming the Brain: The Truth about Drugs and Mental Health.* New York: Free Press.

Van Manen, M. (1984). Practicing Phenomenological Writing. *Phenomenology and Pedagogy, 2*(1), 36–69.

Van Praag, H. M. (1990). The DSM-IV (Depression) Classification: To Be or Not to Be? *Nervous and Mental Disease, 178*(3), 147–149.

Vannini, P. (2006). Dead Poets' Society: Teaching, Publish-or-Perish, and Professors' Experiences of Authenticity. *Symbolic Interaction, 29*(2), 235–257.

Vannini, P., & Williams, J. P. (2009). Authenticity in Culture, Self, and Society. In P. Vannini & J. P. Williams (Eds.), *Authenticity in Culture, Self, and Society* (pp. 1–20). Farnham, England: Ashgate.

Vellenga, B. A., & Christenson, J. (1994). Persistent and Severely Mentally Ill Clients' Perceptions of Their Mental Illness. *Issues in Mental Health Nursing, 15*(4), 359–371.

Verbeek-Heida, P. M., & Mathot, E. F. (2006). Better Safe Than Sorry – Why Patients Prefer to Stop Using Selective Serotonin Reuptake Inhibitor (SSRI) Antidepressants but Are Afraid to Do So: Results of a Qualitative Study. *Chronic Illness, 2*(2), 133.

Wagner, P. J., Jester, D., LeClair, B., Taylor, T., Woodward, L., & Lambert, J. (1999). Taking the Edge Off Why Patients Choose St. John's Wort. *The Journal of Family Practice, 48*(8), 615–619.

Walker, C. (2008). *Depression and Globalization: The Politics of Mental Health in the Twenty-First Century*. New York: Springer.

Wallerstein, R. S., & Goldberger, L. (1998). *Ideas and Identities: The Life and Work of Erik Erikson*. Madison, CT: International Universities Press.

Ward, S., & Wisner, K. L. (2007). Collaborative Management of Women with Bipolar Disorder During Pregnancy and Postpartum: Pharmacologic Considerations. *Journal of Midwifery & Women's Health, 52*(1), 3–13.

Warner, R., Taylor, D., Powers, M., & Hyman, J. (1989). Acceptance of the Mental Illness Label by Psychotic Patients: Effects on Functioning. *American Journal of Orthopsychiatry, 59*(3), 398–409.

Weiner, B., Graham, A., & Chandler, C. (1982). Pity, Anger, and Guilt: An Attributional Analysis. *Personality and Social Psychology Bulletin, 8*(2), 226–232.

Weisberger, A. M. (1995). The Ethics of the Broader Usage of Prozac: Social Choice or Social Bias? *International Journal of Applied Philosophy, 10*(1), 69–74.

Weitz, R. (2001). *The Sociology of Health, Illness, and Health Care: A Critical Approach*. Belmont, CA: Wadsworth/Thomson Learning.

Werneke, U. (2007). Complementary and Alternative Medicines. Retrieved 28 July 2010, from www.rcpsych.ac.uk/mentalhealthinfoforall/treatments/complementarytherapy.aspx#dep.

Westerbeek, J., & Mutsaers, K. (2008). Depression Narratives: How the Self Became a Problem. *Literature and Medicine, 27*(1), 25–55.

WHO. (2017). Depression. Retrieved 17 May 2017, from www.who.int/mediacentre/factsheets/fs369/en/.

Widdershoven, G. (1993). The Story of Life: Hermeneutic Perspectives on the Relationships between Narrative and Life History. In R. Josselson & A. Lieblich (Eds.), *The Narrative Study of Lives*. Newbury Park, CA: Sage.

Widiger, T. A., & Sankis, L. M. (2000). Adult Psychopathology: Issues and Controversies. *Annual Review of Psychology, 51*(1), 377–404.

Wileman, L., May, C., & Chew-Graham, C. A. (2002). Medically Unexplained Symptoms and the Problem of Power in the Primary Care Consultation: A Qualitative Study. *Family Practice, 19*(2), 178.

Williams, G. (1984). The Genesis of Chronic Illness: Narrative Re-Construction. *Sociology of Health & Illness, 6*(2), 175–200.

Williams, G. (1997). The Genesis of Chronic Illness: Narrative Reconstruction. In L. P. Hinchman & S. K. Hinchman (Eds.), *Memory, Identity, Community: The Idea of Narrative in the Human Sciences* (pp. 185–212). Albany, NY: State University of New York Press.

Williams, J. M. G. (1992). Autobiographical Memory and Emotional Disorders. In S.-A. Christianson (Ed.), *Handbook of Emotion and Memory* (pp. 451–477). Hillsdale, NJ: Erlbaum.

Williams, J. M. G., Barnhofer, T., Crane, C., Herman, D., Raes, F., Watkins, E., & Dalgleish, T. (2007). Autobiographical Memory Specificity and Emotional Disorder. *Psychological Bulletin, 133*(1), 122–148.

Williams, J. W. J., Mulrow, C. D., Chiquette, E., Noel, P. H., Aguilar, C., & Cornell, J. (2000). A Systematic Review of Newer Pharmacotherapies for Depression in Adults: Evidence Report Summary. *Annals of Internal Medicine, 132*(9), 743–756.

Williams, S. J. (2003). *Medicine and the Body.* London: Sage Publications.

Willig, C. (2008). *Introducing Qualitative Research in Psychology: Adventures in Theory and Method.* Maidenhead: Open University Press.

Wilson, M. (1993). DSM-III and the Transformation of American Psychiatry: A History. *American Journal of Psychiatry, 150*(3), 399–410.

Wisdom, J. P., Bruce, K., Auzeen Saedi, G., Weis, T., & Green, C. A. (2008). "Stealing Me from Myself": Identity and Recovery in Personal Accounts of Mental Illness. *Australian and New Zealand Journal of Psychiatry, 42*(6), 489–495.

Wisdom, J. P., & Green, C. A. (2004). "Being in a Funk": Teens' Efforts to Understand Their Depressive Episode. *Qualitative Health Research, 14*(9), 1227–1238.

Woike, B. (1995). Most-Memorable Experiences: Evidence for a Link between Implicit and Explicit Motives and Social Cognitive Processes in Everyday Life. *Journal of Personality and Social Psychology, 68*(6), 1081–1091.

Woike, B., Gershkovich, I., Piorkowski, R., & Polo, M. (1999). The Role of Motives in the Content and Structure of Autobiographical Memory. *Journal of Personality and Social Psychology, 76*(4), 600–612.

Wong, Y. J., Tran, K. K., Kim, S.-H., Van Horn Kerne, V., & Calfa, N. A. (2010). Asian Americans' Lay Beliefs about Depression and Professional Help Seeking. *Journal of Clinical Psychology, 66*(3), 317–332.

Wood, A. M., Linley, P. A., Maltby, J., Baliousis, M., & Joseph, S. (2008). The Authentic Personality: A Theoretical and Empirical Conceptualization and the Development of the Authenticity Scale. *Journal of Counseling Psychology, 55*(3), 385–399.

Wylie, R. C. (1974). *The Self-Concept. Volume 1: A Review of Methodological Considerations and Measuring Instruments.* Lincoln, NE: University of Nebraska Press.

Yalom, I. D. (1980). *Existential Psychotherapy.* New York: Basic Books.

Young, M. A., Scheftner, W. A., Klerman, G. L., Andreasen, N. C., & Hirschfeld, R. M. (1986). The Endogenous Subtype of Depression: A Study of Its Internal Construct Validity. *British Journal of Psychiatry, 148*(3), 257–268.

Zinn, J. O. (2005). The Biographical Approach: A Better Way to Understand Behaviour in Health and Illness. *Health, Risk & Society, 7*(1), 1–9.

Zola, I. K. (1973). Pathways to the Doctor – from Person to Patient. *Social Science & Medicine, 7*(9), 677–689.

Index